This book presents a fresh perspective on the epic drama of arctic exploration in the early and mid-nineteenth century, the period that witnessed the search first for a Northwest Passage to the Orient and then for the expedition led by Sir John Franklin which had been lost in that search. Drawing upon a wide range of scientific, technical, social, psychological, and medical data, Hugh N. Wallace surveys and evaluates the activities of the various expeditions organized by the Royal Navy and the Hudson's Bay Company. He views exploration in terms of a metropolitan country, Great Britain, discovering a hinterland region, Canada's Arctic. He is concerned with the problems of initial and follow-up discovery, the choice of entry routes and the techniques of travel along them, the impact of advancing technology upon ships and men, and he shows how these challenges were met with varying degrees of success by naval and civilian explorers. Much emphasis is placed upon the personalities and incentives of those who led the parties and those who sent them out. A central figure is Dr. Richard King, a London surgeon who made a journey to the region in 1833–35 and thereafter became one of the leading advocates of light, indigenous, and inland or coastal means of travel in the Arctic, as distinct from the heavily equipped, deep-sea approach of which Franklin's ill-fated expedition remains the classic example. Rebuffed by the Admiralty, King assumed the role of chorus in a developing Greek tragedy. Had his views been adopted, Professor Wallace contends, Boothia Peninsula might have been fully delineated and a Northwest Passage discovered by the early 1840s, and the Franklin disaster thereby averted; later, King's accurate predictions as to where the lost sailors might be found were similarly ignored. Instead, arctic exploration became an exercise in elaborate multiplicity which eventually led, at great cost and after long failure and frustration, to the discovery of one-half of the Canadian Arctic and three Northwest Passages, as well as the evidence of Franklin's fate.

Professor Wallace is a member of the Department of History at Mount Saint Vincent University, Halifax, N.S.

THE NAVY, THE COMPANY, AND RICHARD KING

British Exploration in the Canadian Arctic

1829-1860

Hugh N. Wallace

McGill – Queen's University Press
Montreal

© McGill-Queen's University Press 1980
International Standard Book Number 0-7735-0338-2
Legal deposit 2nd quarter 1980
Bibliothèque nationale du Québec

Design by Naoto Kondo
Printed in Canada by
Imprimerie Gagné Ltée

This book has been
published with the help of
a grant from the Social Science Federation
of Canada, using funds provided by the
Social Sciences and Humanities
Research Council of Canada

To my wife who waited and
my daughter who interrupted

Contents

Plates

between pages 106 and 107

1. Steam machinery from Sir John Ross's H.M.S. *Victory*
   Department of National Defence

2. Plans for screw propeller, H.M.S. *Erebus*, 1845
   National Maritime Museum

3. H.M.S. *Erebus*
   Scott Polar Research Institute

4. India rubber boat, Rae expedition, 1846–47
   Orkney Natural History Society

5. Profile and plan of steam vessels *Pioneer* and *Intrepid*, 1851
   National Maritime Museum

6. H.M.S. *Assistance* and steam vessel *Pioneer*, 1852
   British Library

7. Extract from the diary of A.B. James H. Nelson, 1853
   Courtesy of Mr. J. W. Nelson

8. Document found at Point Victory in 1859
   National Maritime Museum

9. Aerial view of Montreal Island
   Department of Energy, Mines and Resources

10. View from the King cache on Montreal Island
    From Richard King, *The Franklin Expedition from First to Last* (London, 1855)

11. Colonial Office minutes on letter of Dr. Richard King, 1847
    Public Record Office

Maps

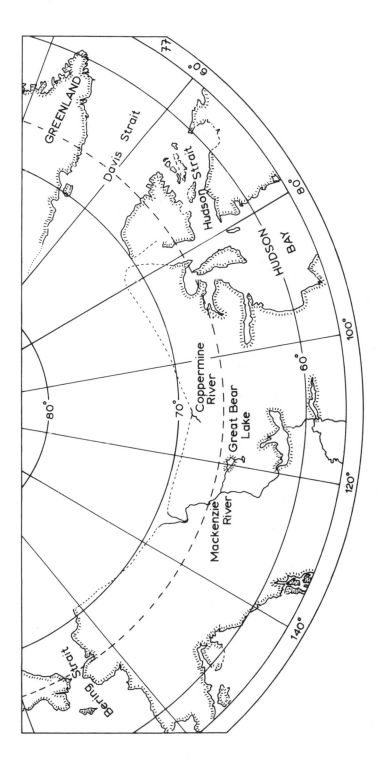

1. The North American Arctic as known in 1818

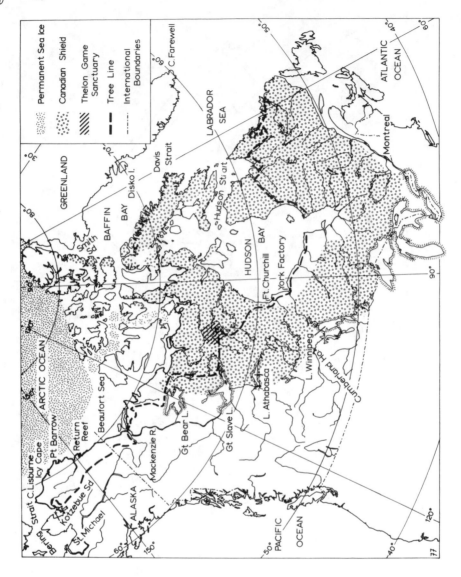

2. Canada: Permanent
   Sea Ice; the Shield
   Structure; the Tree
   Line

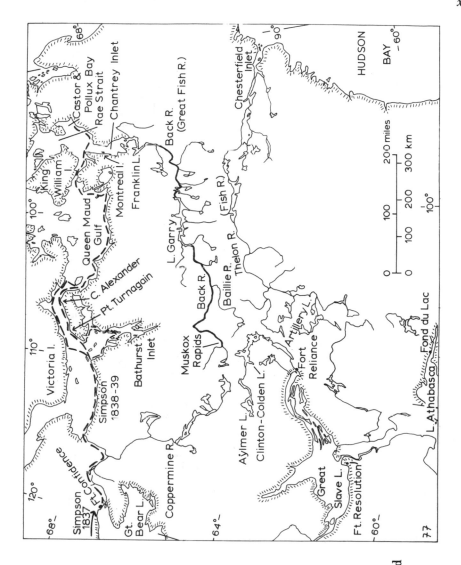

3. The Back River Region and
   Simpson's Routes,
   1838–1839

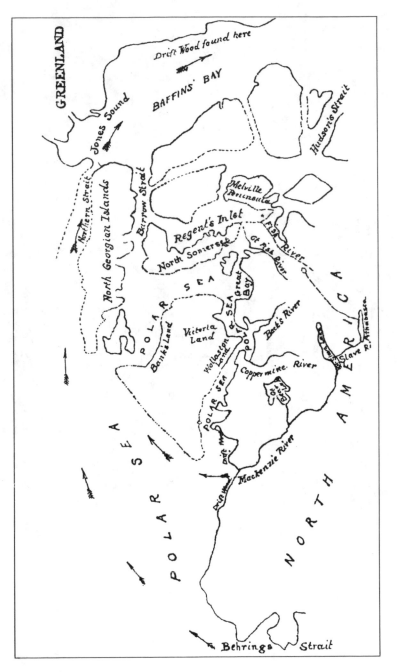

4. Richard King's View of the Arctic, 1845

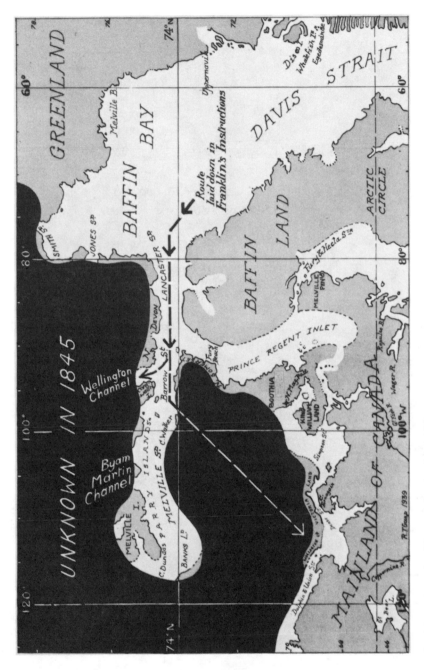

5. The Admiralty View of the Arctic, 1845

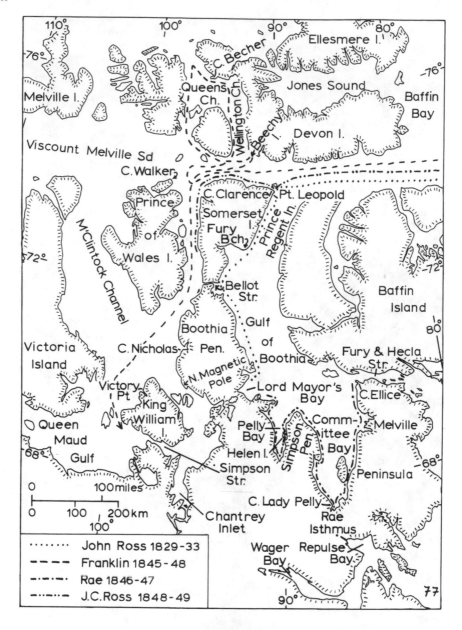

6. The Voyages of the Rosses, Franklin, and Rae

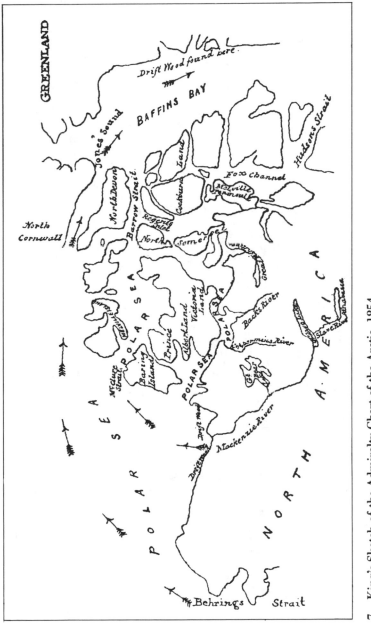

7. **King's Sketch of the Admiralty Chart of the Arctic, 1854**
In 1855 Richard King compared this map with his own map of 1845, claiming that discoveries had justified his projection. The Admiralty still continued to depict King William Island as peninsular; King had correctly identified it nine years earlier.

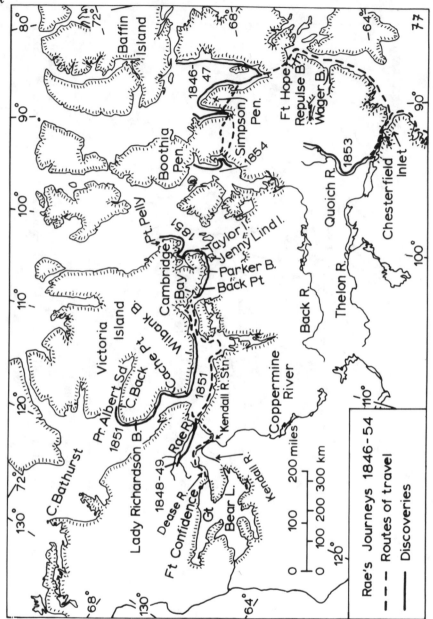

8. Rae's Journeys, 1846–1854

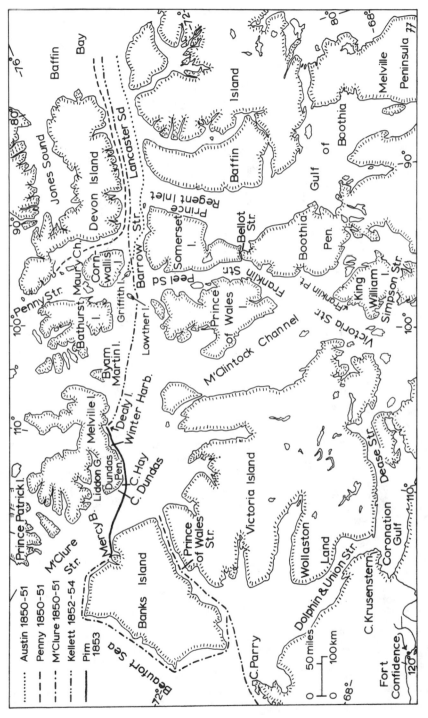

9. Some Voyages of the 1850s

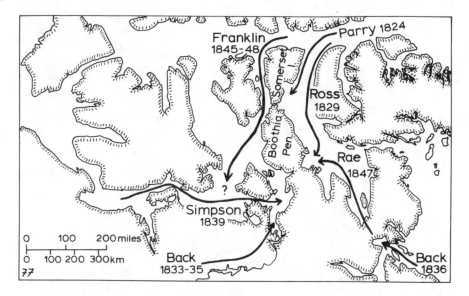

10. Routes leading to Boothia Peninsula, 1824–1848
Boothia was at the end of the line for all the routes, as the Royal Navy searched for a passage and lost Franklin.

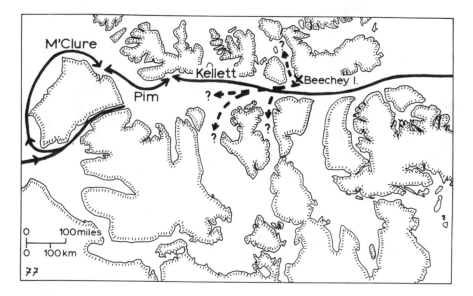

11. Beechey Island and the Completion of the Northwest Passage
Beechey Island was a cross-roads: which way had Franklin gone? The navy had searched for him and found a passage.

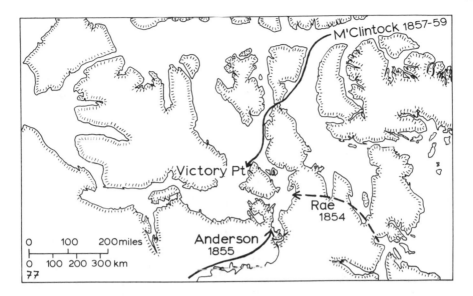

12. The Discovery of Franklin's Fate, 1854–1859
In 1854 the Royal Navy gave up the search for Franklin and learned of his fate, as
Rae found initial evidence, amplified upon by Anderson and M'Clintock.

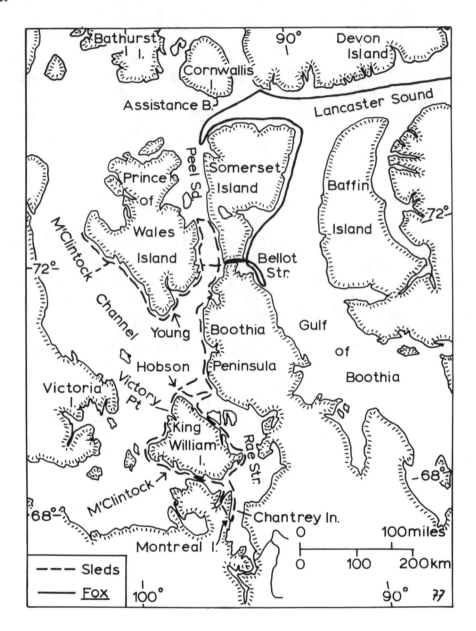

13. M'Clintock's Voyage in *Fox*, 1857–1859

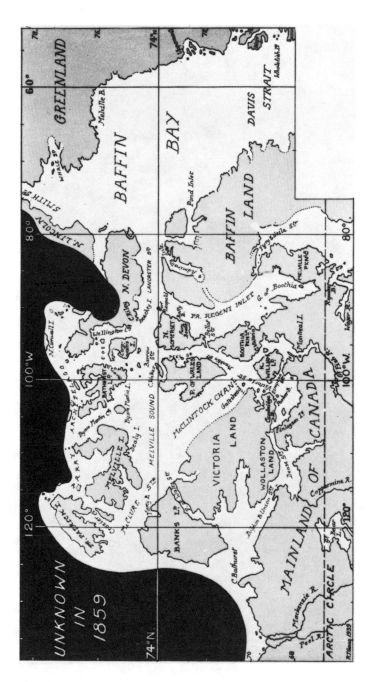

14. The Arctic as known in 1859

Preface

The roots of this book lie in the influence of my father, J. N. Wallace (1870–1941), a Dominion Land Surveyor in Canada's Northwest in the early part of this century. Although the laying out of meridians and base lines brought surveyors at that time only, at most, to the fringe of the Arctic, J. N. Wallace did survey well ahead of settlement more northern boundaries of the western provinces, including a part of the British Columbia–Yukon border. He viewed the surveyor's concern with boundaries as overlapping, so to speak, the boundary of his profession, and reaching into the field of exploration. Development in the Northwest, he felt, occurred first in terms of explorers; then of surveyors who were almost explorers; and then of settlers. Of necessity he had to journey with a certain lightness, and he was sure that it was not always those who got through with great trouble and heroic trials who were the best travellers; on the contrary, a minimum amount of difficulty in the North was a sign of competence. He also had respect and admiration for the Indians' knowledge of their environment and for their adaptation to it. When as an avocation J. N. Wallace came to study the fur trade, the terms "metropolitan" and "hinterland" were not yet in use, but there is a suggestion of such an outlook in his work, *The Wintering Partners on the Peace River* (Ottawa, 1927). For in this he emphasized strongly the pioneering character of the North West Company and yet, imperialist by conviction, referred as well to the more centralized, organized, and large-scale role of the Hudson's Bay Company. He also stressed the part played in this context by two differing types of personality. In short, there is a suggestion in that book of what is called in these pages "initial" and "follow-up" discovery. It seemed to me as I worked that the views and attitudes of J. N. Wallace, taken as a whole, had a bearing upon events further north.

Other influences are also present in this book. It is a pleasure to acknowledge here my debt to Professor Mason Wade who, at the University of Rochester, introduced me formally to Canadian studies. Aware of my background, Professor Morris Zaslow of the University of Western Ontario encouraged my interest in the North. Also aware of it, Professor Gerald Graham, then Rhodes Professor of Imperial History at King's College, the University of London, fostered this tendency. There are emphases in the book which bespeak his influence: that, for example, upon the use of steam at sea. My greatest thanks are due to Professor Glyndwr Williams of Queen Mary College at the University of London. Scholar and writer on Canada's fur trade, expert upon the search for a Northwest Passage and, like Professor Graham, distinguished in the field of maritime history, Professor Williams's encouragement, knowledge, and advice had their influence throughout my research and writing. While opinions and conclusions are mine, my debt to him is central.

I am glad to acknowledge grants of assistance from the Canada Council, which largely financed research in England upon my topic, and from Mount Saint Vincent University, for the preparation of the manuscript, maps, and illustrations. I am grateful to institutions and individuals referred to in the bibliography and in the notes, and to other individuals as well, to whom I have written or with whom I have had conversations, in particular Professor Irene Spry, whose encouragement and knowledge of northwestern exploration were much appreciated at an early stage; Dr. J. E. Caswell, of Turlock, California, whose knowledge of arctic history was also of great use at an early stage; Dr. J. Keith Fraser, of Ottawa, who at the outset gave me information concerning the geology of the Arctic; Mr. G. W. Rowley, formerly of the Department of Indian Affairs and Northern Development, Ottawa, and Capt. T. C. Pullen, RCN (retired), Ottawa. I have exchanged letters with profit on the subject of the "barrens" and related matters with Professor George Whalley, Queen's University, Kingston, Ontario. I have also corresponded with Dr. Terence Armstrong of the Scott Polar Research Institute, and I am grateful for much help from Dr. Alan Cooke, formerly of the same institution, now associated with McGill University's Centre for Northern Studies. Like those of the Scott Polar Research Institute, holdings of the Royal Geographical Society proved a basic source, and I am very grateful for the help of their staff. I am grateful also for the help of the Librarian and staff of the National Maritime Museum at Greenwich, and to those at both the British Museum, now the British Library, and the Public Records Office who gave generously of their time and expertise. My thanks are due also to the staff of the Archives of the Hudson's Bay Company, at the time of my research still located at Beaver House in London.

I am indebted to the Reverend David Martin, formerly of King's College at London, who early assisted in matters of style. I am particularly grateful to Professor G. F. W. Young of Saint Mary's University, Halifax, who read and commented upon earlier drafts of this work; and my debt is large indeed to Professor Murray Beck of Dalhousie University, Halifax, who assisted greatly with the manuscript at crucial stages.

I owe special thanks to Mrs. Ferial Falconer of Dartmouth, N.S., who has worked with skill and care in preparing the maps.

Mrs. Sandra MacDonald of Halifax has typed more preparatory drafts of this book than I care to recall, as with unusual skill, sometimes under pressure of time, she dealt with manuscript and typescript material that often presented a formidable task in "initial discovery." Mrs. MacDonald typed as well the last draft, thus performing a final "follow-up" task.

The author wishes to acknowledge the permission of the Public Record Office, London, to make use of Crown-copyright records in this study. He is also indebted to the following institutions and organizations for permission to use manuscript and/or illustrative material in their possession: the British Library, London; the Department of National Defence, Ottawa; Guy's Hospital Archives, London; the Hudson's Bay Company Archives, Winnipeg, and the Hudson's Bay Record Society; the National Air Photo Library, Ottawa; the National Library of Ireland; the National Maritime Museum, London; the National Portrait Gallery, London; the Office of the Hydrographer, Taunton, Somerset; the Orkney Natural History Society, Stromness; the Royal Geographical Society, London; the Scott Polar Research Institute, Cambridge; the Society of Apothecaries and the Guildhall Library, London; and Trinity College Library, Dublin. For permission to use family or personal papers he wishes to thank Mr. G. E. Banes, Bishops Stortford, Herts; Mr. John McClintock, Ballycarry, Co. Antrim; Mr. J. W. Nelson, Leicester; and Miss Esther Ross, London.

It should be noted that in the period covered in this book the north magnetic pole was located approximately at Boothia's west coast and the words "north pole" and "polar regions" usually referred to this pole and its environs, or quite often simply to the North American Arctic in general, that is to say, an area including approximately the southern two-thirds of the Canadian Arctic today and on occasion the present-day Greenland and Alaskan Arctic regions as well.

During the era of arctic exploration the term "Eskimo" was commonly used in referring to the Inuit, and "half-breed" in referring to people of mixed European and Indian ancestry; for that reason both terms have been employed here.

Hugh N. Wallace

1

Introduction

In the discovery of the Canadian Arctic the period from the end of the Napoleonic Wars to 1860 can be likened to lengthening days in the Arctic itself. Midwinter darkness at noon represents geographic ignorance of the region at the start of the period. An April day in the Arctic when the sun, whatever the northern latitude, is already more continuously above the horizon than below it, describes the wide knowledge of the polar region that had been acquired by 1860.

In 1818 the Arctic map showed peripheral seas near the Atlantic and Pacific Oceans. On the Atlantic side a vague and shadowy outline of Greenland's west coast was known, as were Davis Strait and Baffin Bay; further south, Hudson Strait and its bay had long been in use by the Hudson's Bay Company. If, alternatively, one chose to enter the Arctic from the Pacific, Bering Strait alone was known. Between these peripheral seas the map showed to the west of Hudson Bay two rivers, the Coppermine and the Mackenzie, that reached northward like threads to two points on a polar sea; between the two rivers was Great Bear Lake. All else, either north of or between these water-ways, was *terra incognita*.[1] Known least of all was the fact that there lay in the polar sea one of the world's great archipelagos, including three of its ten largest islands, Baffin, Victoria, and Ellesmere. Yet by 1860 there had been traced many lines along the Canadian Arctic mainland, including its northern coast, the southern half of the vast archipelago beyond this, and three Northwest Passages.

Making these discoveries had been like seeking the light switch in a darkened room. As they sought a Northwest Passage and then the lost Franklin expedition, explorers had groped their way painfully on the mainland, in the Arctic Ocean, and in the archipelago. Proceeding in inky ignorance they had encountered peninsulas thinking they were islands, by-passed straits thought to be bays, and even mistaken open sea for mountains. The analogy of arctic night and a darkened room is heightened by the paradox that the explorers often moved amidst scenes of dazzling white. Universal snow could produce snowblindness and meant real difficulty in distinguishing frozen sea from frozen land. We can clearly see the mistakes explorers made; they, at the time, could not. Yet the analogy of a darkened room should not suggest that tracing the geographic outline of the Arctic was for the explorers a trifling affair. A wrong turning, choice of one rather than another river, or misreading an ocean current, could stunt a career, endanger a vessel, or lose lives.

To understand how, in such peculiar northern conditions, explorers actually succeeded or failed in accomplishing their task and to pose an hypothesis concerning their successes and failures, it is useful to look at the outset at earlier North American exploration. A theme of this book is that exploration most appropriately occurs in a series of phases in which the routes, the methods of travel, and the personalities which are adapted to an early stage are not necessarily those which excel in a later one, and that if this sequence is disrupted trouble may ensue. A small party, for example, of a few individuals with light and simple means of travel, led by a man of great individuality who brings back a limited but crucial store of information may in an early phase of exploration be called for. Later it may be that what is most needed is a larger expedition with more complex means of travel and a more hierarchical organization and leadership which brings back (for these very reasons) a larger amount of information of a more detailed nature. A corollary is that very often on the North American scene the land routes were likely to be propitious for the kind of initial light party here referred to, while coastal, and to an even greater extent sea routes, were likely on the other hand to entail larger and heavier parties.

Indeed, to see discovery in terms of a sequence is to relate two well-known schools of thought in regard to arctic exploration. There have been writers, of whom Stefansson is the best known, who have extolled explorers who "travelled light" and "lived from the land." Another school of writing has tended to extol naval explorers. It has not been critical of the fact that members of the Royal Navy were less aware of indigenous factors than were Hudson's Bay Company men, and tended to travel in larger and more slow-moving parties. The writings of L. H. Neatby fall into this school.[2] The present work suggests that the two schools can be related to each other if one thinks sequentially. One type of travel was more adapted to early and rapid forays, the other to later amplification and elaboration. Indeed, such a sequence between earlier, lighter means of travel and later more developed ones had already been revealed along two access routes to North America, including its Arctic. These were the northwest route and Hudson Bay, which were in turn related to each other by a dominant Canadian feature, the Laurentian Shield.

So influential, indeed, was the Shield that there would emerge eventually a view of Canadian history based upon it as a factor: the "Laurentian School,"[3] whose implications as regards exploration this study attempts in part to extend northward to the Arctic. Almost two million square miles in extent, covering one-half the area of modern Canada, the Shield was composed of precambrian rock, the oldest on the surface of the earth. It was a consequence of retreating glaciers which had left it almost without soil but rich in water and aquatic animals. Lying like a vast U round Hudson Bay, from Ungava and Labrador in the east to the St. Lawrence River in the south, and the Mackenzie River in the far north and west, it constituted, especially along its gigantic margin, North America's basic fur-bearing area. The Shield was penetrated at its core by the bay itself which formed one route into the interior. It had also at its southern and far western fringe, from the St. Lawrence to the Mackenzie River, a four thousand-mile chain of streams and lakes that, like vast emptying pools, formed a second route to the fur country. On the whole, of these two approaches the northwest route was one of lighter, faster, and more indigenous travel. Despite its greater length, it was adapted to initial discovery; indeed, because of this, for it went around hindrances. In the French period of North American history, for example, it had helped the French to discover, ahead of their rivals from Hudson Bay, large regions of the Northwest. On this route especially, prime beaver and birch bark for canoes were found.[4] In addition, Montreal, chief port of the northwest route, was open for seven months of the year, by comparison with an open season of only two months at Fort York on Hudson Bay.

In its use of the indigenous food pemmican the North West Company added still a further advantage to the Montreal route. Praised by Stefansson as one of, if not *the*, most nutritious of all foods, possessed of vitamin C which guarded against scurvy,[5] pemmican was a food indigenous to North America, a means of sustenance of Indians but one whose production was organized by the white man on a very large scale. It consisted of lean meat, or on occasion fish, sun dried, pulverized, and packed with melted fat, sometimes with dried berries, into rawhide bags. It was very concentrated and therefore light and portable. Another advantage was that it did not take long to prepare for a meal. One could eat it as a soup or stew called rubbaboo, take it fried in a form called rousseau, rechaud, or richot, or even chew it cold as one actually travelled. It soon became "the life-blood of the Nor'Westers' fur trade," as "the food fuel for the fur brigades." Pemmican, like the use of the canoe, was a means for light and rapid travel along the Nor'Westers' route.[6] It helped confirm a pattern in which, in the late eighteenth and early nineteenth centuries, the North West Company sometimes conveyed, by its own means along its own route, London news of the Hudson's Bay Company to Bay men in the interior more rapidly than that company conveyed the same news by its own route and means. Finally, with headquarters in less distant Montreal, the North West Company also had a more flexible organization than did the London-based Hudson's Bay Company.[7]

On the other hand, although it had only a short open season, Hudson Bay gave direct sea access to the heart of the Northwest. The Hudson's Bay Company did explore, as for example in the case of Hearne, but its explorers tended to travel in larger parties, as Hearne did when he journeyed with Indians, and to stay closer to the bay than did discoverers who travelled by the northwest route. A *forte*, by contrast, of Hudson Bay and its company was transport. The company could carry trade goods and heavy furs more inexpensively than could its competitors, which gave it an increasing advantage in later stages of development, and so too eventually did its more centralized organization.[8] An example of the Hudson's Bay Company's heavier approach was the York boat. Originally from the Orkney Islands and for coastal not inland use, this was a craft of transport not adapted to exploration or even to the earliest days of the fur trade in a new area. It had to be pulled over rollers at portages; but by the early nineteenth century these were available, and then the boat proved for most purposes more suitable than the freight canoe of the North West Company.[9] In brief, in such matters as opening the Saskatchewan and Peace River countries and the first accomplishment by Alexander Mackenzie of a Northwest Passage by land, a great deal of initial exploration was accomplished along the northwest route. Yet the Hudson's Bay Company's more direct sea access and heavier means of inland transport gave it ultimate superiority.

Even in coalition, however, the old relationship remained. For after 1821, when the two companies joined forces, the northwest approach was used for administration and communication; at Lachine was Sir George Simpson, governor of the Hudson's Bay Company's North American territories, and from Montreal there ranged express canoes through the North carrying personnel, orders, and reports, while through the bay itself came the trade goods.[10] This was a fitting postscript to what seemed to have emerged as a main characteristic: that North American exploration was likely to come at first by small inland scouting parties using light flexible means of travel, derived largely from indigenous inhabitants or those with knowledge of the region. They would find out, in an early stage, the basic topography of an area, and make and bring back what observations they could. Subsequently, others would use this information in more elaborate stages of discovery and development, often coming more directly by sea.

At Quebec the Royal Navy had arrived upon the North American scene in the role of conqueror, after much exploration of the continent had been done. Now, conqueror also at Trafalgar and guarantor of peace, from 1815 the navy was in search of new ways to expend its energies. If there was a navigable Northwest Passage to the Orient this would obviously increase British power and world commerce. England had been searching for a Northwest Passage for three centuries. In the late sixteenth and early seventeenth centuries Frobisher, Davis, Weymouth, and Foxe, as part of the general quest, had sought a passage in the Arctic. The eighteenth century, however, had witnessed the end of the search in temperate latitudes, so that after 1815 it was argued anew that there might be a strategically and commercially useful passage in the polar regions. National prestige would be served if Great Britain completed the quest, and harmed if some other nation did so. Russia was already a competitor in the Arctic and the United States might be increasingly so. Naval service amidst arctic snows would be good for the national character. It would also give a new officer class an avenue to promotion. To these factors were added a widening geographic and scientific interest, in earth magnetism for example. It was also observed at this time that arctic ice conditions were especially favourable. All these were reasons why the Royal Navy now took a hand in arctic exploration.[11]

The navy, of course, was interested primarily in deep sea routes. Centred in London, it was an even older and more continuous institution than the Hudson's Bay Company; even more than the company, it was "of the establishment," monopolistic, and an agent of authority. Product of an hierarchical service discipline, its purpose was war and the keeping of peace and order. In the days of Frobisher and other Elizabethan explorers, vessels had been small. Now the navy tended to take pride in size, and would soon take a growing interest in technology, the use of steam for example. Even more than the Hudson's Bay Company, not to mention the North West Company, it was composed of salaried people who were interested in their careers but for whom practical means of survival and travel in North America had not the same central concern as they did for the fur traders.

No doubt the navy's Hydrographic Office, under whose direction discovery vessels were sent out, believed itself to be organized for exploration.

Yet this might prove a contradiction in terms. For that Office had the purpose primarily of charting and aiding navigation in regions already known in outline; its kind of exploration, therefore, was likely to be closer to surveying than to discovery. The Office might not recognize any necessity for a special initial stage, exploration *per se*. It might view discovery as an exercise in heavy transport and orderly progress rather than in travelling light by way of rapid forays. Its parties might be characterized by many members, elaborate organization, the latest in European technology, and officers with sophisticated training in navigation, hydrography, and magnetism. Without full consideration of indigenous conditions, the navy might show a bent instead to seek elaborate and massive information about the environment of a more theoretical kind. If there were difficulties, it might meet them by still greater determination coupled with still more elaborate techniques and a still larger number of vessels, in a desire to make the new environment match that of the sailors' homeland or of some ocean already known to them.

There was a possible exception. Discovery on the mainland had tended to come in a sequence first of communication and then of transport, but if the Arctic was open perhaps the two functions could be combined there. Ships could carry a larger number of men and more equipment than was possible in land travel, and if unobstructed could move quickly. The navy, therefore, might perform two tasks at once, exploring and surveying. On the other hand, obstructions such as ice or land could necessitate, even for the navy, an earlier lighter party (perhaps by land) and a later more sophisticated one. In fact in the North American Arctic there were, as yet unknown, both an archipelago and a complex continental coastline. From the days of Frobisher, in addition to a short season and polar ice, explorers had been confronted by these two land barriers.

The land obstructions were related to each other in part by the Laurentian Shield. Geologically the archipelago is primarily of a different structure than the Shield. Yet a precambrian formation does underpin much of it, giving the islands in this way a relationship to the mainland. Second, despite its general absence on the surface of the archipelago, a precambrian structure does fleck the eastern arctic islands. The southern side of Baffin Island, for example, is precambrian; there is much of this formation on Ellesmere Island; and the banks of Fury and Hecla Strait are "outworks" of the precambrian structure. Furthermore, Boothia, the northernmost portion of the mainland, is a peninsula of Shield composition. It consists of a very narrow isthmus near its base, after which it thrusts far into the archipelago, marking a division between the eastern and western Arctic of North America. West of Boothia there is a more regular mainland shore as far as the Pacific; here a precambrian structure does not appear on the surface of the islands; and here, although there is a Shield structure on the mainland to an area near the Mackenzie River, it is one often overlain by moraine.[12] Yet a precambrian structure does not simply demarcate at Boothia two Arctics which differ in these ways. Forming at Boothia the Cape Horn of North America, the Shield structure also conceals this fact. For the precambrian spur does not end at Boothia; after a brief mile-wide, canal-like interruption at Bellot Strait it continues northwards for still another two hundred miles, as the western side of Somerset Island. Because Somerset Island could so easily give the impression that it was continuous with Boothia, and Boothia the impression at its narrow isthmus that it was an island, together these two features made the Boothia–Somerset complex the last and largest bar to the discovery of a coastal passage, and a potential death-trap for the navy.

There were two main approaches by deep sea: Baffin Bay and Bering Strait. On the other hand, the northwest route, which had already played an express role further south, could also serve as a path of "first arrival" at the Boothia–Somerset complex. It led not only to the Athabasca region but beyond that by the Mackenzie, Coppermine, and Back Rivers to the Arctic itself. It had, as well, a more "southern exposure" than the deep sea approaches and thus a longer open season. Personnel and communications for polar discovery could enter the Athabasca region by the northwest route; equipment for the same purpose could reach it by Hudson Bay,[13] a traditional transport route. Perhaps Hudson Bay could now play a new role also. Stimulated by naval activity and coastal in its own emphasis, the company was in fact destined soon to identify discovery of the continental shoreline with the finding of a Northwest Passage. In the eighteenth century company exploration had ruled out the possibility of a strait between Hudson Bay and the Pacific.[14] Now, however, both the navy and the company hoped that through Foxe Channel or Basin a route to the Pacific might be found. The company, in short, by the very fact of being coastal in its emphasis, had interests, incentives, and routes which would make it in the new era an agent not simply of secondary but also initial discovery. Boats, its particular craft, were very good in coastal travel; thus its emphasis would place it in a relationship of both competition and cooperation with the navy in Arctic discovery. In short, in arctic exploration there was a sequence of three kinds of routes, inland, coastal, and deep sea, by contrast with the twofold sequence of the earlier period.

Several of the incentives for naval travel in the Arctic and of its potential characteristics found expression in one man. John Barrow (1764–1848) was second secretary of the Admiralty for forty years. He had had as a

younger man technological interests. Possessed of a training in land surveying, he had a long-standing interest in the Office of the Hydrographer.
In younger days a great concern of his had been China, which he had
visited as assistant to Lord Macartney on that diplomat's famous Chinese
mission (1792–94), and he continued to write much upon this country. He
had matured in the eighteenth century when a Northwest Passage to the
Orient in temperate latitudes had still seemed possible. As this hope had
faded there had emerged in him a new illusion: that the Arctic itself was
temperate. He had been there, but only on a summer cruise to Greenland
at the age of eighteen when he had seen no icebergs. Polar travel seemed
heroic to him but in general he underestimated difficulties at sea, and of
the Arctic in particular (it becomes apparent) he took a facile view. Quite
unaware of the archipelago in the North American polar regions, yet at the
same time more averse than others to coastal as compared with deep sea
travel there, Barrow looked at the Arctic more in terms of an easy route to
China than in terms of itself. Over fifty, his attitudes largely formed, a man
of worldwide experience yet of no special practical expertise in North
America's Arctic, of a type to urge battling through a *terra incognita* with
great determination rather than to feel the need for coming to terms with a
new environment, underestimating (as a part of this) hardships in the Arctic, Barrow became in the postwar period an enthusiastic projector of polar
expeditions to find a passage. He advanced a number of the arguments
already enumerated for arctic discovery and was instrumental in launch-
ing voyages for this purpose. Lobbyist and administrator, he acquired the
title of Father of Arctic Exploration.[15]

The first of the expeditions in which Barrow was influential was that of
1818 under the future Sir John Ross (1777–1856). Born and brought up in
the eighteenth century, Ross had served with the East India Company and
had had a colourful career in the navy in the Napoleonic Wars. On this
journey Ross penetrated Baffin Bay and entered Lancaster Sound. There,
however, he turned back when he thought he saw the famous "Croker
Mountains." These proved to be figments of Ross's own imagination and
the event was one which alienated him from Barrow and the Admiralty, so
that Ross's twenty-eight-year-old second-in-command, Edward Parry, now
came to the fore. In 1819–20 Parry extended knowledge of what he himself was to call a broad and magnificent channel[16] westward from Lancaster
Sound through Barrow Strait to Viscount Melville Sound and Melville
Island. He had probably been fortunate in encountering so open a season
on his first voyage;[17] to the end of the nineteenth century only one other
expedition would sail from the Atlantic as far as Parry's Winter Harbour
on Melville Island. The young commander had come close in fact to

M'Clure Strait, one final link of a Northwest Passage; and he could see from Melville Island the "loom of land" of Banks Island to the south, where lay Prince of Wales Strait, a more navigable final link of the same passage. Yet M'Clure Strait was blocked by ice; and such an early success as detecting Prince of Wales Strait was probably precluded to Parry at this time by a lack of capacity so early in arctic discovery for extensive sled travel. Otherwise a Northwest Passage might have been found long before the actual M'Clure–Kellett discovery of 1850–53.

On the other hand, although untrained in sled travel, Parry had great capacity as a marine navigator. Yet this, paradoxically, turned his attention away from deep sea travel towards the continental mainland, for he had shown that progress could be made in the face of polar ice by hugging a shoreline. There in the summer the ice broke up more readily and floated off with the tide, affording a precarious passage to the pilot with skill and daring.[18] On subsequent trips he stayed close to the shoreline of the main-land itself, and he also demonstrated that the western exposures of bodies of land that ran at all north and south were prone to be relatively ice-free. On the first of these trips (1821–23) Parry sought a Northwest Passage through Hudson Strait.[19] Yet, although he wintered twice in the Foxe Channel and Basin area, he could not get through the solidly ice-blocked Fury and Hecla Strait. He was one of the navigators who demonstrated the impassibility of a sea route westward from Hudson Strait itself. The Baffin Bay route was the sole Atlantic entry to the Arctic. On his second coastal attempt (his third expedition, 1824–25) Parry sailed through Baffin Bay and Lancaster Sound to Prince Regent Inlet. Yet once again he seemed to have reached a cul-de-sac; for from that inlet there is no exit to the south save the very narrow Bellot Strait, which Parry did not find. Besides, this was a year in which ice conditions were especially bad. *Fury* was wrecked, its stores cached at Fury Beach on the western shore of the inlet, and the crews of both vessels brought to England in *Hecla*. Once again, however, Parry had approached a crucial area, this time as regards a coastal North-west Passage. In entering Prince Regent Inlet and encountering Somerset Island he had come to the Boothia–Somerset complex, already referred to, which separates the eastern from the western Arctic and is a central obstruction in the arctic maze.

Yet the factor which had driven Parry home was not shipwreck but scurvy. In the twentieth century, partly from the evidence of arctic expeditions of the nineteenth, it has become apparent that this illness is a deficiency of vitamin C resulting from a lack of fresh meat and other fresh foods. It was already well known in the eighteenth century to be connected with a dietary lack and there was considerable knowledge of the proper means for its prevention. Yet in the nineteenth century there was back-sliding. The navy had widely used with good effect the true lemon from Europe and Africa as a substitute for fresh meat and hence as an antiscor-butic, but it had called this true lemon a lime, a semantic imprecision which led to trouble. For in the nineteenth century West Indian limes came to be used as antiscorbutics, even though they do not retain scurvy-preventative elements as effectively as does the true lemon. The fact, how-ever, that both fruits tended to go by the same name meant that the real difference was obscured as the navy made its conversion from one to the other. The change would come especially in the latter part of the nine-teenth century, yet, because of the problem in nomenclature, it is some-times hard to know what form of fruit, the less effective limes or more effective lemons, were by mid-century being given to arctic crews.[20] Lack of fresh meat and defective antiscorbutics were reasons why scurvy might attend any long icing-in of a ship and its crew.

The navy, in short, in its first decade of arctic activity (1818–27) had been to a considerable extent filling the role of "first discoverer." Parry, in particular, had with great rapidity and skill found the extreme limits of open sea travel from the Atlantic. Under him there had been "a miracle of navigation" in handling sailing ships as they twisted and turned through the pack ice at the mercy of winds and ice.[21]

Yet, by comparison with methods of inland and coastal travellers, the navy's deep sea expeditions had used heavy transport. Ross's vessels *Isabella* and *Alexander*, for example, had been 368 and 252 tons with complements of fifty-eight and thirty-seven, respectively. They had been transports chosen for the task of discovery over "Men of War" as being "better adapted to this service ... from their greater capacity for stowage." There had been, too, a wish to strengthen vessels for the Arctic by such means as double planking, deadwood in the bows, and iron plates to sheath them. The expeditions had also had a surveying aspect. A portable astro-nomical observatory, for example, had been set up aboard *Isabella*. Built of wood, of octagonal form with a conical top, watertight, six feet ten inches high, the observatory was "easily turned upon rollers," so that it could be directed "towards any part of the heavens," and it could also be carried ashore. Furthermore, there had been a wish to carry the home environment with the expedition. Naval crews had played cricket with Eskimos on the ice, but had not learned to rely on Eskimo igloos or sleep-ing methods. Instead the vessels were "provided with Deals, Russian Mats, and Tarpaulins for ... building huts on shore," and every man had, in addition, "a bed-cabin, so contrived that each consisted of a separate box which might be taken out and removed on shore should it be found necessary to leave the ships during the winter, and sliding-doors were attached to close them up and increase as much as possible the warmth within." Indeed, in the equipment of the vessels complete attention had been "paid to the comfort and accommodation of both officers and men" so far as "human foresight could suggest, or a liberal Government provide."[22]

Ships in the Arctic, however, were operating in unique circumstances. The only real wonder, Parry had said of the wreck of *Fury*, lay in the fact that such a calamity had not occurred sooner. When it did happen, *Fury* was like a stranded whale, a sea animal forced by reason of all-encompassing pack ice to operate in land or semi-land conditions. He could cope, Parry said as regards detention in the Arctic, with ice that was "fairly in motion ... but ... *hermetical* sealing-up I do not understand."[23] One looks in such circumstances for a sense of amphibiousness. In effect, slowly, this had developed. When iced-in Parry pioneered the use of ships not as direct means of initial discovery but as forward wintering bases from which discoveries could be made by sled. Although at the outset naval uniforms were of standard pattern, more appropriate to Portsmouth than the Arctic[24] (officers even wore top hats as they coasted near arctic shores in ships' boats), nevertheless by the time of Parry's trip to Fury and Hecla Strait polar clothing was improved. By then his men wore long fur-lined "pea-jackets" of blue box-cloth closely woven so as to be almost impervious against wind and rain; and in 1824 Parry experimented with the water-proof material of Macintosh of Glasgow.[25]

These, however, were indications of adaptability as regards European means of travel. As regards indigenous means, Parry had at first represented a very rudimentary stage in arctic travel.[26] He did not take at the outset to the native sledge but carried his supplies, rather, by means of a cart on a trek across Melville Island. Later, it is true, he became the first European to use sledges in the Canadian Arctic as a means of travel, and he acquired on his voyage of 1821–23 dogs from the Eskimos for this purpose.[27] On that voyage Parry also took an interest in handling a kayak; and in 1824 he experimented with pemmican, destined to become a staple of polar travel by the navy. Even so, his land journeys showed only a limited degree of progress. He was not equipped to set out early enough in the year on sled journeys and he lacked, in particular, an economical fuel.[28] Despite some awareness of Eskimo means he and his officers tended to consider that Europeans had a natural superiority for survival.[29] Sailors, M'Clintock would claim, "inured from boyhood to dragging at ropes" were especially capable of heavy haulage,[30] and certainly officers and tars alike under Parry did perform herculean tasks in dragging heavy boats made into sledges across the ice and snow.[31] They had not as yet learned, however, to rely upon the means at hand in the region they explored. Parry, "the beau ideal of an Arctic officer,"[32] and his methods, were well adapted to large-scale group effort at sea but not so well suited to small parties on land or ice and the use of indigenous means. Yet employment of those means was perhaps more urgent as he moved southwards to explore near the main-land. Here the Hudson's Bay Company might prove superior.

Certainly members of the Hudson's Bay Company did feel superior in relation to the chief land explorer of the Royal Navy in this period. Admiralty strategy was to use a land as well as sea approach, and in this regard John Franklin was, like Parry, a "co-operator" attuned to group endeav-our but not necessarily to more solitary travel with a great emphasis upon the local environment. Born in 1786, child of an earnest religious home, a man who impressed all with his honesty, energy, good humour, openness, and ability as a naval officer, Franklin, like many naval men concerned with arctic exploration at this time, had been at Trafalgar. As did other naval officers, he looked upon arctic discovery as a road to promotion in the post-Napoleonic period. He served as a subordinate on an arctic trip from Spitzbergen in 1818, and then entered the North American Arctic as leader of the first of his own expeditions, a land journey to and along the continental coast in 1819–22.[33] Journeying from York Factory with voy-ageurs in boats,[34] his party progressed to Great Slave Lake, went down the Coppermine River to the Arctic and then eastward along the mainland coast to Point Turnagain, arriving there in July 1821. An object of his trip was to aid Parry, then on his journey westward to Melville Island. It was, however, the Franklin party itself which suffered greater privations, due to some extent to trouble between the rival fur companies. Ten of Frank-lin's men were lost in the barrens, and when, much later, he made his last arctic voyage people at home would render a crucial judgment, that he and his party would never choose a retreat from the polar sea by that region. For now, in 1821, the party was reduced to the expedient of literally making soup from their shoes, and after his return Franklin would often be called, "the man who ate his boots."

On his second trip (1825–27), Franklin and his fellow officers reached Fort Cumberland on the Saskatchewan River by Montreal and the tradi-tional northwest route while boats and supplies came through York Factory. Part of the object this time was to explore westward from the Mackenzie delta to Icy Cape, Alaska, where a naval vessel was expected from Bering Strait. Franklin and his men, however, turned back at Return Reef six days before a party of H.M.S. *Blossom* reached Point Barrow by boat. Other members of his party went east to the Coppermine River, discovered Dolphin and Union Strait and part of Victoria Island, and entered Coronation Gulf, from which they returned to Great Bear Lake. Some of the expedition returned to England by Montreal and the rest by York Factory.

Although Franklin and his parties had used as means of travel canoes, sledges, dog teams, and snowshoes, Franklin himself was not a huntsman; he had tried to perpetuate the old environment, or to dominate, not adapt to, the new one;[35] and, in contrast to other arctic commanders in the period 1819–60, he had lost a large number of his men. His methods were the subject of criticism by George Simpson, shortly to become governor of the Hudson's Bay Company's North American territories. Simpson had seen his own men in the days of Franklin's first expedition go for three days without food and had himself travelled for eleven days on little or nothing. When, therefore, an appeal came to him through George Back, midshipman, from the Franklin party at Great Slave Lake for food, supplies, and clothing, because, in the words of the appeal, "Officers (not to mention the men) ... are destitute of the most common articles of Dress, such as Spirits, etc.," Simpson rejected the request. It had come from a party which he thought badly planned and poorly commanded by a man who could not walk more than eight miles a day, who needed his three meals a day, and for whom, "Tea is indispensible [*sic*]."[36]

Yet whatever the feeling about Franklin was in the Northwest, and however much he may have been the author of some of his own difficulties, he nevertheless became a hero to the British public. Fur-trading professionals had experienced hardships in North America for generations, often getting through to their destinations without great disasters or attention. Even when there had been much hardship, as in Sir Alexander Mackenzie's successful feat in reaching the Pacific, attention had not been fully forthcoming at home until some years had passed. Yet now the British public enjoyed hearing of naval amateurs in, for them, strange surroundings. On his return to England after his second land trip Franklin was knighted and Oxford University awarded him an honorary degree. Years later John Rae was to write of Arctic discovery: "The way to get into credit ... is to plan some ... scheme ... and after having signally failed, return with a lot of ... reasons—sufficiently good to gull John Bull—for your failure."[37]

The point is unfair if applied too strictly to Franklin. Nevertheless, Sir John had run into great trouble on the first of his two trips and had not completed his mission on either; and while public acclaim could further arctic discovery, relative unawareness at home of North American conditions might, on the other hand, prove a danger. Yet Franklin's parties had explored a fairly extensive section of the northern coast of North America by way of the northwest and Hudson Bay routes, and this coast was emerging, apparently, as a major part of a Northwest Passage. Franklin's route was propitious even if his methods of travelling it were not.

This cursory examination of the initial period of naval activity leads to a double preliminary conclusion. As long as it could operate in open sea the navy might accomplish initial discovery. When hemmed in by ice or on land, however, its bent was not so much early discernment as to amplify in a methodical manner knowledge of regions already discovered. The navy, with Barrow as an important home figure, was conforming to Parry's own description of himself: it could cope with ice so long as its ships were "fairly in motion," but it did not understand so well "*hermetical* sealing-up," whether by ice in the ocean or out of its own *métier*, on land.

2

Boothia and the Back River
(1829–1835)

Franklin's second expedition ended in 1827. Probably influenced by a decline in Russian arctic ambition, the Admiralty was by that time itself losing interest in polar exploration. In 1828 an Act of Parliament repealed the awards which had formerly been offered for arctic discovery.[1] Nevertheless, Parry's unfinished investigation of Prince Regent Inlet was taken up by private sponsorship using the newest of European techniques, namely, steam. It was hoped that this would expedite discovery of a passage and make it commercially navigable. A privately financed expedition with a small vessel and crew, but led by the naval officer John Ross, entered the Arctic in 1829.

In 1828 Ross had published the first edition of one of the earliest studies on the use of steam at sea, in which he presented among other matters a system of visual signals which would do away with the need for "bawling out" from bridge to engine room.[2] He wrote also upon steam as a means of reaching India, as useful in wartime convoy duty, and as a new factor in tactics in war. Technically, he discussed high pressure engines, the new safety valve, and the difficulties that beset steamers with side paddle-wheels when they were used at sea rather than in fresh water. Behind Ross's technological interest in steam was another incentive. Involved at one time with his brother, George Ross, in a British railway scheme, he was caught up in the promotional and financial fever that came with steam. Now, in ill-favour with the Admiralty because of his earlier arctic trip, he hoped that after three centuries of inconclusive search by sail, steam would at last open a Northwest Passage and thereby his own way to fame and fortune. He had found a sponsor in his friend Felix Booth, a sheriff of London and Middlesex, founder of the Booth distilling firm and the man after whom Boothia Peninsula was soon to be named.[3]

Ross's attempt to use steam in arctic navigation in 1829 was revolutionary. It was not likely to have been attempted at this time under Admiralty auspices, for the navy had but few steamships in 1829. The ship *Victory* which Ross chose to use was a yacht which had been on the Dover–Calais run.[4] The famous Swedish engineer John Ericsson had recently had successes as a designer of boilers, and this attracted the attention of Ross. Ericsson held a joint patent for a new boiler with the manufacturer John Braithwaite of London. Felix Booth knew the partners and introduced Ross to them. Ross asked that they fit his newly acquired *Victory* with steam, but he practised a concealment that was traditional in polar exploration. Wishing to hide his arctic destination from whalermen as well as from Ericsson and Braithwaite, he told the partners that he was engaged in experimentation for war, was "going to fire red hot shot!" and would "require furnaces for the purpose." He continued to conceal *Victory*'s destination until the trials of the engines.[5]

Ross's installation of steam in *Victory* showed a combination of ineptness and foresight. The machinery had "high pressure boilers, surface condensers, forced draft apparatus, and many other novelties."[6] Part of Ross's own description is as follows: "There was no flue; instead of which, the fires were kept in action by bellows, and it was, of course, a high pressure engine, the boilers of which were heated by pipes passing through them in a manner now sufficiently familiar."[7] These bellows themselves became one of the subjects of contention which later arose between Ross and Ericsson. As already indicated the boilers were the part of the Ross machinery specifically supplied by the partners; but a Maudslay engine of two cylinders was also installed to run the side paddle-wheels. Of these and their connection with the engine Ross wrote that the machinery formed "a patent contrivance; and the paddle wheels were so constructed that they could be hoisted out of water in a minute." In favourable navigational circumstances the paddles could be positioned to propel the vessel. If there were ice or heavy seas they could be lifted out of the water. In another innovation Ross tried to cope with the alternating deep dip into and high rise out of the water by the paddle wheels consequent upon the sea's roll. He supplied box-like covering devices over the upper half of either wheel. Here we see Ross's concern, whether he was an engineer or not, with inadequacies of the paddle-wheel at sea. He was coping with one of the problems for which the screw propeller was the answer. Ross's solution, however, particularly drew Ericsson's scorn as showing an absence of even the most rudimentary mechanical sense.[8]

Final preparations were hurried. The engineer assigned to attend the trial of *Victory* and her engines at Limehouse, in order to present a report under Admiralty orders, almost lost his life in the process. *Victory*, indeed, sailed before her engines were thoroughly reliable, and on the voyage an astonishing series of accidents occurred, with Ross entering in his journal bitter comments about the machinery. The vessel under steam power never made more than three miles an hour. Despite the use of dung to keep them from doing so, the boilers leaked; pumps failed; and the engines gave out.[9] It was during these mechanical misadventures that *Victory* sailed down the same Prince Regent Inlet which Parry had entered on his third voyage and came into the Gulf of Boothia. As *Victory* did so, Ross unfortunately failed to notice the one exit leading westwards from this gulf, Bellot Strait, halfway down the Somerset–Boothia complex at its wasp's waist. The strait forms a part of the coastal passage as it is used today. Otherwise, the gulf is a dead end.

Ross had got himself involved in the last major conundrum which the mainland Shield posed. He had made for the first time in these marine voyages (without knowing it for certain) a landfall on the North American mainland. He named it Boothia Felix after his sponsor, and by October 1829 was wintering at Lord Mayor's Bay on its eastern shore. Arctic explorers of the first half of the nineteenth century found that among Eskimos, women especially were cartographers. Basing his decision upon a map in whose drawing an Eskimo woman played an important part, Ross concluded that Boothia was a peninsula, without water connection at its foot to the west.[10] He confirmed this view himself as far south as Lord Mayor's Bay, and considered the evidence of the Eskimo map to be further strengthened by the fact that, according to his calculations, the sea on the east side of Boothia was at a different level from that on the west side of it.

By contrast, Ross's nephew, Comdr. James Clark Ross, RN (1800–62), serving on the expedition under John Ross, had a different idea. Unlike his uncle, James Ross believed that Boothia was an island but, also unlike his uncle, suspected the existence of Bellot Strait. He made as well good use of the time available to the expedition by studying Eskimo dress and igloo-building. He sledged across Boothia Peninsula and crossed the ice to reach Point Victory on the western shore of King William Island, or King William's Land as he calld it, for he thought it likely that it was joined to the mainland. On another sled trip James Ross also reached the north magnetic pole, on 1 June 1831 at Cape Adelaide on Boothia, and built a cairn there to mark the existence "of one of [nature's] great and dark powers."[11]

Upon two important matters, namely, the existence of Bellot Strait and of Boothia Isthmus, the two Rosses, James and John respectively, had come to two accurate and important conclusions. They had also (taken the other way round) come to two wrong ones; and, ironically, it was in due course the wrong conclusion of each Ross, not the right one, which would become most current. Opinion would in the future tend to ignore James Ross's accurate suspicion of a strait in the Brentford Bay region and tend to ignore also John Ross's equally accurate opinion that there was no west-ward outlet from the Gulf of Boothia further south.[12] Upon a third issue, that of whether or not King William's Land was an island or a part of the mainland, the Ross expedition (as John Ross's chart reveals) had tended to come to the wrong conclusion, that it was joined to the mainland both in an eastward direction towards Boothia and also, as James Ross believed, in a westward direction in such a manner as to make the shore at Point Victory on King William's Land continuous with Point Turnagain of Franklin.[13]

Meanwhile the Ross expedition had come to one decision: it had had enough of the steam equipment. Not long after arrival at Lord Mayor's Bay, John Ross had thankfully taken the larger portion of both the engines and boilers out of his vessel, placing the dismantled parts on the ice. "The enemy ... was at last at our feet," he was later to write, adding, "I believe there was not one present ... ever again wished to see, even its minutest fragment."[14] Two years later when *Victory* was finally abandoned at Victoria Harbour other heavy items were left ashore. The ship had become simply a sailing vessel.

A first landfall on the mainland and the discovery of the magnetic pole were accomplishments, but we begin to see emerging a pattern of danger in arctic exploration which was not new. Ships became iced-in so that escape was cut off, leading in consequence to a danger of scurvy. Ross's ship was, in fact, beset in Felix Harbour in the winters of 1829–30 and 1830–31, and the vessel was able to move only slightly in the following summer. By the third winter (1831–32) scurvy had begun to appear amongst Ross's men. In the summer of 1832 the party pulled boats to Fury Beach on North Somerset, as it was then called, where it had access to *Fury* suppiles. Parry's loss of *Fury*, an early premonition of the eventual Franklin dis-aster, was thus being used by Ross to prevent such a disaster to himself. From Fury Beach the party sailed to Lancaster Sound but had to turn back and spend a fourth winter at *Fury*'s cache. In August 1833, in the fourth year of their trip, the party was picked up by the Hull whaler, *Isabella*, in Lancaster Sound, the same vessel in which Ross himself had sailed to the Arctic in 1818. If Ross had been unfortunate in missing Bellot Strait and getting himself beset in a cul-de-sac, he had had what some have con-sidered great good fortune in the way in which things had ultimately turned out. The *Isabella* brought the missing party back to England and Ross, who had spent four years in the Arctic without loss of life to his party, was knighted; he and his men were granted a £5,000 prize.

It is easy to understand Ross's anger at the failure of the first use of steam in the Arctic, and no doubt it was only human to blame the misfortune upon Braithwaite and Ericsson. In a famous pamphlet duel which almost became one of actual weapons, he and Ericsson laid charge and countercharge. Yet, though the story of *Victory* does not appear to be to the credit of either Ross or Ericsson, *Victory*'s machinery had in fact contained the germs of many improvements in marine steam which were later brought to perfection.[15] However, although the experiment had brought Ross to the last barrier which the mainland Shield interposed, it had not got him round or through the barrier. The experiment had not solved the question of a Northwest Passage. On the other hand, an element in Ross's story did stand out. Though advanced in technology by naval standards, Ross's party had been very much a light one. *Victory* had been small, only 150 tons all found, and her tender *Krusenstern* had been only 16 tons, by comparison with Parry's vessels *Fury* and *Hecla* which had been 375 tons each. Ross's party had also been few in number, twenty-four, by comparison with complements ranging round sixty each on successive voyages of *Fury* and *Hecla*.[16] The party had certainly not been one of full naval organization; yet this had not hindered a successful use of *Victory* as an advance base for further discovery and some use by James Ross of indigenous means of travel. The Ross party had stimulated, finally, its own antithesis: an approach to the central part of the North American Arctic by land.

When the Ross expedition had been in difficulties a party was sent to rescue it by the Back River. Like the Mackenzie and Coppermine Rivers, the Back is an extension of the Northwest route. It had been suspected since the days of Hearne but was as yet undiscovered. The expedition that now went down the river was a private one, though a government grant was the largest single contribution to its total funds of £5,000. Money came from many contributors and the Hudson's Bay Company donated food and canoes. The party was a consequence of concern by George Ross, father of James Ross, for the safety of his son. It was an early example of the paradoxical fact that in arctic discovery the humanitarian aim to find a lost expedition might be a much stronger incentive to explore than was exploration itself. Officially, orders were given to the expedition by Lord Goderich at the Colonial Office on 4 February 1833; in fact, as was often the case, the instructions had been written by the party leader himself.[17]

This was Capt. George Back (1796–1878) who had entered the navy as a midshipman at the age of twelve, seen action against the French in northern Spain, and spent the years 1809–14 as a prisoner-of-war. He had served with Franklin on the voyage from Spitzbergen in 1818, and under him as his subordinate on both Franklin's land expeditions. Present, as part of this service, with Franklin at his furthest east at Point Turnagain, Back had like his commander gained a hero's reputation through his northern travels. Socially very active, something of a Georgian dandy, possessed of a capacity for descriptive writing and, like a number of other naval "Arctics," of marked talent as an artist, Back had learnt to paint while a prisoner-of-war, and had improved this capacity by further study in Italy in the years after service with Franklin.

Just as smallness in matters of craft and the size of a party could prove an asset in the exploration of the Canadian Arctic, so too, perhaps, could a small physique. Back had commented at the outset of a journey in 1820 from Cumberland House to Fort Chipewyan that Franklin had "never been accustomed to any vigorous exertion" and besides, "his frame is bulky."[18] Back by contrast was of such small stature (perhaps five feet or even less) as to have been carried in a pannier on a sumpter mule across the Pyrenees when a prisoner-of-war, and on his northern travels his snowshoes were only three feet long by comparison with a usual length of four to six feet.[19] Perhaps physical smallness was an asset to Back as an explorer. There was also another factor. Under Franklin the navy's attitude in the strange surroundings of land exploration had been overly rigid. Perhaps in social relations Back went too far the other way. He "was popular with all sorts of natives and half-breeds, with whom he talked easily in their various patois." This marked affability and familiarity have been criticized as detrimental to command; on occasion he had trouble with morale. Yet it has also been said of Back that there was in him a contrast between a pleasant appearance and an underlying hard reality. It seems that Back, "courageous and persevering in urgent and demanding situations," was at other times vain and self-indulgent.[20]

A naval man, now aged thirty-seven, Back had with him a contrasting subordinate. Richard King, a central figure in this study, was a 23-year-old civilian who had recently qualified as a surgeon. The only other "officer" or leader of the Back party, chosen from a wide range of applicants as surgeon-naturalist to the expedition, the young doctor had been, if anything, over-eager as a candidate. Although paid a salary, he had volunteered at first to go on the expedition without remuneration, and when selected was elated at the opportunity to save lives in the Arctic.[21] Born in 1810, he was the son of another Richard King, of Pimlico, employed at the Ordnance Office in the Tower of London. In 1820 at the age of nine the junior King was enrolled at St. Paul's School in London. His father, however, had destined him for a medical career and from August 1824 he served a seven-year apprenticeship with the Society of Apothecaries in

Lower Grosvenor Street, qualifying for the Licentiate of the society in April 1832. By this time King had also had nine months as a student probationer at Guy's Hospital in London and soon afterward qualified there, becoming a member shortly of the Royal College of Surgeons.[22]

From his reading even before he arrived with the Back party in North America, King had already come to suspect that the best way to discover a Northwest Passage was by land. Early in the trip he placed himself self-consciously in the tradition of fur-trade travel, emphasizing small land parties and the means of journeying of North America's indigenous peoples. Naturalist under Back as well as surgeon, he studied not only the flora and fauna but the weather and other aspects of the continent. Upon his return he wrote the botanical and meteorological appendices to Back's *Narrative* and reported in his own *Narrative* a great deal about the physical environment and the Indians and Eskimos of North America; he also became a co-founder of the British Ethnological Society. He believed that a medical training was an important asset in exploratory travel in the Arctic, and he was "hailed with delight" on his trip for his healing ministrations. Thus, while Richard King stressed fur-trade methods of travel and knowledge of North America's environment and peoples, he brought to bear upon these the developing empirical approach of the natural scientist and a growing humaneness that belonged to his own century.[23]

King has been described as "a fine looking fellow," "resolute," and "just the man for such a task" as leading an expedition up and down the Back River. Indeed, although he was only second-in-command and new in the North, he early showed a tendency to attempt himself to decide upon a route for the Back party. Besides impetuosity, self-confidence or egoism was a part of his personality. He could on occasion speak in so rapid and clipped a way as to be difficult to understand, and his arctic writings show that he could be rudely blunt. In spite of these characteristics (perhaps because of them) he appears to have got on well with the men he led.[24]

The barren lands, or "Barren Ground" as Hearne called it, through which the Back River flows, is a "triangular-shaped area of the continental mainland" lying "west of Hudson Bay, south of the Arctic coast, and north of treeline." A "gently rolling plain developed on the precambrian Shield but with bedrock often deeply buried" beneath rocks brought down by glaciers, the territory has to this day "an aura of romanticism and mystery." To those, nevertheless, who were willing to accept hardship and respectful of the difficulties, the barrens were not necessarily the horror they had been depicted. Whoever, it has been said, called the tundra of this region the barren lands "could not have been an ornithologist, botanist, entomologist, or naturalist at all"; "even a dendrologist would [find] something of interest in the dwarf trees." The lands, that is, are not really barren; instead of grass, there are lichens on the rock and on the stony surface, while along the banks of streams are spruce and larch of stunted growth, except along the Back River whose banks are treeless.[25]

Certainly from Hearne in the 1770s to Anderson in 1855 the evidence is impressive. The former described the Back River as flowing through a country abounding in animals. The Back party itself saw on its journey down the Great Fish River thousands of reindeer and many musk-oxen, and Simpson found an abundance of reindeer, musk-ox, salmon, and seals at its mouth. Both Back and Anderson reported flocks of geese along the river and in a shallow bay in Lake Aylmer, Anderson was to find "a whole shoal of splendid salmon trout" of which "three or four were captured by the men with their hands."[26] Although the annual precipitation in the barrens is low, so too is the rate of evaporation, and there are ponds and lakes "in great profusion." In the summertime there arise swarms of mosquitoes and black flies, making travel especially unpleasant. The general elevation of the area is about 1,200–1,300 feet. There arise within a short distance of each other the three main rivers of the region, the Coppermine, the Thelon, and the Back which is "the largest river contained entirely within" the barrens. The distinctive feature of the region is certainly not that it is lifeless but that, as both Indian and Eskimo names for it indicate, it is treeless. It was this aspect which had given the area a particularly formidable reputation. Furthermore, Indians shunned it because this was a region where they might encounter their enemies, the Eskimos.[27] Indians spoke also in strong terms against going down the Back or the Great Fish River, by contrast with a trip down the Fish or Thelon River, and tended thus to avert attention from the former. Finally, while the barrens did not lack fur-bearing animals, the Hudson's Bay Company also shunned the region because it was destitute of wood.

Without doubt to this country, if to any, light-party techniques were appropriate. Yet the Back expedition was by later standards elaborate. Composed of twenty members, it was not only a large but a mixed expedition in manner of recruitment and organization. Just as Back and King were respectively a serviceman and a civilian, so the crewmen included Woolwich naval yard carpenters, Royal Artillerymen, and voyageurs and others of the Hudson's Bay Company. The party also had a variety of craft. For the trip inland there were two bateaux and two canoes, the latter taken apparently in consequence of advice by Sir John Richardson (1787–1865), the naval medical officer who was Franklin's brother-in-law and had served as second-in-command on his two land journeys.[28]

With Back ahead by canoe, making arrangements for the expedition and King bringing up the rear in charge of transport in the bateaux, the travellers arrived from Montreal at Lake Athabasca by way of the usual northwest route and then went down the Slave River to Great Slave Lake. At the eastern end of the lake, reached by Back in August, Fort Reliance was built as a wintering quarters, probably according to a plan by Back but under the active leadership of Chief Trader Alexander McLeod. Designated by George Simpson as the company man most fitted to help the Back party and promised early promotion to a chief factorship if he undertook to do so, McLeod hunted for the expedition as well as constructing the winter establishment. "To his indefatigable exertions and extraordinary activity," in King's view, was "to be attributed," so far as it occurred, "the ... success of the expedition." King himself did not reach the new post until 16 September when, Back found, despite King's "inexperience in the country" he had brought in "his heavy cargo in a very good state of preservation."[29]

Associated as he had been with Back yet seeing his commander often go ahead by canoe, Richard King had become by this time an advocate of canoes in contrast to boats. Despite one inconvenient experience when he had fallen behind while he himself was using a canoe (an occurrence he did not consider typical), the young surgeon had come to the conclusion that travel by the native craft was faster than by boat, chiefly because one could portage canoes much more easily. Now King was also a believer in the small, light, and civilian party in contrast to the large, service type. And he showed as well his wish, already referred to, to give direction himself to the party. For he had heard of an alternative wintering site and route (as he regarded it) to the Arctic, namely the Fish River, or Thelon as it is known today.[30]

The Back or Great Fish River has its headwaters to the north and east of Great Slave Lake. For 300 miles it follows a course generally eastward and then, after a sharp turn, flows north a final 150 miles to the Arctic. The Thelon or Fish River, for its part, flows eastwards from a region east of Great Slave Lake and runs generally parallel with the Back for 300 miles. Unlike the Back, however, the Thelon continues eastwards until it enters Hudson Bay at Chesterfield Inlet. It is less tumultuous than the Back and, although it too lies beyond the general tree line, it nevertheless has wooded banks on part of its middle and upper reaches, within what is today the Thelon Game Sanctuary. The Thelon also has wild life, whereas at Fort Reliance at the eastern end of Great Slave Lake, where Back wintered, conditions in the winter of 1833–34 were those of starvation. What meat the Back party did obtain in fact came from the Thelon. That region, King argued, would have afforded better provisions than Fort Reliance; wintering in it would have saved the food consumed in transporting game from the Thelon to Back's headquarters, a march of five days each way. Besides, a lake whence the Thelon River was said to take its rise might, King said, have afforded the expedition an ample fishery. In addition, he also claimed, the Copper Indians remained in the winter of 1833–34 in one group at Fort Reliance, to Back's detriment. The Chipewyans, by contrast, wintered in small separate groups, some in the Thelon region, where they were better able to survive and would have been a help rather than a drain upon the Back party. Had the Thelon been the wintering area, in the early summer of 1834 the boat "would have been launched at once ... and the laborious duty of travelling over two hundred miles of ice [from Artillery Lake near Fort Reliance to the Back River] ... which ... occupied four weeks, would thus have been saved."[31]

Yet there was a flaw in one aspect of King's view. The long parallel courses of the two rivers and native reports that both of them entered salt water where there were Eskimos gave to King the mistaken notion that the Thelon as well as the Back flowed into the Arctic Ocean, not Chesterfield Inlet. It was an idea in which he persisted for many years, holding that the Thelon joined the polar sea to the east of Boothia just as the Back did to the west. It is hard to discern in this connection whether in the spring of 1834 he would have liked the whole of the Back party to go all the way to the Arctic by way of the Thelon. Without doubt, however, he at least regretted that the Thelon was not used as a subsidiary route by which an extra party might aid a main one. Back, too, had heard accounts of the Thelon route. Before leaving England he had read a paper on his proposed travels and he felt now that an account of wooded territory and moose along the Thelon argued a distinctly more southerly course for it than for the Back. He judged, rightly, that the Thelon flowed into Hudson Bay, and so decided that he would adhere to his "original plan" of employing the Back. King's advocacy of the other river must, however, have added at this time to Back's many concerns.[32]

This matter determined, Back scouted ahead from Fort Reliance in search of the headwaters of the Great Fish River. He did so in August 1833 in a half-sized canoe which was both lighter to carry and in other respects more convenient than a larger one for the shoal streams he expected to encounter. The outward foray, primarily north but a little to the east, was completed in August and the return made by the early part of September. The veteran explorer had found that by way of three lakes—Artillery, Clinton-Colden, and Aylmer—one could reach the headwaters of the Great

Fish River. Returning to Great Slave Lake, Back joined Chief Trader Alexander McLeod of the Hudson's Bay Company at the new site at Fort Reliance, where McLeod was contructing the winter quarters. The buildings were of an elaborate nature, including as they did an observatory, a large structure with a "spacious hall" for the Indians, and separate rooms, apparently, for Back, King, and McLeod; in addition, there were houses for the men. According to King the main building or "mansion" was too large, and the establishment as a whole too difficult to keep warm.[33]

Because of ice in Hudson Strait during the difficult winter of 1833–34, Back's letters could not reach England by Hudson Bay and had to go out instead by Canada. It was by the same northwest route that in the spring of 1834 there were brought to Back, with express service speed, news that John Ross and his party had been rescued, Ross's chart, and a further set of instructions. At the time of Back's preparations in England, Sir John Richardson had written of an Indian report that there was "a Peninsula projecting far to the North" from the coast of the Arctic where Back was going; but this information must have been disregarded, for where the party had "expected to find water," they were now surprised to discern, in Ross's chart, land, "under the appellation of Boothia Felix."[34]

The new instructions directed Back to turn his "whole attention" to the task of "completing the coast line of the North-eastern extremity of America." A difficulty was, however, that the Arctic Land Committee in London accepted James Ross's belief that King William's Land was a part of the mainland both to the east, in the Boothia direction, and also to the west towards Point Turnagain. The committee thus felt that to join Point Turnagain of Franklin with Point Victory of James Ross was all that was needed to complete discovery of the continental coastline. It was for this reason that it neglected, in its instructions to Back, the very area east of Point Victory which had been explored by the Rosses but inadequately, and which therefore still needed clarification. For in that very region there did in fact lie, unknown to the committee, proof of two key features, the insularity of King William's Land and the peninsularity of Boothia, which, taken together, made Boothia the projecting "Cape Horn" of the continent and its west coast the final link in a passage. Thus, failing to recognize this incompleteness, the committee concentrated in its instructions upon what lay to the west of Point Victory rather than to the east of it.[35]

There is a contrast between the speed with which word of the Ross party and the new instructions had come to Back and the slow start of Back himself in 1834. His party did not leave its quarters at Fort Reliance until early June. This was because boatbuilding for Back's party, done at the western shore of Artillery Lake some days' march from Fort Reliance, was not started until late February. Back's Woolwich-trained carpenters were not used to building coastal craft and the very idea of carrying a boat was new to Back who in descending to the Arctic used, in any event, only one of the two craft built for him. This was a consequence, he says, of the fact that the expedition had now ceased to be a rescue mission and become purely exploratory. King says, however, that the reason was that the expedition was unexpectedly short of food, as a result particularly of the winter hunting trips to the Thelon and the large-scale efforts of the woodcutters at Fort Reliance to keep Back's stockade-like winter quarters warm. There was, King says, only enough pemmican for eight men (additional to Back and King) to go down the river.[36] In any event, in an action very indicative of his own emphasis, Back chose the heavier of the two craft available to him.

Thirty feet in overall length with a twenty-four-foot keel, this boat weighed a long ton and a half, exclusive of masts, sails, and other accoutrements. The lower part of the vessel was carvel-built, so as to eliminate overlapping edges which would strike against stones or sunken rocks in rapids, and to facilitate repairs in the event of accident, a precaution especially important because the carpenters would not accompany the boat on its journey. The upper part of the vessel was clinker-built. The complement consisted, in addition to Back and King, of two half-breeds, two Highlanders, and an Orkneyman, all from the company, and three of the Royal Artillerymen. Yet, because of its weight, these men were quite incapable of portaging the boat; instead, it had to be run or lowered down many dangerous rapids and reached the Arctic in a damaged condition. At the single place on the Back River where it was absolutely necessary to carry the vessel, a friendly tribe of Indians "most fortunately situated" supplied the vital help needed. At a crucial point on the shores of the Arctic itself, however, where a portage was also essential, similar Eskimo help was not forthcoming, for a reason referred to below. Had there been Eskimo help at this hindrance, King claims, the party would have had it "most decidedly in our power" to finish the exploration. Purportedly built for both river and ocean travel yet not really equipped to reach the Arctic or once there be dragged over ice along the shore, Back's boat was in fact too heavy for either of its tasks. Although the total of ten occupants formed a light party, that, ironically, was just what was not appropriate in the circumstances. Now, with a boat too big in any event, there was as well a party too small to carry it.[37]

Yet the fact that only one portage was absolutely necessary along the Back argues that the difficulties of that river have been overstated. Concerning it, Back himself has written a well-known passage. The stream, he says, is

"broken into falls, cascades, and rapids to the number of . . . eighty-three."
It reaches the Arctic, "after a violent and tortuous course of five hundred
and thirty geographical miles, running through an iron ribbed country,
without a single tree on the whole line of its banks." The large lakes into
which the river expanded had, Back claims, "clear horizons, most embar-
rassing to the navigator." Further exploration by the river "would be as
rash as its results would be fruitless."[38]

Richard King, by contrast, found the barrens to his liking. "In preventing the growth of trees Nature has indeed deprived these parts of their
softest beauties," he wrote. Nevertheless in that country the "gigantic
features . . . amply repay the loss of the pleasant feelings arising from
[trees] . . . by calling forth emotions of a far higher order."[39]

The river, King also said, was "by no means so formidable" as it had
been represented. He certainly did wish in the future to avoid as much as
possible its rapids and cascades, especially those on its upper reaches. Yet
there was only the one portage, already referred to, and on much of its way
to the sea the river "coursed its meandering way" through "luxuriant
plains" which gave food and security "to vast herds of ruminating animals." The men performed well; King had a rapport with them. In sum,
physical difficulties were less than Indian predictions had suggested, and,
despite some earlier warnings, the Eskimos proved on the whole peaceful,
as Sir John Richardson had predicted.[40]

Having arrived by the end of July at the complicated mouth of the Back
(Chantrey Inlet), Back at first expected to link this quickly with Point
Turnagain. Yet he soon became aware that he was in a long inlet of salt
water where there was much ice. Working its way along the western shore
of the inlet the party found it very flat. Looking across, however, at the
inlet's eastern shore, Back saw there a chain, "bold and mountainous."
He had encountered the mainland Shield base from which there projects
the Boothia–Somerset spur, forming in all the remarkable coastline that
stretches northwards from where Back stood for nearly 450 miles, with its
sole interruption at the very narrow Bellot Strait. Yet Back thought this
shore ended within sixteen miles. The chain, he concluded, terminated "in
a . . . huge projecting cape" which he named Cape Hay.[41]

The party continued to work its way along the flat western shore of the
inlet past Montreal Island to Point Ogle, the shore's northern extremity.
Here the expedition was stopped by ice from taking the boat westward. A
further attempt to proceed in the same westward direction by dragging the
craft across a sandy neck also failed when Back found himself again
blocked by ice in Barrow Inlet. From a vantage spot near Point Ogle
(Mount Barrow) Back observed two features, King William's Land on the

north side and an island on the south side of what Back correctly discerned to be a channel westward, namely Simpson Strait. From Mount Barrow Back also looked to the northeast where he saw "a vast stretch of water and ice" and beyond this "a water sky," gray and considered to indicate open sea.[42]

Observing Cape Hay, as he now did for the second time, Back felt that at it the mainland indeed "rounded suddenly off ... to the southward and eastward." Had there been more land running northward from the cape, he would now, he said, have seen it. In fact he did see land to the north but misjudged it to be separated from the continent and gave it the name Ripon Island. Later Thomas Simpson would prove this to be another main-land cape and would rename it Cape Britannia. Back, however, was all the more sure of a channel eastward because he also mistook what lay to the north and northeast. Ross's chart supported, in Back's view, Back's own feeling that in those directions a single island was formed by King Wil-liam's Land and Boothia. As in Simpson Strait to the west, so also to the east there was, in Back's judgment, a waterway: not the actual one of Rae Strait that led northeast and then along the western shore of Boothia, but an illusory one which, passing as Back believed to the south of Boothia, led to the Gulf of Boothia and Sir John Ross's machinery. There were, Back wrote, "strong inferences" in favour of such a channel; and, he added, had "it ... been our duty to follow the eastern rather than the western passage, there seemed no obstacle to prevent our doing so."[43]

Yet, ironically, the revised instructions (concerned as they were with what lay to the west) were silent in any specific sense about going eastward; as regards that direction there were at most only the very general preamble that Back should complete the coastline of the northeastern extremity of America and (if one went back to the original orders of 4 February 1833) the instruction that Back should direct his attention to "mapping what yet remains unknown of the coasts" which he would visit. Convinced as he was, Back evidently believed that this preamble and the original instruc-tion had no eastward import, in the situation in which he now found himself; and he disregarded as well the Eskimo claim that Boothia was peninsular, now embodied in Sir John Ross's chart, a view essentially the same as that of the Indian report that there was "a Peninsula projecting far to the North." Instead, Back would write after his return to England that he would not attempt to describe his feelings at finding he was "baffled in every quarter but the one with which (however interesting as regards the trending of the land)" he had no concern.[44] Thus he did not investigate and at the same time misconstrued what would thereby prove, in due course, the last and most inaccessible shoreline in the discovery of a coastal passage.

Had King possessed a marine rather than a landsman's point of view, had he been a serviceman more used to subordination, and had he been older and less enthusiastic, he might have seen (figuratively and literally) more eye to eye with Back. On 11 August, with a telescope from Mount Barrow, he too accurately assessed the existence of Simpson Strait. However, at an age (twenty-four) when one's eyesight is normally good, King also "distinctly saw" from Point Ogle "land far to the north of Cape Hay." From it, he states, "the land blue in the distance trended north-north-east." He rightly surmised that what Back had named "Ripon Island" was part of a mainland that we know includes Boothia, and he would write later of Back's "optical illusion." King reported to Back his assessment, and Back sent three men with telescope and compass for their opinions. However, while two of these men agreed with King, one did not; and the men allegedly became involved in an affray with Eskimos. Hitherto these had proved quiet; but now three of them were killed, according to information of which King was apprized only after his return to England. It was an incident which arose, King felt, through a misconception between the men and the natives, and he believed it would not have happened had the men been accompanied by either King or Back. As it was, while Back's opinion of the trending of the land remained unchanged, coastal Eskimos, King avers, henceforth out of fear allowed themselves to be seen only at a great distance from the Back party. Most deplorable in itself, the loss of life was, in addition, King claims, the reason why Eskimos were not available to Back and his party at the crucial portage referred to above, which was thus of necessity forgone; it was also the reason, he says, why the men disagreed amongst themselves as to what they had seen from Mount Barrow.[45]

A coast in the direction of Boothia running north and south as King's observation tended to suggest, bore directly upon the question of a Northwest Passage. At home, Richardson had suggested leaving the arctic coast as late as September, and King believed the party should have remained in the region where it was a short time longer; he would criticize later the setting by officialdom of too rigid return dates. Apparently he urged Back to investigate eastward; it would have required, he wrote later, no more than a trip of 116 miles—one day's sail or two days' rowing—to have examined at this time the insularity or otherwise of Boothia. Such a journey, carrying Back's party to Rae Strait, might, it is true, have refuted and clarified Ross's chart in a manner indicating that Boothia's western coast was the last link in a passage. Back, however, had been ordered to commence his return between 12 and 20 August, and had been cautioned against endangering the lives of his men. In addition, through a combination, perhaps, of bad weather, indecision, the shooting affray (which King says much depressed the men, although he admits he himself did not notice the depression at the time), and differences between Back and King, the morale of the men was now as poor as their health. The commander concluded that there was nothing further to investigate and that the time was ripe for retreat, for which the party was assembled on 15 August. Already King had left at Montreal Island in Chantrey Inlet near the foot of the Back a cache as a marker and as food preparatory to another trip down the river.[46]

On the return the Back party saw, far up the river at Lake Garry, seventy or eighty Eskimos with only four kayaks. Because this was a very small number of vessels for so large a party, King felt that the Eskimos had arrived from the sea by a short overland trip; and from this he deduced that there was likely to be a deep bay on the arctic coast reaching southwards towards Lake Garry, in the manner of Bathurst Inlet but to the east of it. Continuing up the river the party wintered in 1834–35 at Fort Reliance and, much to King's disappointment, set out for England in the summer of 1835. Back left King to conduct the party home while he himself, once more by canoe, hurried on ahead by way of Montreal to reach Liverpool on 8 September. King reports of his own return trip that he was not likely to forget "the transport of the baggage across Great Slave Lake and the boat over Portage la Loche." On 20 September 1835 King sailed with eight other members of the expedition from York Factory in the Hudson's Bay Company vessel *Prince Rupert*, and he reached London on 28 October. The St. Lawrence route had, once again, performed the function of rapid communication while the Hudson Bay route had provided a transport service.[47]

The Back River expedition had given one more point of reference on the arctic coastline and had tended, in Back's and King's discernment of a channel at Simpson Strait, to refute James Ross's feeling that King William's Land was joined to the mainland in the direction of Point Turnagain. The Back party had also provided a map of the difficult Great Fish River. It was "really a shame to the Hudson's Bay Company," Thomas Simpson said, that the company "knew nothing of this river till Back came to find it for them." Above all, the descent and ascent had been accomplished; this route to Boothia was now a known one, demonstrating, at least to King, that the Back River gave the most ready access to the Boothia region. "It must be apparent to all persons," he wrote later, "that the Isthmus of Boothia cannot be approached more readily than by the [Back River, as there] ... the difficulties to be contended with are known, with the exception only of two or three days' march beyond the limit of our late expedition."[48]

He was also convinced of the paramount importance of the Boothia region in delineation of the final link in a passage, through the discovery there of one or another set of features.

3

Boothia Remains Elusive (1836–1844)

Besides contributing to the scientific appendix to Back's *Narrative*, King also wrote his own account of the Back River trip.[1] Not only does his work show that strong interest in means of travel, geography, natural history, and native peoples already referred to; parts of King's book may be described as good-humoured and amusing. Yet he also now made public his criticism of Back. He was quite sure by this time that the query as to whether Boothia was an island or peninsula was itself the question of a passage. Indeed, because this was so and because Back and Ross differed upon this important matter, "neither of them should be employed to settle the point."[2]

King had placed his cache at Montreal Island in preparation for a future expedition. After Back had said he did not intend to return to the Back River, King envisaged a party of his own. From the time he reached England he studied mathematics and navigation, and when James Ross planned to rescue whalers beset in Baffin Bay King attempted to join him. He hoped to reach York Factory in Hudson Bay and thence the Back River, but the Admiralty referred King to Ross who turned him down. King tried to bring to public attention the plan he had formulated "in the Indian country," but was unsuccessful in getting Colonial Office assistance. He produced for the project a copy of a map drawn by a métis, advanced his plan in his *Narrative*, and had printed 500 pamphlets which "were most extensively distributed throughout the country." At the same time King opened a public subscription for £1,000, the amount he felt he required for his project. His proposal "was no sooner made public" than he "was congratulated on the certainty of so small a sum being immediately provided." He was, he said, "assisted by a few sincere friends," the chief of whom was Dr. Hodgkin, discoverer of Hodgkin's disease, a member of the Royal Geographical Society, perhaps a former teacher of King at Guy's Hospital, and shortly to be a co-founder with him of the Ethnological Society. Among the subscribers was the famous Dr. Michael Faraday.[3]

Save for facts brought to its notice the press would have remained dormant as regards King's project. He protested early in 1836 against criticism of his plan in *The Times* and the *Naval and Military Gazette* without investigation, rather than on real demerits. He won over the editor of the latter, Sir John Philpot, and he obtained backing as well from what he described as several other influential newspapers, "in particular the Sun, Atlas, ... and Leeds Mercury." The *Naval and Military Gazette* had stressed the fitness of James Clark Ross to complete the discovery of a Northwest Passage. King disputed the capacity of a naval officer for the project. The Back party, he wrote to Sir John Philpot, had "consisted of two officers only, yet the quantity of baggage and necessaries was sufficiently considerable to cause a failure." The "number of persons forming the land Expeditions," King wrote, had "been a source of great error; experience having shown the larger the party the less the change of success." King felt strongly that it was necessary to have a leader who had a knowledge of ascending and descending rapids, of portaging, trading with Indians, and of canoe and sledge travel. This was knowledge, he said, that only a person who had experience in the interior of North America could possess. The leader of a further survey of the North American coast "should comprise within himself Commander, Medical Officer and Naturalist." It would be madness to go "through the inhospitable regions of the North" without a medical officer.[4]

Meanwhile a committee of the Geographical Society was established to examine proposals for further exploration for a Northwest Passage and of the north coast of North America. The society published individual proposals for a future polar expedition from five naval "Arctics": Barrow, Franklin, Richardson, John Ross, and Sir Francis Beaufort, hydrographer of the navy. Barrow was president of the Geographical Society and King described in person to him the route he proposed, and also applied for society support in a written paper. As no notice was taken of his application, "Dr. Hodgkin, as a member of that body kindly undertook to address its committee" on King's behalf.[5] King proposed a land expedition that would travel from Montreal to Fond du Lac at the eastern end of Lake Athabasca. From this King would pass due north with an Indian guide and, by a chain of small lakes and portages well known to the Chipewyans, reach the Thelon

River. Here he would winter because not far from the source of the Thelon there was said to take its rise a tributary to the Back River, most likely Baillie's River, which was said to "disembogue" into the Back below Musk-Ox Rapid. Early in the spring King's party would proceed down this to the Back itself. Thus his party would avoid 200 miles of lake and river which the Back party had travelled on the ice before its boat was even launched, and King in consequence would reach the coast a month earlier than Back. Having ascended Chantrey Inlet to Cape Hay, King's party would coast along until the Isthmus of Boothia was either met with or proved not to exist, and the problem of a Northwest Passage in the Boothia–Somerset region settled. As already stated, King said that his was the most accessible route and the one which gave ample time, because it was known for almost its entire extent. Claiming that sea expeditions had often been unsuccessful or risky, he predicted that it was to land travel that England would "in all probability be indebted for the survey of the coast now unexplored, and for the knowledge of any Passage about Prince Regent Inlet."[6]

Not only did King argue for a land expedition but for one of a small party and civilian type, composed of a leader and six men and using canoes. This was in contrast to the service type of land party of twenty or more men and officers. The latter, King's argument ran, needed boats, which were too easily damaged and too cumbersome for portage. Its members would be inexperienced, too numerous to feed from the land, and time, "the most important element in northern travel" would inevitably be lost. These were not theoretical views but facts "proved by fearful experience." The canoe and the small party had numerous precedents in their favour. Hearne and Mackenzie had made their discoveries by these means. The canoe had also been used by Franklin, to survey from the Coppermine to Point Turnagain. This was a spot which, King pointed out, had not again been reached with heavier craft, even though two parties had sailed from England, one at great expense.[7]

The party, said King, should use native and fur-trade means of subsistence, and should cultivate good relations with the natives. The spot chosen for wintering should not only be close to the summer season's work but provide the best conditions for the health of the party. The leader should have a capacity "for doing and suffering" united with talents for science. Land parties were inexpensive, Mackenzie and Hearne having already accomplished much at very trifling cost. It was not the size of a northern expedition nor the money spent upon it that was the criterion of success but the skill and experience of the leader.[8]

There was, in fact, a strong bar to the acceptance of King's plan. Back was a founding and for many years a governing member, and also a gold medallist, of the Geographical Society to which King was appealing for sponsorship. Most of the other leading men of the Geographical Society at this time were also naval men, whereas King, a landsman and civilian, was not even a member of the society. The attitude of Back and other naval "Arctics" seems to have been that King was a very commendable surgeon and a naturalist and as such had nothing to do with naval operations or, that is to say, exploration; certainly Back viewed King as a tyro, a green-horn in the North.[9]

Besides a clash of land and sea points of view, and of civilian and serviceman, this was also one of youth and age. With a tact which King himself would probably not have shown, his mentor, Dr. Hodgkin, gently suggested to the Geographical Society that Back and his contemporaries had now earned their laurels and should yield the arena to younger men. Another clash of youth and age involved the second secretary of the Admiralty. Now knighted, Sir John Barrow was seventy-two, and the criticism was already heard that he had been too long in his naval post.[10] King, twenty-five years of age, a man who knew and seemed to have an affinity for the barrens, who had a newer kind of scientific training than Barrow, and who did not have the same eighteenth-century attitude towards the Northwest Passage as Barrow, was stressing a passage which might be of doubtful interest or use to the navy. If King was right there was an implied refutation of the kind of navigable passage the navy had hoped for.

Ironically, it was Franklin himself, whose later disaster might have been forestalled by King's plan, who was the instrument by which it was turned down. Asked by the Geographical Society to comment, Franklin said that the plan was based on information that was not new, relied on Indian testimony, was too meagre in detail, and would entail "the acknowledged difficulties" of "travelling the barren grounds for nearly 300 miles."[11] The Thelon, he said, did not flow northward, as King imagined, but eastward into Hudson Bay. Franklin did not see, moreover, how King could winter on the Thelon as that part of the country was destitute of wood, nor was it likely to yield fish for a winter's supply. If King got to his proposed wintering place early in the autumn, before the caribou left, he might be able to kill a sufficient number for wintering, but this was improbable. Finally, the only ultimate aim of the proposed expedition was evidently to find out whether beyond Cape Hay "the isthmus of Boothia" existed or not. He felt the plan should be turned down.

The Geographical Society did not even acknowledge King's plan, and only long afterwards did King see Franklin's strictures and reply to them. Conciseness, King then said regarding Franklin's claim that the plan was too meagre, should apply to arctic writing no less than arctic travel. Indian testimony, King said, was of a very high order; in Back's *Narrative* the Thelon was clearly stated to be known to fur traders; the whole route from Lake Athabasca to the Thelon region was not through treeless barrens; on the contrary, both it and the wintering area were well wooded, as Back's own *Narrative* indicated. Franklin, said King, had read the plan carelessly in assuming that King had thought of going down the Thelon. He would be mad to do so, since the whole course of the Back was known and the river fell "into the sea most conveniently" for arriving at and tracing "the west coast of ... Boothia Felix, where I imagine the passage lies." Of course there would not be a useful fishery in any river; it was in the lakes King would look for fish. He had "yet to learn" that the caribou quit the barren lands during the winter; he knew "to the contrary." In any event, the country to which he wanted to go "is well-wooded and therefore abounding in animals of every kind." On evidence garnered from his own wintering in the North, he expected other animals than just caribou—moose, for example, which was a less migratory animal than the caribou. Franklin, King continued, ought to have made himself more familiar with Back's *Narrative* which, it was evident, he had not consulted. As to the assertion that King's ultimate object was merely to determine whether the isthmus of Boothia existed or not, King replied, "and quite enough when the problem of a north-west passage ... would by that means be solved."[12]

The Colonial Office, the Admiralty, and the Geographical Society all having failed to support a trip by King, only the Hudson's Bay Company remained as a potential aid. In his *Narrative*, however, King had not simply been critical of Back but of the fur trade as well. Medical practitioner and ethnologist, he had written of it as the destroyer of the native peoples of North America. In other words, he had cut himself off from the land as well as the sea "establishment." Besides, even had the company been sympathetic to King, it probably felt there was some unreality in his approach. Alexander Simpson, biographer of his brother, Thomas Simpson of the Hudson's Bay Company, says that even if King's party had reached the mouth of the Back River, it was evident a "bark canoe" was "quite unfit for navigating the Arctic Ocean." King's progress would in all likelihood have been little better than Back's. As it was, Richard King did not have the support of the company, while on the other hand, "Mackay, Sinclair, and all the men experienced in the navigation of the Arctic rivers" were in company service, "and no Canadian voyageurs could have been procured in Canada adequate for such an enterprise."[13]

By January 1837 the fund which King hoped would reach £1,000 stood at only £400. Disregarding the earlier snub, King again addressed the Geographical Society (now become the Royal Geographical Society), this time in a letter to Captain Whittington, RN. He was sure that the remaining £600 would be "instantly forth-coming" from other donors, if the society would "countenance the plan by a small grant." If they would simply promise their assistance King felt confident that "the Sanction of the Government and cooperation" of the Hudson's Bay Company would "ultimately be obtained." However, wealthy patrons of discovery were for the most part friends of Back and as support was not forthcoming from the society King's project failed.[14]

Frustrated in arctic endeavour, King turned to the practice of his profession, in Piccadilly until 1847 and after that in Savile Row until the last decade of his life when he moved to Manchester Square. The strong urge to save life that is evident in King's arctic activities arose naturally out of the ethos of his profession. He played, indeed, a pioneer role in the remarkable lowering of infant mortality in the nineteenth century. Specializing in obstetrics, he held a number of medical appointments, and in this field as in arctic matters wrote in an independent manner. As part of his founding work with the Ethnological Society, he wrote monographs on Indians, Eskimos, and other groups, and was a copious contributor to the *Ethnological Journal*, of which, as in the case of the *Medical Times*, he was for a while editor. He became a member of the Councils of the British Association and the Statistical Society.[15]

Subsequent events lent a good deal of support to King's views, save mainly in the matter of craft, on which King himself changed his outlook. Certainly he had been wrong in believing that the Thelon River flows into the Arctic while Franklin and Back had been right in believing it enters Hudson Bay. Nevertheless, this did not invalidate King's basic plan. Such a chain of communications as King had in mind did exist between Lake Athabasca and the Thelon, and the chain did lie through an area which is today wooded save for a short distance, and which may have been entirely so in King's day. King's plan to establish himself at the western end of what is today the Thelon Game Sanctuary was also realistic. King had discerned (as Franklin had not) the one largely wooded area north of the general treeline; he recognized this as preferable for wintering as such, and also as being in greater proximity to the Arctic than Back's wintering site, Fort Reliance. Secondly, while evidence today does agree with Franklin that caribou usually winter in wooded areas, nevertheless the winter ranges of the caribou "may be on the tundra," and formerly may have been more so. In any event, King's point was, precisely, that he was not writing about the tundra at all, but about a wooded area where other game than caribou was available, moose, for example, which King had correctly assessed as less migratory than caribou. Further, despite Alexander Simpson's remark, King had obtained promises of enlistment by Hudson's Bay Company men who had formerly accompanied him on the Back. He has claimed as well (although this may be the afterthought of a subsequent year) that he did plan that his party should go westward to Point Turnagain as well as eastward to Boothia. As it was, even Simpson said of King's scheme that it "was ... undoubtedly the most feasible that could have been projected" as a "self depending" one not reliant upon company help.[16]

Perhaps more important as regards King's accuracy is the story of a sea expedition whose failure King predicted and which did, indeed, fare badly. After examining the plans of the naval men the Royal Geographical Society approved a second expedition by Back. He was to sail in H.M.S. *Terror* through Hudson Strait to Foxe Channel and Basin and winter at Repulse or Wager Bay in 1836–37. Thereafter his expedition was to complete a coastal survey, in an attempt to find a passage from Fury and Hecla Strait to Point Turnagain. By contrast with King's approach from the southwest by canoe, this was a sea approach from the southeast by Hudson Strait which tended to presuppose that Boothia was an island. King did not think Back would reach the Gulf of Boothia, let alone the Back River estuary or beyond. Those who were sanguine about the expedition, he said, "would be grievously mistaken" and "should that insane portion of the instructions, the crossing of the isthmus dividing the waters of Wager Bay from Regent Inlet, be attempted, the most disastrous results might be expected."[17] In fact *Terror* was beset in ice in Foxe Basin near Southampton Island in 1836; crippled, she spent a winter drifting in great danger and was only released in July in Hudson Strait, from which she was brought back and beached on the shores of Ireland. For several years thereafter Back himself was not well and he did not explore again. Retired on half pay at forty-one, after a lapse of time he became active at the Royal Geographical Society and for many years was consulted as an arctic expert.

Back's experience supported King's wariness as to travel by sea in the initial search for a passage. The Hudson's Bay Company now, in its turn, supported his positive assertions about the advantage of travel by continental routes and lighter parties. It is likely that King's plan had helped to stimulate the company to efforts of its own. In polar discovery in this period success came to explorers who in most instances were not past their mid- or late thirties. Born in 1808, almost of an age with King, Thomas Simpson of the Hudson's Bay Company did all his exploring by his early thirties. A cousin of George Simpson, he was (it has been suggested) the first explorer "able in all the Arctic arts," including the basic one of living off the land. He duplicated or exemplified in a number of ways characteristics and emphases of King, including that of a difficult egoistic individuality. Yet Simpson had the advantage that he was the effectual and accepted leader in the Arctic as King had not been, while on the other hand he also had, in Chief Factor Peter Warren Dease, who was nominal leader of his expeditions, a man whose good nature shielded Simpson from the effects upon his men of his own authoritarian personality.[18]

The Hudson's Bay Company, said King of Thomas Simpson's explorations, had adopted King's "principle of a small overland party" and used McKay, Sinclair, and Taylor, three of the ablest men who had accompanied King in the search for Ross, in order to clear up the most important matters with which King had wished to deal in his plan of 1836. Certainly in the years (1837–39) that followed Back's reverses in *Terror*, Simpson did extend, by journeys in which individual distances of as much as 1,400 miles were traversed, Franklin's discoveries along the coastal mainland, both to the east and the west. Yet in one respect these travels did not seem to vindicate King. For, except that in 1838 Simpson accomplished alone in an Eskimo craft an important final dash to Point Barrow, his explorations were by boat, not by canoe or kayak. On other points, however, King's views seem to have been confirmed. This "intelligent traveller," as King called Simpson, showed, for example, that from Cape Alexander eastward to Simpson Strait "the coast was composed of one spacious bay," named by Simpson Queen Maud Gulf. In a letter of 5 June 1840 to Dr. Hodgkin, of the Council of the Royal Geographical Society, King recalled the return trip of the Back party up the Back River in 1835, and the Eskimos whom that party had met near Lake Garry who had come from the sea with relatively few kayaks. He pointed out that the forecast he had then made, in regard to these Eskimos, of the existence of a deep bay had been justified by the actual discovery of Queen Maud Gulf. Parry, he went on to say, had clearly demonstrated that western aspects of lands of a north–south trending were usually less ice-encumbered than their other aspects. Applying this to the Eskimos and Simpson's travels, he reasoned that, had the coast eastward from Point Turnagain formed several capes "to the eastern portion of which the ice would cling so long as any remained in the surrounding sea," then "insurmountable obstacles might have presented themselves" both to the Eskimos coming to Lake Garry in relatively few kayaks and to Dease and Simpson in their arrival from the west. It was Queen Maud Gulf, whose discovery he had thereby predicted, which had in both cases, King now argued, forestalled this possibility.

Secondly, contrary to Back's firm opinion, and again, said King, as he himself had predicted, Simpson had found "a bold projecting bluff named Cape Britannia two points more northerly than Cape Hay," correcting the mistake which had probably been a chief deterrent keeping Back from Boothia in 1834.[19] In all, King considered that, just as Back's failure in *Terror* in 1836 to reach Boothia by sea had fulfilled King's dire predictions in that regard, so the excellent results of Simpson's travels by land and coast had equally "proved the correctness" of his "most sanguine hopes" in this second regard. Moreover, predictions and results had in both cases occurred, said King, in contradiction to "all the great northern authorities."[20]

Certainly, in travelling from Point Barrow on the Alaskan coast in the west to Castor and Pollux Bay (named after Simpson's vessels) beyond the Back River estuary in the east, Simpson had very nearly completed discovery of a Northwest Passage. He had now capped the work of Parry, the Rosses, Franklin, and Richardson in such a way that a Northwest Passage lay revealed to the east and west of Boothia. All that was needed to complete the discovery was to find a way past the Boothia–Somerset spur: by circumnavigating it to the north, going through it at Bellot Strait (as yet undiscovered), or (if the Boothia part of it was an island) south of the whole complex.

Finally, King's views did seem to have been borne out as regards the Back River route. Simpson had started and closed his vogages by the Mackenzie and Coppermine Rivers, not the Back, so that he had been overextended when he arrived at the Boothia region, and in consequence had been unable to assess it fully. Thus the last of the three possibilities (that Boothia was an island) was precisely what Thomas Simpson mistakenly believed he had demonstrated. He thought he had proved a direct water channel from Chantrey Inlet to the Gulf of Boothia.[21] Yet in fact, as at the close of Back's trip down the Back, so also at the close of Simpson's travels the nature of Boothia, which King felt was crucial, remained unknown, while at the same time it was thought to be proved.

This was a central point in King's letter of 5 June 1840 to Dr. Hodgkin.[22] King admired Simpson's work but the company plan, he urged upon Hodgkin, had serious defects. Using the Coppermine, Dease and Simpson had left Boothia's nature unsettled and hence, also, the question of "communication of the Polar Sea with the North Atlantic Ocean by the Fury and Hecla Strait." King's own "intended track," commencing from the Back River, would have embarked on new discoveries "immediately on reaching the sea"; he would have explored first from the Back River to Point Turnagain and then, returning to Boothia, traced either its western shore or the coastline from the Back River estuary to Fury and Hecla Strait, depending upon whether Boothia was an island or not. Now, still not accepting Boothia's nature as determined, King felt there was a further task that could only be accomplished by the Back River. If Boothia was a peninsula its west coast (pre-eminently accessible by the Back) was the final link in a passage; if not, the Back was also the right means to demonstrate Boothia's insularity. The company itself had learned the need as regards the central region of the North American Arctic of "a starting or retreating point much nearer to the scene of operations" than the wintering grounds hitherto of Dease and Simpson. It had, said King, "determined upon" another land journey and for this might use the Back River, King's "precise route."

King had rightly heard that the company was considering further exploration and had rightly deduced that it would use the Back River; but he was wrong in thinking that this was to test, what the company thought already proved, a channel south of Boothia, much less to investigate, as King wished to do, Boothia's west coast. Nor were Thomas Simpson or the company directors interested in the logical consequence of their own claim: a passage all the way from Bering Strait through the Gulf of Boothia, Lancaster Sound, Baffin Bay and Davis Strait to the Atlantic. For this would be a deep sea passage on the Atlantic side, not one by the continental shoreline into the company's own Hudson Bay and Strait. The directors and Thomas and George Simpson wished, rather, for a full survey of the northern coast of North America, which Thomas called carrying the company flag "fairly through and out of the Polar Sea"[23] and probably thought of as completing a Northwest Passage.

On 18 October 1839, Thomas Simpson asked permission to complete a survey of "the Gulf of Boothia the only section of the Arctic coast . . . now unknown."[24] The Back River, he wrote, fell "into the sea in the vicinity" of the Gulf of Boothia, giving it thereby an "immense superiority" over the Coppermine River as a "starting point." It could bring a future expedition "upon the field one month earlier" than had the Coppermine, and had an even greater superiority over a route from Churchill as a means for arrival in the Gulf of Boothia. It was clearly "the best egress to the scene of operations," and without doubt, "Fort Reliance ought to be the wintering ground" for the proposed party. With fourteen members, the expedition during its first winter should construct "two small boats" at Artillery Lake, and in these in the following summer the main party should proceed by the Back River to the sea. For this Thomas had retained "the services . . . of MacKay and Sinclair, the only steersmen in the country . . . acquainted with the long and dangerous navigation of the Great Fish River." Provisions could be secured at Athabasca, "trading goods brought from the depot," and the expedition proceed in 1840 or 1841. Simpson, however, must have discretionary power to employ a second season on the arctic coast if necessary and either to fall back on the Back River or (as he much preferred if practicable) push on through Fury and Hecla Strait to York Factory.

The response of the governor and committee was positive. In March 1840 they declared they were "exceedingly anxious to complete the survey of the [arctic] coast into Hudson Bay," and on 3 June accepted Simpson's project to do this, "from the mouth of the Great Fish River to the Straits of the Fury and Hecla," at the same time ordering cooperation with it throughout the country.[25] The governor of the company's North American territories (in London at the time) was also well disposed and impressed upon his cousin that "the completion of the survey to any of the inlets leading into Hudson's Bay is the great and important object in view; — an object which the Hudson's Bay Company are determined ... to accomplish." Eskimos might tell Thomas as he travelled whether there was any channel nearer than the Straits of Fury and Hecla to the large bay Thomas had seen eastward from the mouth of the Back River. The governor's "own belief" was "that such a channel does exist, probably from Repulse Bay; and if so it would greatly shorten the voyage."[26]

Not only, in other words, did George Simpson accept Thomas's idea that Boothia was an island; he also believed that Melville Peninsula was one. Unaware of the eighteenth-century work of the company's own explorers, which should have dispelled all thought of Hudson Bay as part of a passage, and of Captain Lyon's exploration in 1824, which had specifically ruled out Repulse Bay as a strait, Governor Simpson represented a company hope, dying hard, that the bay was part of a passage. That Thomas's "enterprising and arduous task might be crowned with the most complete success" was George's most fervent wish. Indeed, by the coastal survey Thomas would now accomplish what had "baffled ... numerous Government expeditions ... during ... the past three hundred years" and his cousin's trip, the governor trusted, would "immortalize" Thomas's name.[27]

In tactics as well as other exploratory matters George Simpson had shown little regard for the navy or for "naval gentlemen." It meant little either to the company as a whole or to him that Back considered the Back River unnavigable and without further use in exploration.[28] If, George Simpson now wrote to Thomas, the necessary steps had already been taken for exploration in the summer of 1841, Thomas's proposal for use of the Great Fish River was good. If, however (as the governor apprehended), they had not, then York Factory was a better starting point because it would save, in that event, a year. Thomas could choose either route, depending upon which one he felt was best for the "speedy and successful accomplishment" of his mission. If he proceeded from York, in the fall of

1840 there should be sent north by small decked craft a depot as far as open water allowed. There should also be sent to Great Slave Lake instructions for deposit by the Back River and at its mouth of still another depot by the summer of 1841. The exploring party itself and supporting personnel should start from Churchill "in March or April of 1841, taking two North canoes or very light boats on sleighs as far as ice travelling" permitted. From the depot set in the preceding fall, a small quantity of provisions should be taken forwards by the explorers toward Boothia. If successful, Thomas would, in the depot at the foot of the Back, have an ample supply to make his retreat by that stream to Great Slave Lake in the autumn. If unsuccessful, he could fall back on the first depot in the Hudson Bay region. In either event, the party should number only seven or nine in all, as it might have to winter with Eskimos upon whose limited means of assistance, even of blubber, the crews of two boats might place a strain.[29]

There had arisen, in short, as exploration had neared Boothia from the west, a sensitive situation analogous to the question aboard a sailing vessel as the time approaches for a new tack of just when to "come about." Thomas's plan visualized holding the old tack longer than George's did, for his intention was to use the Back River as the route of entry and Hudson Bay as that of retreat, while George's proposal was the exact reverse. George had also emphasized a smaller party and craft, perhaps even the canoe, than had Thomas. In either event, the company had a bias to avoid Boothia and arrive as soon as possible in the bay; coastal in its emphasis, it was interested in all shorelines but that of Hudson Bay in particular, as it wishfully identified a tracing of this and of coasts leading into it as completion of a passage. Although it was not sceptical of the Back River as a practicable route, the river was, nevertheless, to be used in a way which did not stress its most notable feature: that it led directly to the west coast of Boothia where (despite company thinking) completion of the coastal passage lay. Once again there had come into play, on a small yet pivotal matter, a longstanding company tendency to explore within a certain range of the bay itself. Had Thomas Simpson's plan matured this emphasis would not perhaps have mattered; for in that event he would have encountered, willy-nilly, the peninsularity of Boothia and its west coast, which might have led to the discovery of Rae Strait and the final link in a passage. However, events were to forestall Thomas's plan and put into operation that of George Simpson.

On 6 June 1840, three days after the committee's acceptance of Thomas's plan, two after George Simpson had written from London to Thomas, and one after King had written to Hodgkin regarding further exploration,

Thomas left the Red River settlement by way of the United States for England. In 1833 at Norway House he had said that Back seemed a "very easy affable man; deficient, I should say, in that commanding manner with the people so necessary in this savage country."[30] This was not the bent of Thomas. He had on an early occasion offended half-breeds and was detested for his arrogance by voyageurs from their ranks; that is why George Simpson had placed Dease in official charge of Thomas's expeditions, in which capacity Dease had "kept the men in good humour and responsive to the most exacting demands" of Thomas.[31] Now, however, Dease was on leave and Thomas Simpson, little appreciating the role his associate had played, was "overwrought and possessed of a morbid fear that Dease would receive the credit" for Thomas's discoveries of 1839. Thomas had said, "Fame I will have but it must be *alone*," and he was aware of an initial reservation by George Simpson towards any plan for further exploration that did not include Dease.[32] He was not aware of London's support for his project or, latterly, of the support of George Simpson himself, as he hurried to company headquarters to plead in person a case already won. No information (George Simpson wrote in September) had reached London relative to Thomas, "beyond the appalling statement contained in ... the 'St. Louis Bulletin' ... from [which] ... no doubt exists that Mr. Simpson has met with an untimely end; but the whole of the tragic and extraordinary story is shrouded in so much mystery and obscurity that I am lost in conjecture."[33]

In territory today part of North Dakota, Thomas Simpson had died a violent death in circumstances still obscure. The facts suggest that he was murdered by half-breeds travelling with him, or that in a fit of manic depression he may have committed suicide.[34] Events, in short, reveal that George Simpson's reluctance to allow Thomas to travel alone with half-breeds was well-founded. Thomas, a man of highly strung temperament, in a situation entailing geographical and psychological tension, had been a casualty in part, perhaps, of failure to use the Back River much earlier. For had he explored with vigour (and with Dease) when fresh by way of that river, then features of the central Arctic might by this time have been known and only the easier portions of a passage have remained to be dealt with. The decision to send out Franklin on his last expedition might not thereafter have been taken, or a different course charted for him. Certainly, at all events, Thomas Simpson had failed in the discovery of the most difficult link in a passage. George Simpson wrote that Thomas's death terminated "for the present, all hopes" for the projected "survey from the Great Fish River to the Straits of Fury and Hecla."[35] Once again exploration of Boothia's west coast had been left unfinished.

There was a lull in the search for a Northwest Passage but early in 1842 Richard King took up again the matter of the Arctic. For the colonial secretary, Lord Stanley, he traced his involvement in its affairs. After 1836, King wrote, he had retreated into the shade, but Thomas Simpson's plan of 1840 had been ended by his death so that now King could come forward without intrusion. His project was the same as that of 1836, save that a part of the earlier plan had now been accomplished, causing to rise "into importance" "a new line of coast." Once again King proposed wintering at the headwaters of the Thelon with a party of six men led only by himself. Arriving by this wintering ground at the eastern boundary of the estuary of the Back, there would thereafter be "no difficulty in reaching the land of Boothia ... or in case of its insularity, the Hecla and Fury" strait. "In the latter case the northern configuration of America" would be complete. In the former (Boothia's peninsularity) it would be necessary to test whether King William's Land was a part of Boothia; if a strait of any size separated the two lands, "the grand problem of a practicable" passage was "solved." The Colonial Office replied that the government contemplated no such expedition.[36]

King turned his attention once more to the Royal Geographical Society. In his statement to the society, as in the one addressed to Lord Stanley, he named elements in the region of Boothia and its gulf (including Boothia's west coast) which remained to be explored in order to complete knowledge of North America's northern coast "and ... determine the existence and practicality" of a passage. These features might be investigated by ships through Barrow Strait or by making in boats "via the interior lakes of America" to "the Great Fish River Estuary" and so proving the insularity or otherwise of Boothia.[37]

In an article in a learned journal King made a similar statement as to the problem involved and declared the unknown coast might "be explored in one summer at the very trifling outlay of a thousand pounds." Once again he stressed the relative ease of tracing western coasts of lands and quoted Parry in support of a claim that bays, as well, were relatively free of ice. In his projected journey there were "two western coasts and one bay." Presumably King meant the west coasts of Boothia and Melville Peninsula, and Committee Bay; the "form and aspect of the unsurveyed lands" made them, he wrote, favourable to discovery. There remained only the question of approach. Quoting verbatim the objections of Franklin to his own plan of 1836 and giving a reply to these, King advanced his proposal and spoke of the rewards in commerce and science already produced by the search for a passage. A practical channel might yet be found. As with King's earlier proposals for exploration, there was no positive response. Yet it is important to notice that King had gradually switched his emphasis from one on canoes in 1836 through a silent neutrality on the subject or slight favouring of boats to, finally, a full espousal of boats in his communication to the Royal Geographical Society in 1842. Evidently the example of Thomas Simpson had convinced him of the efficacy of these for the tasks he had in mind, provided that like Simpson's they were boats capable of portage.[38]

Richard King had been wrong upon a number of matters, as for example, the location of the mouth of the Thelon River, a suggestion that Lake Franklin was a mouth (the chief one) of the Back River, and the suggestion that Committee Bay had little ice in it, a statement shortly to be disproved. A polemicist, King had shown a tendency to exaggerate, as in comparing his own leadership of the Back party across Great Slave Lake to Parry's attempt to reach the North Pole on the ice, or in saying that his project for a journey down the Back River involved no more danger than did one's daily occupation.[39] On the other hand, King had shown discernment with regard to two major matters, the first of them the so-called barrens. Throughout most of the nineteenth century, it has been said, explorers would continue to think of "the mighty tundra wilderness" as "an obstacle to be crossed en route to somewhere else"; only in the last decade of the century would there come a "new breed of tundra travellers" who dealt with "the people, the animals, the very nature and quality of the tundra ... in detail for their own sake." Yet King, a naturalist and student of native peoples, had already anticipated this new attitude. It was in this context that he had advanced in its most notable form, that of going down the Back River, his fundamental view that one should use inland and coastal approaches first and only afterwards explore by deep sea.[40]

King's second major discernment was with regard to the Arctic itself, and the archipelago there. His letter of 24 January 1842 to Lord Stanley, posing as it did the joint possibility of the peninsularity of Boothia and insularity of King William's Land, had advanced in effect the possibility of Rae and James Ross Straits. In 1840 he had also urged a sea expedition which would have, among other aims, that of sailing westward along "the land of North Somerset" so as to feel out its coastline,[41] advice which might, if taken, have led to the discovery of Peel Sound. By 1842, that is, there were signs that King had already anticipated both Franklin's route in 1846 by Peel Sound and also the route by James Ross and Rae Straits which Franklin would thereafter have been (had he known of and accepted them) wise to follow. In short, the surgeon had anticipated delineation of the coastal passage which actually existed but whose contour would not be known or accepted in London until 1854 or even 1859.

Moreover, King had also looked northward, to still another passage, or even two. In 1836 he had written that, in the event of certain findings, there should be sent "a sea expedition, to try for a Passage about the broken land around Melville Island," and in 1840 he had suggested that the Hudson's Bay Company should send a party down the Mackenzie River which would "trace Victoria Land with relation to Bank's Land of Parry"; for there, King said, there might lie "a practicable passage." These are terms which point possibly to M'Clure Strait and certainly, in the phrase "Victoria Land with relation to Bank's Land," to a passage at Prince of Wales Strait. King rightly felt, in addition, that a northern passage would likely be more navigable than a coastal one.[42]

There had now come towards Boothia expeditions from four directions. At the peninsula's east coast there had arrived in 1829 a deep-sea party led by Sir John Ross from the Atlantic and carried in sailing craft with auxiliary steam. Secondly (in terms of clockwise rotation), there had come from the southeast, via Hudson Strait and Foxe Channel, Captain Back in *Terror* by sail in 1836. Thirdly, there had come from the south to a region near the western foot of Boothia, by the inland route of the Back River in 1834, the boat party of Back. Finally, from far west by boat and the mainland coast, there had arrived at Boothia in 1839 Thomas Simpson of the Hudson's Bay Company. In these developments it had taken four years for Ross to reach Boothia and return home by deep sea, and even this had been by good luck; and the intended Back expedition by Wager Bay, also a deep sea attempt, had got nowhere near Boothia. On the other hand, the inland and coastal parties of Back and Simpson had taken, respectively, somewhat over and distinctly less than two years, a speed that was due to the advantages, for initial communication, of boat by comparison with ship travel, and of the inland and more southerly northwest fur route, in contrast to more northerly approaches by sea. Boothia, at the end of the line for all the routes, was approachable for preliminary investigation most rapidly and profitably by boat from the south and west.

Besides a contrast as regards varying routes and craft, there had also appeared by now—in the explorers themselves on sea, coast, and river—a set of differences of temperament, emphasis, and training. Leaders differed in their degree of espousal of indigenous means, in their wish either to dominate a region or come to terms with it, and in their inherent preference for travelling alone or in a large group. Edward Parry, for example, less individualistic and less a light-party man than John Ross, had also shown less confidence than Ross that indigenous peoples had unique awareness of their surroundings. Possessed of technical ingenuity, he would, as hydrographer and then head of the Steam Department, prove reasonable and coherent. Ross, rebellious and egoistic by comparison,[43] had shown, however, an emphasis upon small parties, indigenous information with regard to Boothia, and a bizarre but innovative way with European technology. On the coastal approaches there had appeared the same contrast. Franklin, trained like Parry for the navy and adapted to group hierarchical endeavour, had shown a "stiffness" and "exhibition of fortitude and power" that were prone to produce the very horrors in the midst of which naval discipline had seemed all the more necessary and had come all the more into play. Thomas Simpson, making considerably longer and more rapid coastal journeys than Franklin, had emphasized small parties, indigenous means,[44] and, in contrast to Franklin's form of discipline, a haughty solitary authoritarianism. Franklin's demise would occur in a search for the passage and fame by a large-scale, elaborately organized project; Simpson's had already happened as he travelled with the same intent, accompanied by a small group of half-breeds but remaining very much a solitary figure or, in his own word, "*alone.*"

These contrasts in temperament, training, and attitude had been repeated upon the most inland route of all. On the Back River there had travelled in 1834, cheek by jowl, a "heavy transport" man, George Back, RN, and a "rapid communications" one, Richard King, MD. Back aimed to win a victory, as if in battle, over the region in which he found himself, for example in his choice of the heavier of his two boats to descend and ascend the river, and in a martial determination to bring the boat back up it. Yet, confident initially, by the time he had completed this return journey Back was convinced that the river was not susceptible of travel; he had allowed it and the barrens the final word. At home, knighted and very active in London society,[45] he may already have had a retarding influence upon discovery of a passage. For Back's argument had the effect of presenting an unwarrantedly harsh view of the river, of the country through which it flowed, and of what might be found by it. He confirmed rather than amended a company tendency to underrate the potential of inland treeless country. Unwilling himself to go again down the Back River to the west coast of Boothia, he was also active in keeping others away from the river, particularly his former subordinate.

King, on the other hand, had shown a greater interest in, and awareness of, the nature of the barrens than had Back. Earlier the only real questions regarding the Back River and its region had been those of transit and survival. These, however awkwardly, the Back party had now answered. Uncertain at the outset of the trip down the river as to whether or not the Back party would ever reach the Arctic by it,[46] King was now confident he could again achieve the polar sea and make good his return by the Back. The very inadequacies of the naval officer's expedition were in King's view a warranty, once they were discerned and corrected, that the river would in the future prove more, not less, manageable. Even the company, both in London and in North America, now judged the river usable. Meanwhile, the contrast between Back and King, first demonstrated on the river, continued at home. The London surgeon went frequently in the 1840s to the treeless broadlands of Norfolk known as the "Wells Fields," where he shot "*barefooted* no matter what weather" and was considered "a great oddity."[47] Yet such activity may be further evidence that King had a more accurate grasp and greater aptitude and fitness than most in regard to what was needful now to complete a Northwest Passage. The more one pressed towards the heart of the Arctic, the more it appeared that a small land party led by a man of indigenous and "lone wolf" stamp might have advantages.

Of sand-flies in the Northwest Back had written that, scarcely visible individually, they could rise collectively "in clouds actually darkening the air," causing agony to his party.[48] It is a picture not inappropriate to the situation that was now developing. Apparently small, even insignificant, as an influence upon the scene at this time, there were nevertheless certain arctic realities which were capable, cumulatively, of "darkening the air." To these King gave expression at home. On the one hand, his own society was a complex metropolitan one, elaborately organized, technologically advanced, and confident of the ability of the Royal Navy to conclude a marine search begun three centuries ago. On the other hand, King himself was at variance with a number of these features. An extreme hinterland and small-party man, stressing the techniques of faraway native peoples, he had his eye not on the ocean but upon a rugged inland river flowing through vast tundra. Convinced, by the experience of having travelled on it, that he could explore and find a passage by the river, King was a voice crying literally about certain things in the wilderness yet also one crying figuratively in the wilderness. From one point of view "a great oddity," he was, from another, the chorus in a developing Greek tragedy.

4

The Franklin and
Rae Expeditions (1845–1848)

In 1845 the Royal Navy attempted the completion of the 300-year-old search for a Northwest Passage. Believing the last step was simple, it sought to accomplish its aim by means of a deep-sea party under Franklin more elaborate than any before, without benefit of land or coastal assistance. It thought in terms of a route plotted through an as yet uncharted quadrilateral which lay to the west of Boothia and north of the continental coast, reaching to Barrow Strait and Melville Island.[1] (See Map 5.) Sir John Barrow, anxious to see the final expedition launched before his retirement at eighty-two, said that as both the eastern and western approaches had been penetrated there remained nothing to do but "pass the thresholds." A passage had been discovered; all that remained was to sail it. Not very aware that a good deal of polar exploration had been done by land and coastal approaches and a number of discoveries made by explorers outside naval aegis, Barrow wrote in terms of a deep-sea expedition by the navy cruising through the Arctic at thirty miles a day and of a passage requiring in the future only fourteen days to navigate. He was as unrealistic as ever.[2]

A special concern of the navy was earth magnetism. On Parry's first arctic voyage there had sailed Capt. Edward Sabine (1788–1883), an army man who was now an expert in terrestrial magnetism and who formed an important link between this and polar exploration. A world program of observations on the subject was now nearing completion and Sabine urged that securing magnetic data would be reason enough for a polar expedition.[3] Yet he also wrote optimistically about finding a passage at this time. The Russian explorer Baron von Wrangel, Sabine reasoned, had shown in

1820–23 that there was much open sea off Siberia's shore; by analogy, the sea north of the Parry Islands and between Melville Island and Bering Strait must also be free of islands. While he had assessed in this way the existence of Beaufort Sea, Sabine nevertheless underestimated ice as a barrier in that sea, and his analysis had the effect of minimizing North America's vast arctic archipelago. Sir John Barrow, in particular, misapplied Sabine's analysis to mean that there was open sea much further east than Sabine argued, in the quadrilateral that engaged Barrow's own interest.[4] Naval men placed further emphases upon an iceless polar sea far to the north; upon steam as an adjunct to sail in arctic navigation; upon relatively large vessels and large-scale provisioning; upon arctic service as excellent training for seamen and officers; and upon commerce, strategy, and national prestige as reasons for finding a passage, especially in the face of competition from other countries in these matters.[5]

The choice of Sir John Franklin as leader of a sea expedition at the age of fifty-eight rested upon his record as a land explorer many years before, and upon a feeling of compassion for him. Franklin had recently been suddenly retired from the governorship of Van Diemen's Land, allegedly for lack of energy and initiative, but really, it has been argued (perhaps over-argued), as the result of the manoeuvrings of a subordinate.[6] Despite a naval tradition that explorers write their own instructions, Franklin's were a cooperative product in which views that he himself held were not fully apparent. His own thinking showed a continental stress. He already suspected before he left England the existence of Peel Sound and in conversation emphasized, with a map before him, that to link his expedition to the western end of Simpson Strait would complete a passage.[7] Nevertheless, the instructions, as actually written after a canvass of naval arctic opinion, had at their core Sir John Barrow's extensive quadrilateral to the west of Boothia.

The veteran explorer was directed to hurry through Barrow Strait. Because ice found by Parry off Cape Dundas at Melville Island made a search in that direction unpromising, Franklin should sail southward and westward from Cape Walker as directly towards Bering Strait as ice or land permitted, that is diagonally across the quadrilateral from its northeast to southwest corner. Yet there was also added to the orders, in a different hand and almost as if in afterthought, a suggestion of Sir James Clark Ross. If, Franklin was told, his way was obstructed in the area of the quadrilateral and he had noticed that the mouth of Wellington Channel was open, he was to consider whether it offered an "outlet from the Archipelago" and a "ready access" to an open sea to the north where "neither islands nor banks [would] arrest and fix the floating masses of ice." In this way the idea of a northern open polar sea entered into the instructions, while, on the other hand, there was in them no specific incorporation of Franklin's own expressed coastal interest.[8]

At the same time as the navy sought to complete a Northwest Passage by deep-sea means, the Hudson's Bay Company aimed to do so through coastal travel by boats, and with a strong emphasis upon indigenous and light means of travel. Semi-maritime itself, the company was like the navy over-optimistic, in its case as regards topographical questions slighter than those which concerned the navy but nevertheless crucial. In 1846 the company had, unlike the navy, a new and youthful explorer for whom joining his exploration with that of Thomas Simpson was a specific, not as in the case of Franklin merely a possible, aim. At the age of thirty-two, Dr. John Rae was sent by the company to "complete the geography of the northern shore of America ... from the Straits of the Fury and Hecla ... to the ... discoveries of ... Dease and Simpson."[9] The instructions embodied Sir George Simpson's recommendations to Thomas Simpson in 1840. Using Hudson Bay and its Foxe Channel extension as the route of entry, Rae was to make the Back River his means of retreat if, as the company hoped, Boothia turned out to be an island.

The instructions implied that the problem of North America's shoreline from Hudson Bay westward was the same as that of a passage, and this was also the burden of a conversation which Rae himself had with the future novelist R. M. Ballantyne, then in company service, when the two men passed each other as Rae travelled to York Factory. For the new company explorer hoped that there existed a channel, of which he told Simpson there was an Eskimo report, connecting Repulse Bay with the Arctic and "converting Melville Peninsula into an island." The names of Rae's two boats, *Magnet* and *North Pole*, bespoke, one judges, both an interest in magnetism and also a hope of clear sailing from Repulse Bay to the magnetic pole, west of Boothia. In short, both Simpson and Rae thought it reasonable to assume that Boothia was an island and that, despite past disproof, Melville was also. As in the 1830s the company hoped it could complete, from its own bay in one operation, discovery of the continental northern shore and a Northwest Passage, the latter an aim which Simpson well knew had great public attraction.[10]

Yet certainly, even though it was like the navy over-hopeful, the Hudson's Bay Company had set itself a simpler goal than that of Franklin. Its quest was not through what has since been called an "extensive blank area" but, rather, the more certain one of finding a continuous, or almost continuous, coastline. Nor, of course, did Rae plan to sail a passage in its entirely but only, at most, to find and report the last link in one. Again, Simpson alone had chosen and instructed Rae,[11] a simple procedure unlike the complicated group method by which Franklin had been chosen as leader of his party and his route selected.

John Rae (1813–93) was born in the Orkneys, near Stromness, and grew up there, in what he called a paradise of northern travel for boys. Whereas from boyhood Franklin was a deep-sea sailor for whom the post-Napoleonic period was one of adjustment from war to peace, for Rae the same period gave an opportunity to become an expert coastal sailor. Shipping had learned during the late wars to pass to the north of Scotland, to avoid trouble further south; the pattern persisted in peacetime and Rae and his brothers would race their boats against those of the professional pilots of Stromness to meet this shipping. Another contrast was that Rae was a solitary youth, unlike the sociable Franklin. Naïve and diffident and the butt of his companions, he early took to wandering alone in his native habitat. Again, Franklin had never been a huntsman, but Rae learned how to handle a gun before his earliest memories. When Franklin left the Arctic for sea service in warmer zones, Rae, recently qualified in medicine, came to North America as a company doctor in the severe winter of 1833, and at Moose Factory broadened his capacity for hunting and travel.[12] The choice of Franklin had been much influenced by reasons of compassion; Rae was chosen as leader of the new company expedition because he had recently demonstrated a capacity for rapid travel and because of his prowess as sportsman. Finally, if Franklin and other naval officers were trained and sophisticated in navigation, of which magnetism was an integral part, Rae was a tyro in these skills and was delayed, from 1845 to 1846, because he travelled to Toronto to learn their elements under another army expert, Lefroy. His modest training completed, Rae made his way to York Factory in October 1845 and was ready to commence exploration in the following year.[13]

There were further differences beyond those between individuals. A contrast existed, for example, as regards organization and discipline. The Franklin party was not only much larger than Rae's; its structure was hierarchical, unlike the more simple arrangement for the company party. Franklin's complement of 134 at the outset included twenty-five commissioned officers, making a ratio of between five and six members of the party for each officer, or twice the officer–man ratio of the Rae party, which consisted of only one leader and eleven men including the later addition of the Eskimo, Ouligbuck. Besides, the very presence of warrant in addition to commissioned officers in the Franklin party not only increased the number of officers in relation to men, but also indicated a ranked gradation of command by comparison with Rae's less complicated system of a single leader and the rest as followers. Again, the Franklin party was to observe "everything from a flea to a whale," a task in which each commissioned officer was encouraged to take one branch of science under his immediate care, while Franklin's own task was "more the training and overlooking of these gentlemen than doing the work itself." Rae, by contrast, was instructed to keep only a single journal on his expedition and, as the sole officer of the party, he was of necessity a jack-of-all-sciences. Whereas the navy's method stressed the amount of scientific information which was to be acquired, the company's stressed the importance of getting home again with what information one did have.[14] Moreover, the company's method, adapted to smallness, was likely to place preservation of life itself before preservation of discipline. The naval method emphasized unbroken ranks in the most extreme circumstances, the company's the avoidance of such circumstances.

It was Richard King, however, who most of all looked at the Arctic in terms of its own nature, and least of all saw it as an area through which to reach the Orient or in which to make magnetic observations or engage in commercial enterprise such as the fur trade or whaling. He was concerned with a science of the Arctic itself. For although like the company he stressed the importance in exploration of getting home with what scientific information one could, he went further than this, using in a particular way science itself as a means to assess where to go. Ethnology, for example, was for him a means to help discover topography. He argued that on the evidence of similarities in the cultures of Eskimos in the west and east of North America's Arctic, in contrast to a wedge of cultural difference in the region between, there must be an ocean current flowing north and east from Alaska, before it turned southward to approach the mainland of the continent again at Baffin Bay. By this route and means, King reasoned, there had occurred a migration of Eskimos from a more Pacific to a more Atlantic region of the Arctic. In our own day King's views have been borne out by archaeological findings on Greenland and Ellesmere Islands; in his day he used his observations to discern a more northern passage, just as he had once trusted direct information from Eskimos themselves in order to perceive a coastal one.[15]

As regards a coastal passage, King was now more convinced than ever of the peninsularity of Boothia, of its west coast as the locale of the final link in such a passage, and of the Back River as the most effective way by which to reach that locale. In short, he alone advocated the very inland Back River as the principal route of entry, not of retreat, for arctic exploration at this time, and he also spoke and wrote of the west coast of Boothia as the appropriate destination if one wished to complete a passage. He produced a rough sketch map which revealed his views upon a more northern passage, upon Boothia, and upon other matters.[16] (See Map 4.) This map shows that, contrary to the general naval outlook, he thought in terms of a solid impervious territory where Franklin's instructions and Franklin himself presupposed that the expedition of 1845 could sail. It portrays a solid land mass where, as we know today, Victoria Island lies, and accurately shows Wollaston Land as part of this, although it is inaccurate in making Banks Land a part of the same land mass. The map does not show Bellot Strait, but does depict, accurately, King William's Land as an island.

Richard King's judgments of the 1830s had now been proved correct, and there was a new acerbity in the manner in which, on the basis in part of his map, he gave blunt, unsolicited advice to the Admiralty and Colonial Office against the sending out of a maritime arctic expedition. If the Admiralty plan was pursued, King wrote, Franklin would have to "'take the ice' as the pushing through an ice-blocked sea is termed."[17] In public he told Sir John Barrow that he was sending Franklin to the Arctic "to form the *nucleus* of an *iceberg*."[18] To Lord Stanley at the Colonial Office King wrote that he had "contended against the present attempt by sea from an honest conviction of its impracticability in the present state of our knowledge of Arctic lands."

The sending of a sea expedition would not lead, King continued, to the discovery of a passage but to the search for it being "actually . . . in abeyance" unless there was support by land. If, despite his warnings, a sea expedition must be sent by the navy, then a land expedition would raise the "moral courage" of the projected naval party and provide a support which was "requisite in pushing an adventurous way through an unknown sea." King, however, did not confine himself simply to support of the Franklin party by the Back River. He advocated, rather, an inland expedition which would send two boat parties to the Arctic in the spring of 1846, one down the Coppermine and one by way of the Back. There were many, he said, who could conduct such a party, but if no one came forward, he was willing "to volunteer the whole command or part of [it]," providing only that the leader he served under should be of his own age and equal vigour. He was willing to do his own exploring as well as planning. He, like Rae, stressed smallness of party and of expenditure. With typical sharpness he observed that if Barrow had in the past sent out land instead of sea parties to accomplish the same ends, he would thus far have saved the country £200,000 and so would deserve from a grateful nation a peerage rather than a knighthood.[19] He had also long stressed the role of the single-minded energetic leader. In conclusion, the choice of Franklin and the writing of his instructions had been, in effect, by a committee; the choice of Rae and of his route had been by a single authoritarian leader, Sir George Simpson; King, however, had combined all three functions, choice of leader, choice of route, and actual exploration along the route in a single "do-it-yourself" individual, himself. Even more than Rae or Simpson, he was a "loner," to the point of an extreme but, if accuracy is the test, justified egoism. Sir John Barrow reacted vigorously, however, and neither the Admiralty nor the Colonial Office accepted King's plan.

Recently returned from an antarctic expedition under James Ross, and now intended for service with the Franklin expedition, were the bomb vessels *Erebus* and *Terror*, built in 1812 and 1820 and of 340 and 370 tons respectively. After alterations to install steam machinery, the vessels were approximately 107 and 110 feet long. Their bows were without figure-heads and were a mass of timber about eight feet thick, cased with strong sheet iron. As protection against ice the vessels had ice-boards with chains, projecting as far as the shrouds. Adapted for steam and with rudders capable of being unshipped, the vessels' sterns were perpendicular.[20] Sir John Ross felt that under both Back and James Ross *Terror* had proved herself "totally unfit" for arctic travel. His own vessel *Victory* had been much smaller than either *Erebus* or *Terror* which, he wrote, were too large, and were rendered still less fit by the addition of steam machinery which brought them even lower in the water.[21] The Admiralty thought of sailing through relatively open sea between Cape Walker and the continental coast, or in open sea far to the north; even Franklin, relatively conscious of the mainland, did not, for example, contemplate sailing close to Boothia. It was to such routes, or imagined ones, that the size of the vessels was matched; they were of the weight which Sir James Ross had asked for, for arctic service, a decade earlier,[22] and would ask for again in 1847; and they were almost twice the tonnage of *Fox* in which M'Clintock would sail successfully to Boothia in a later period. Aboard *Erebus* and *Terror* were nineteen boats in all, consisting of whalers and galleys, each thirty feet in length, pinnaces twenty-eight feet long, and, in dwindling scale, cutters, gigs, and dinghies, the last of twelve feet.[23] Finally, there was one Halkett boat, referred to below. There was also Silvester heating aboard, with hot water conveyed in pipes to warm the officers' cabins and men's berths.

Rae, for his part, had rejected the larger and more comfortable means which he had been offered at this time of "a handy little schooner" in favour of two boats, built, by contrast with Franklin's vessels, near the Arctic and specifically for their task.[24] Waiting for Rae when he arrived at

York Factory were *Magnet* and *North Pole*, strong, clinker-built craft twenty-two feet long by seven and a half feet broad, each capable of carrying a load of between two and three tons. They had aboard one oiled canvas canoe and "one of Halkett's air boats," the invention of Lt. Peter Halkett, RN, son of John Halkett, a governor of the Hudson's Bay Company. This boat was an inflatable india rubber craft, called by its inventor his "Cloth-boat." Roughly oval in shape, eight or nine feet long by three or four feet broad when inflated, it had a cockpit, suitable attachments such as mooring rings, and could seat two or three. Covering the boat with canvas, Rae used it and pronounced it a great success.[25]

Richard King's plan was to have his party build the craft they needed during the expedition itself. One of the boats for his suggested expedition, to be twenty-eight feet long, was to be built in three weeks at Lake Athabasca by a boat carpenter and two other men. The same three men were to build the second boat still further inland, on the Thelon River. However, during the winter the boats were to be transported, in the manner of Simpson, to the points on the Coppermine and Back Rivers respectively, from which exploration would commence in the spring.[26]

Apprehensive that its adoption by the French Navy was a threat to British security, the Royal Navy was now converting to steam and it showed, in particular, an interest in the Archimedian screw.[27] Parry, now head of the Steam Department, said to the first lord that he could quote a hundred instances in which, in calm weather or light contrary winds, the power of taking advantage by steam of occasional temporary openings in the ice might have gone far towards giving arctic expeditions complete success. That is, in twentieth-century language, auxiliary steam would give navigators a means of taking advantage of brief green traffic lights during otherwise extended ice-jams. For conversion to steam the keels of *Erebus* and *Terror* were extended to give the required vertical alignment to their stern posts, and to do this a false keel was added to each vessel, giving it, incidentally, extra hold space and also the opportunity to strike ice or ground without damage to the main body of the vessel. Each stern post had a well, up and down which the newly installed propeller could be lowered and raised, as the presence or absence of ice might demand.[28] As Thomas Maudslay and Company did not have time enough in which to supply new engines, an engine for *Erebus* was secured from the London and Greenwich Railway and one for *Terror* from the London–Birmingham Railway. They were high pressure ones, making *Erebus* and *Terror* somewhat novel at this time among vessels fitted with screw propellers; each engine had two cylinders, direct gearing, and a nominal horsepower of 30. In April and May there was a series of trials off Greenhithe and

Greenwich in which *Terror* on one occasion travelled under her own steam at three knots.[29] While Capt. James Fitzjames was enthusiastic about starting with "three years provisions and the engines," he fully appreciated the cost: "We are now full—very—... The deck is covered with coals and casks, leaving a small passage before and aft, and we are very deep in the water."[30]

The size of Franklin's ships was matched by the size and scale of his provisioning.

> Enormous quantities of provisions and fuel were carried; china, cut glass, and heavy Victorian silver encumbered the wardrooms; each ship had a library of 1200 volumes ranging from treatises on steam engines to the works of Dickens and Lever and volumes of *Punch*. Franklin was particularly concerned for the educational and spiritual welfare of his men while isolated in the Arctic wastes. Slates and arithmetic books, pens, ink, and paper were provided for classes during the winter; testaments and prayer books were available for all; and a hand-organ playing fifty tunes, ten of which were psalms or hymns, was purchased for each ship. Of special Polar equipment, except for scientific research, there was none apart from large supplies of warm underclothing and a few wolf-skin blankets. The Arctic clothing of the Franklin expedition was the stout blue cloth of Her Majesty's Navy.[31]

In all, the approach, by comparison with that of Elizabethan days, was one of "floating palaces"; it was that of carrying as much as possible of one's home environment with one, rather than emphasizing the environment which was being explored. Outwardly the very massiveness of this method engendered optimism. There was a feeling of confident pride among both the public and officials concerned with the party. In the background, however, was some disquiet. Sir John Ross promised Franklin he would search for the party if February 1847 came without word of it, and in private a veteran explorer of the Arctic and Antarctic, Comdr. Archibald M'Murdo, RN, doubted that Franklin would return.[32] The only public and strident voice of concern, however, was that of Richard King. Indeed, as it set sail in 1845, the Franklin party was in the long tradition of illusory hopes in the search for a Northwest Passage. Nor, as it launched its own expedition, was the Hudson's Bay Company fully realistic. By 1845–46, vis-à-vis both the company and the navy, Richard King, more realistic upon a number of important points than either institution, had placed himself at the centre of a developing arctic blizzard.

Shortly after Franklin got under weigh in May 1845, he spoke disparagingly of Lord Stanley to Captain Fitzjames, second-in-command aboard *Erebus*, and seemed bent upon disproving the charge the colonial secretary had made against him of inactivity in Van Diemen's Land. Never, an observer remarked, had he seen ships carry so much sail as *Erebus* and *Terror* did on their way to Stromness. Before the vessels had arrived at Lancaster Sound members of the expedition were already taking "short cuts through North America," and some of them expected to reach the Pacific in a season.[33] Having tried to go southwest from Cape Walker, but apparently having been blocked in that direction, Franklin passed between North Devon and Cornwallis Islands to sail north along Wellington Channel for about 150 miles, to latitude 77°. It is not known to what extent an open season, or the use of steam, aided Franklin in making this major foray, although as regards the latter a deduction has been made. In the ice, it has been said, an aim was to have the vessels as light as possible; yet, despite this, only a very modest amount of cast-off lumber was later found at the various sites of the Franklin expedition. From this it has been reasoned that lumber may have been used to fire the steam machinery of *Erebus* and *Terror*, which suggests that it operated effectively.[34] Nor is it known whether the boats which Franklin and one of his officers, Le Vesconte, had suggested for dispatch from the vessels were used for this purpose. It is known that Franklin did return to Barrow Strait by way of Crozier Strait, which separated Cornwallis Island and Bathurst Land, perhaps because he had encountered impenetrable ice, perhaps because he had found the channel leading too far northward.[35]

The winter of 1845–46 was spent at Beechey Island, which had an excellent harbour and was in a crossroads position for commencing discovery in 1846. Presumably the ships were housed over for winter with awnings. Washing places, an observatory, a carpenter's shop, a forge, and a large storehouse were built on shore within easy reach of the ships. No doubt school and scientific work went forward daily. On the basis of earlier and later naval habit, it may be presumed that a special day of feasting and holiday mood was managed on board for Christmas. A sense of a small community and its ramifications attaches to Beechey Island in the winter of 1845–46. While some excursions were made into the interior of the island, ten to twenty miles was probably the limit. Stone walls with a paved floor for a tent were built at one site, and several tent locations were marked with stones. A member of a search party was later to view with foreboding the form of the cooking-places and the deep ruts left by the sledges at this first winter quarter. One can see, he writes, how little Franklin's men appreciated the importance of making travel equipment light and portable when their ships were immobile.[36]

The party probably left Beechey Island during August, or, at the latest, in the first days of September 1846. The signs point to a hurried sailing from the island, presumably to take advantage of an unexpected disruption in the ice. Indeed, it was to the haste of a sudden departure that there was later attributed the strange lack at Beechey Island of a written record. No doubt, the subsequent suggestion went, Franklin wished to leave the latest intelligence and therefore delayed until the last possible moment in making a deposit; but the ice suddenly opened and it was decided to forgo the two-hour walk required to plant a record at the cairn which the party had built at the top of Beechey Island, the logical place for deposit of a message.[37]

In any event, the party now followed the course in which Franklin himself had shown an interest before leaving England. Finding Peel Sound, it proceeded south along that channel to King William's Land. By the close of the season of 1846 it had come "within 90 miles of the known sea coast of America" and had already "in two seasons sailed over 500 miles of previously unexplored waters."[38] In addition, it had probably accomplished those scientific investigations which were an important although subordinate concern. Yet at this point disaster loomed. Franklin had found Peel Sound and Franklin Strait navigable, as they sometimes are in summer. Had he now taken the continental side of King William's Land, he would have entered James Ross Strait, which leads to Rae Strait—both of which are usually open in summer—and he might, in 1846, have seen the final link in a Northwest Passage and even have completed the transit to Bering Strait.[39] The Franklin party would then have been the first to navigate and report a channel from Atlantic to Pacific, and thus would have become the undisputed discoverers of a Northwest Passage.

Yet this postulation becomes increasingly implausible if its suppositions are reviewed in reverse, from Bering Strait eastward. Both Amundsen's *Gjoa* and the RCMP's *St. Roch* required two seasons, not one, in order to travel this distance on this route; and presumably Franklin's vessels would have also, even without mishap. The party would probably, therefore, still have suffered from those ravages of scurvy that occurred in the winter of 1847–48, though perhaps with a better chance of rescue in the spring, because they might then have come closer than they actually did to the Coppermine or Mackenzie Rivers and hence both to Hudson's Bay Company posts and to the Richardson and Rae party which was on those rivers in 1848. Secondly, both *Erebus* and *Terror* were of much greater tonnage than *Gjoa*, 47 tons, or *St. Roch*, 8 tons,[40] and had definitely not been designed for the kind of coastal sailing which this passage required. Indeed, even if the Franklin party had entered James Ross Strait, it is unlikely that, with its relatively cumbersome vessels, it could have got so far as seeing by ship the last link in the passage. Even in what may be called open waters—open but nevertheless encumbered by islands and ice—*Erebus* and *Terror* could have been seriously delayed or altogether stopped.

The basic question, however, is whether there was any possibility at all that Franklin would turn towards the continent at King William's Land. No Admiralty chart available to him showed this land to be an island: Rae Strait, making it so—missed by Back in 1834 and Simpson in 1839—was yet to be discovered. All Franklin's charts would make him presume that achieving Simpson Strait, already designated as his main goal in this direction, required his turning westward, not shoreward, and thus passing into Victoria Strait. Only one book left open the possibility, and only one sketch map showed that King William's Land was an island. That book was Richard King's *Narrative*, which Franklin had aboard and the map was King's Conjectural Chart of 1845, which Franklin was unlikely to have with him.[41] In any event, both the book and the map were the work of a man whose views on the Great Fish River and the Boothia area Franklin himself had turned down a decade before; besides, Franklin's instructions, as well as the build of his vessels, were against his hugging the continent.

Franklin therefore entered Victoria Strait, which "offered in any case the shortest and most direct route" to Simpson Strait. Sailing into this relatively large ocean body which, by contrast with James Ross and Rae Straits, was almost always blocked with impenetrable ice, the vessels became hedged in by ice in 1846 and drifted helplessly, at the rate of about a mile a month, until 1848.[42] They had had to "take the ice" as Richard King had so insistently warned they might have to. There is also the possibility that the steam machinery had contributed to the loss of Franklin by helping to lodge him more quickly and deeply than would otherwise have been the case in the central Arctic. Certainly he had by this time proved the existence of a continuous channel from Barrow Strait to the upper part of Victoria Strait, and all that was required to complete the search for a Northwest Passage was proof that Victoria Strait joined Simpson Strait. The party has been called "the most record-shy"[43] of all arctic expeditions and one of the reasons for this may have been its apparent inability to travel extensively by sled and thereby to leave records. Nevertheless, in May 1847 there was sent out a small group commanded by Lieut. Graham Gore which reached at least as far as King William's Land.

A number of inferences may be made about this trip. First, part of the coast of King William's Land was a shore of Simpson Strait which, to repeat, Franklin had pointed at on a map as the place to complete a passage. Secondly, the actual day when Gore's party left *Erebus* and *Terror* was 24 May, late by exploring standards for starting a spring trip but the Queen's birthday and an appropriate date, therefore, to launch a project of national and international importance: the completion of the last link in the British search for a Northwest Passage. Thirdly, the discoverer of the document by which we know of Gore's journey, Capt. F. L. M'Clintock, believed it likely that Gore was sent to prove a passage.[44] Further inferences concern scurvy: arctic experience, both before and after Franklin's expedition, suggests that this disease was likely to appear at the close of a party's second winter, and it was found as well that scurvy weakened memory;[45] moreover, at a later date arctic experience would also suggest that when men are in precarious health (whether because of scurvy or for any other reason), even good news can kill. These are factors to bear in mind regarding Gore's journey and events subsequent to it.

Four days out, on 28 May, Gore deposited a message near Victory Point on King William's Land which stated[46] that Franklin's party had wintered at Beechey Island in 1846–47 (not 1845–46), a mistake in dates which suggests that Gore had already suffered loss of memory as a result of scurvy, and if so, that others had developed this disease as well. Indeed, it is certain that scurvy did become epidemic during the Franklin party's third winter and we also know that by April 1848, less than a year after he deposited his message, Gore himself was dead. Yet in his message Gore wrote, "All well," and specifically stated that Franklin was in command; we know, in short, that in May 1847 Franklin was alive and apparently well.

Finally, there are upon this document superinscriptions written in April 1848 by two of Gore's fellow officers, Fitzjames and Crozier; and from these we know not only that Franklin died on 11 June 1847, but also that Lieutenant Gore (as he had been when he had affixed his signature in May 1847) was now "the late Commander Gore." From this evidence it may be deduced, not only that Gore's spring journey of 1847 was in all likelihood successful, but also that it was probably completed while Franklin was still living. For, it has been argued, only Franklin would have had the authority to promote Gore to the rank of commander, and the most likely reason for such a promotion was that Gore had not only seen at Simpson Strait the last link in a passage, but had also returned with this news to *Erebus* and *Terror* in time for recognition by Sir John.[47]

This in turn leads to a final if more tenuous inference. The evidence is that Franklin died suddenly and not specifically of scurvy. All had been

well when Gore had left the vessels on 24 May 1847; nineteen days later
Franklin was dead. Taking into account the probability that, like Gore but
at the comparatively advanced age of sixty-one, Franklin was suffering
from incipient scurvy, it is possible that intelligence of a Northwest Passage, crowning in Franklin's mind his life's work and creating in him great
emotion, was a factor in his death. In any event, by mid-June 1847 Capt.
F. R. M. Crozier was the new commander.

There are animals in the arctic area, particularly seals, which can support human life, and had the Franklin party understood this fact and been
able to capitalize on it, they could probably have remained healthy.[48] Yet
the party was relying mainly on food brought with them and, as already
stated, scurvy became epidemic, so that in April 1848, with twenty-four
men dead, the rest weakened, and the three-year supply of food running
out, *Erebus* and *Terror* were abandoned.[49] The Franklin party was now
repeating in more extreme circumstances to the west of Boothia a story
already enacted by Sir John Ross's expedition on the eastern shores of
Boothia–Somerset in 1829–33. Members of the party knew that an expedition had been sent down the Back River on the west side of Boothia to find
Ross in 1833–34, but that he had been rescued by accident in 1833 on the
eastern shore where, incidentally, there lay the *Fury* supplies. Perhaps
scurvy had produced in Crozier a lack of mental alertness; and this may
explain what some have thought his poor judgment in not heading eastward. On the other hand, he and his party may have hoped that, as in
1834, a rescue party would be sent down the Back River. He could even
have made a "split" decision, sending some of his expedition in one direction and some in the other. Instead, under Crozier the party marched as a
whole to the Great Fish River, probably in order to secure, as the chief
incentive of all, fresh game along the Back River that would help cure the
scurvy. Other motives were, perhaps, the hope of reaching the nearest
Hudson's Bay Company post, Fort Resolution, and of getting help from the
Eskimos.[50]

But the party was not adapted in training, equipment, skill, or size to the
escape that was planned. As the boats and sledges were prepared for the
abandonment, even with all lives at stake and perhaps all the more because
of dulled faculties, the method by which the expedition had originally
been equipped in England persisted, so that in one case, a "boat and
sledges, very heavy in themselves, were overladen with a mass of things ...
entirely superfluous."[51] The party had had aboard a copy of King's *Narrative*, and it is possible that this was placed on one of the sleds so as to
furnish information for the intended journey up the Back. In it King had
warned against heavy burdens, heavy boats, large parties, and men inexpe-

rienced in travelling through northern regions.[52] His views, written but rejected twelve years before, had now been placed on file again in London, in June 1847 and in succeeding months, in yet another attempt by King to go down the Back River. Perhaps the only chance of rescue for Crozier's party lay in the acceptance of King's project; yet, as we will see, that had in fact once again been turned down.

Its commander dead, its numbers decimated, and its survivors emaciated by scurvy, the Franklin party was nevertheless large enough to frighten away Eskimo help near Cape Herschel. Already it had left its own superinscriptions upon Gore's message at Point Victory and now it painfully made its way on foot over the west and south coasts of King William's Land, like a travelling hospital in which attendants were fast becoming patients. It was this party which proved, if Gore's party of 1847 had not already done so, the existence of a Northwest Passage. Yet in either case the proof was only for themselves; for the dozen books which they carried with them (records, presumably, of the party's findings since 1845) were to perish at the hands of Eskimo children,[53] unless some remnant of them was deposited elsewhere, possibly although not likely at the King cache at Montreal Island in the Back River estuary, which some of the party may have reached as the expedition's most southerly point.[54] At all events, although certain members of the party did return to one of the vessels and may have lived there until the spring of 1849, none of the shore groups survived 1848. As officers and men proceeded southward they followed ordered naval discipline. It is "a magnificent tribute to the spirit of the men," it has been written, "that discipline and order were in no way impaired."[55]

The accomplishment of large magnetic and other scientific surveys had ended with no studies reaching London. The purpose of finding a far northern passage, or of sailing diagonally across a more southerly one, had resulted in a retreat to the shores of the continent. The use of steam had ended with the men walking. The attempt to sail without simultaneous cooperation by land had concluded in the party seeking escape, and possibly incoming assistance, by the most inland route of all. Objections to an inexpensive support party had led to a dénouement which, it would turn out, would cost between half a million and two million pounds. Reliance almost entirely on canned and preserved foods had ended in what was likely a desperate search for fresh food. The attempt to carry a whole community in miniature had resulted in the survival of not one member of the community. The aim of the expedition to train officers and men for naval service elsewhere had ended in their being unavailable, trained or untrained, for the Crimean War. The preservation of service discipline and unbroken ranks was at odds with breaking up into small groups and "going native," and hence with preservation of life itself. Instead of the Franklin expedition forestalling an American search for the passage, it was to lead to an American entry into the Arctic to search for Franklin. For, finally, if this was discovery, it was by a *reductio ad absurdum*. The location of the expedition that had found a passage was now itself unknown and the members of the party were deceased. Unable to tell its own tale, the expedition would itself become an object of search.

In short, as exploration had advanced towards the centre of the North American Arctic it had been thrown out of focus. Normally, discovery vessels were not only a means of finding new lands but were also surveyors' platforms and scientific laboratories. Now, however, ice and the archipelago in the central Arctic had forced a separation of these two elements, placing marine discovery and marine surveying in conflict. The navy had ignored the possibility that the prompt and realistic way to find a passage might be to send to the Arctic a scouting party by land or small vessels to test and sail it. The Franklin expedition had, in consequence, gone into the Arctic in the manner of hydrographers, land surveyors, military map readers, or even settlers, not of discoverers, and the results had matched the method. The party had surveyed a Northwest Passage, not discovered it; seen it, not reported it. News, that is, had not been conveyed to London. Indeed, now it was necessary both to find the discoverers and also, so far as possible, what it was that they had found. The search *of* Franklin had been for a passage within an "extensive blank area"[56]—a search, so to speak, for a rope through a haystack. The search *for* Franklin resembled the search for a needle in an even larger haystack, inasmuch as it meant finding a single spot that might, or might not, lie within the original area. An entirely new and much more difficult task than the first one, it would induce a still more elaborate survey in succession to the original one by Franklin, and would delay for more than a decade the actual discovery of the coastal passage.[57] Brilliant but disastrous, magnificent but not discovery, a gallant failure which appealed much to the sporting sense, the Franklin expedition was the charge of a heavy brigade from which none had returned. A decade ahead of the army the senior service had produced its own Balaclava.

By contrast with the maximum lading of *Erebus* and *Terror* when they sailed from England, the boats of the expedition that set out from Churchill in 1846 were lightened as a result of John Rae's decision to leave behind a quantity of articles he considered not absolutely essential, such as tobacco and salt. Indeed, the total lading of his boats was less than the amount of tobacco alone, totalling more than three tons, that was carried on Franklin's vessels.[58] In his first season Rae, like Franklin in his first season, made a foray northward, but again on a smaller scale. Arriving at Repulse Bay late in July, he crossed to Committee Bay, discovering Rae Isthmus, named after him, and so proved that, contrary to expectations, Melville was peninsular. He found in addition that the tides in Committee Bay made it likely that Boothia would turn out to be peninsular also; and, finally, he found that Committee Bay was too ice-clogged for him to employ boats there.[59] As perhaps in the case of Franklin, an early reconnaissance had quickly dispelled illusions.

Returning to the head of Repulse Bay, newly discovered by him, Rae now proposed to do what had not been done before on these northern voyages: winter without a ship and beyond the treeline; yet he had only four months' provisions, all his boats could carry.[60] The house which Rae built for his shelter, commenced in August and finished early in September, was reminiscent of shelters of Thule Eskimos who had at one time lived in stone houses in this region, for the walls of Rae's house were also of stone, although its roof was of sails stretched across oars. The structure proved clammy and it was placed in a poor position where heavy drifting of snow weighed down the roof. Despite these failings, it was a wintering quarter, a base, and, technically, a fur-trade post, named by Rae "Fort Hope."[61] Indeed, the very hardships which its inadequacies engendered may have helped the health and morale of the party, by comparison with the effects of confinement, although in relative shelter and warmth, upon Franklin's crew. Certainly the need for Rae's party to procure its own food did contribute to the health of the expedition. Stationed at a height of land (between Hudson Bay and the Arctic) which led to Melville Peninsula, Rae was advantageously placed for an autumn and spring migration of caribou. In contrast to Franklin's party, Rae's group, and not least its leader, was already trained to provide for itself. By the end of November 162 reindeer and 200 partridges had been shot, and a few salmon caught.[62] This meant not only that the party could travel more lightly than the Franklin party but also that its members were not subject to scurvy.

Christmas and especially New Year's were spent in merry fashion, when on each day a "spirited game at foot ball" stimulated an appetite for "fat venison steaks and plum pudding" and, in addition to these, the men were given a "small supply of brandy." Yet the winter, in which the lowest temperature was −47°F., was extremely stormy, with prevailing winds from the northwest; frequently one "could not move fifty yards from the house for several days together" and at such times the party had only one meal during each day.[63] By February the party's stock of oil was so low that they were forced to keep early and late hours, "lying occasionally fourteen hours in bed, as we found that to sit up in a house in which the temperature was some degrees below zero, without either light or fire, was not very pleasant."[64]

Knowing now that he could not use boats in Committee Bay, as the spring approached Rae made two sledges. On its final trip the Franklin party would use boats of heavy structure placed on sleds; Rae's party now used the boats' battens themselves, the only wood available, to make sleds. Three of these nailed together formed runners on sleds which, like the Eskimos', were six to seven feet long, seventeen inches broad, and seven inches high.[65] There were many Eskimos in the area with dogs for sale,[66] and Rae bought four for each sled. Well poised for his spring journeys, owing to Fort Hope's geographic position, Rae commenced the first of these on 5 April. Travelling with a party of six, including an Eskimo, Ivitchuk, Rae rose daily as early as 3 a.m. and built at night a snow hut, whose method of construction he and his men had practised during the winter. Inside the hut one bed was made for all the men. Supper could be pemmican and water, or there might be "pemmican seasoned with a handful of flour, a very nourishing and not unpalatable dish."[67] Of a later arctic trip Rae was to write: "The breakfast my party found it best to work upon was a pint of tea, a piece of frozen pemmican and half a biscuit. We never stopped to eat or drink [but] put a small piece of our breakfast allowance of pemmican in our pockets which we munched at our pleasure . . . during the ten or twelve hours we were travelling."[68]

Rae early increased his speed on this trip through the adoption of the Eskimo practice of icing the sled runners. However, he soon decided he had made a mistake as regards his sleds. For going over hummocks and rough ice it would have been better, he was now sure, to use the Indian or toboggan-type sleigh, broad and flat-bottomed, rather than his present Eskimo type with high runners. (See Appendix 2.) Rae had previously broken his chronometers and, to compensate for this, he measured with a stretched line for some days at the outset of his trip the exact distance he travelled. Gaining thereby a basis by which to estimate his travel rate, he now daily determined longitude as well as latitude. He also daily observed magnetic variation, and acquired in addition knowledge and samples of the geology, as well as of the flora and fauna of the areas through which he passed.[69]

One of the worst days on which Rae had ever travelled was 15 April as he made for Helen Island in Pelly Bay. The cold stopped his watch; a dog had to be abandoned; and the whole group, the Eskimo Ivitchuk included, was frostbitten.[70] By 18 April Rae, wishing to reduce his party, had left behind two men, and on that date, knowing he was near his destination, he ordered the remaining men to stay behind also. Setting out alone, within an hour's walk he came to what he was sure was Lord Mayor's Bay. He had forecast very accurately his time of arrival and, besides familiar landmarks from Ross's chart, his longitude agreed with that of Sir John Ross, so that, it was later argued, all his intervening longitudes between Lord Mayor's Bay and Repulse Bay must also have been accurate. Later James Clark Ross attested he was sure by Rae's description that this was indeed the bay. By seeing continuous land from Committee Bay to this point Rae had proved the peninsularity of Boothia. He found that here at Lord Mayor's Bay Boothia's isthmus was only a mile wide and that the location appeared, by the stone markers on it, to be a favourite resort of the natives.[71]

Rae was now 150 geographical miles from where the Franklin party lay, beset. Ignorant of Franklin's proximity, he turned back, rejoined his men, and made for his base, satisfying himself on the way that Pelly Bay south of Lord Mayor's Bay was not a strait. The bay extended, Rae later reported, sixteen or eighteen miles from the position where he had viewed it from Helen Island on his return trip, and he was convinced that from it there was no continuous water route westward to Simpson Strait. When outbound, Rae had travelled directly across Simpson Peninsula. He now traced its full coastline as he completed, within a period of two and a half weeks, his return to Repulse Bay. Reaching Fort Hope on 5 May, he successfully concluded the longest journey by foot yet made along the arctic coast.[72]

The second of Rae's journeys was begun from Repulse Bay on 13 May, a week after the return to Fort Hope, with a party of five including Rae. It was to explore along the other, eastern arm of the Y whose base was at Fort Hope and whose two arms stretched up either shore of Committee Bay. The western shore and arm of the Y had been completed, and Rae's instructions required him now to reach the Straits of Fury and Hecla by the bay's eastern shore. This time the hindrance was warm weather, and Rae did not take sleds with him except at the outset. Not only was the snow melting; he considered that the sleds had proved impractical on his first trip because of their high runners, and his dogs had failed in strength. Provisions were similar to those on the earlier trip: two bags of pemmican, each weighing 90 lb.; seventy reindeer tongues weighing a total of nearly 30 lb.; and 36 lb. of flour. Rae also took a little tea, chocolate, and sugar, as well as a gallon and a half of alcohol and a small quantity of oil.[73] With long hours of sunshine available, this time a night's journey could end, not start, at 3 a.m. and "supper" be eaten, after the snow hut and small kitchen had been prepared, at 6 a.m. The ice, however, made for some of the roughest travel Rae had experienced: "Walking became most difficult. At one minute we sank nearly waist-deep in snow, at another we were up to our knees in salt water, and then again on a piece of ice so slippery that with our wet and frozen shoes, it was impossible to keep from falling."[74]

Once again as he approached his furthest point, Rae travelled with a reduced party. By 27 May he had with him only two men, and at 9:30 p.m. on that day he set out with one of them, snow falling fast. At 4 a.m. they reached a point near Cape Crozier, from which Rae could see Cape Ellice, and from this in turn, he was sure, the Straits of Fury and Hecla were not more than ten miles distant. "If Arrowsmith's Chart be correct," he wrote, "I joined my discoveries to those of Sir Edward Parry." Having built a cairn, the two men commenced their return to Repulse Bay.[75] They rejoined the other members of their party and the whole group reached Fort Hope on 9 June. At Repulse Bay the party had to await the going out of the ice; they set sail on 11 August and reached the Churchill River towards the end of the month.

Rae and his men had composed (excluding Ivitchuk, the Eskimo with Rae on his first trip) a party of eleven. They had secured by their own exertions, during a fifteen months' expedition, food for a year. The first of Rae's spring journeys had been 712 English miles, performed in thirty-two days at 22¼ miles a day; the second had been 572 English miles in twenty-seven days at a daily average of 21¼ miles. Rae had discovered about 655 statute miles of new coastline[76] which had, he said, baffled Parry, Lyon, and Back in expeditions that had cost the British taxpayer £60,000 to £80,000. His own party, Rae wrote, had conducted its exploration for the "comparatively trifling expense of 1,000 or 1,200 Stg." In topography Rae had "as far as practicable" attained the objects of his expedition. He had also brought back with him a modest yet useful (and unlike Franklin's, usable) set of scientific findings.[77] Rae had maintained discipline, not only among his own men, but in meeting Eskimos, upon whose way of life and travel he had, on the whole, patterned himself. In brief, he had accomplished his aim after the manner of a scouting expedition, just managing to reach various destinations, often short of food, yet never in serious danger. He had not lost a man and, other than his interpreter Ouligbuck, who had suffered a wounded arm and had had to stay at Fort Hope, no one associated with the party had been injured. Indeed, perhaps the only question was whether it was all quite sporting: could not anyone succeed in arctic travel by such means as these?[78]

Sir John Ross was delighted to find himself proved right in regard to Boothia, but Rae's demonstration had a different effect upon Richard

King. Although there was in many ways a community of outlook upon polar travel between King and Rae, it was obvious the former did not admire Rae as he had Thomas Simpson. While the London surgeon claimed (wrongly) that Rae had now shown that the Thelon River ran into Prince Regent Inlet, making, said King, Boothia's peninsularity all the more likely, he did not agree that Boothia's nature was now finally proved. Rae, King averred, had done no more than demonstrate that Boothia's peninsularity was highly likely; conclusive proof would have to come at Boothia's western shore.[79]

In contrast to King, Sir George Back wrote to Rae in "a kind and obliging" tone,[80] commencing a cordial acquaintanceship of many years. Thus, closer though he was in many ways to King's attitude, Rae was aligned personally with Back, and was all the more likely, therefore, to imbibe in the future something of Sir George's rather than King's view of the Back River, a matter of potential importance.

King had reacted explosively to Rae's trip; the navy showed a certain condescension mixed with indifference. The manuscript of Rae's *Narrative* was "sent by request to the Hydrographer of the Admiralty and allowed to remain more than a year in his hands, although he had no right to have it." In fact, Sir Francis Beaufort forgot he had it, while the secretary of the company was too diffident to request its return. When publication did at last occur, in 1850, not only had "any interest" in Rae's exploration "passed away"; worse still, the book had been so edited at the Hydrographer's Office that Rae himself did not recognize his "bantling."[81] In 1850 there appeared also an Admiralty chart representing the greater part of Pelly Bay not by a firm but by a dotted line. Thus the Admiralty, still cherishing the old hope for a channel eastward from Simpson Strait, yet barred now from believing that Boothia, further north, was an island, looked hopefully instead for a continuous water route further south to Pelly Bay. Rae responded vigorously. He and one of his men, he wrote, had in 1847 distinctly seen the whole of Pelly Bay from the summit of Helen Island. His observation was confirmed by the charts of the Eskimos, who spent "their summer on its shore"; they had pointed to where two rivers fell into the bottom of the bay, from which Rae had taken bearing. He had got his information through his interpreter who spoke "both Esquimaux and English fluently," yet, had it occurred to him that anyone would doubt the existence of the bay, he would have put the matter beyond question since he had had "four powerful dogs" and a free day in which to travel, one of his men being laid up for a day after hard travel.[82] Discovery, Rae himself was discovering, did not consist simply in bringing information home; it required also that the information be accepted.

For all that, because Repulse Bay was not a channel and Boothia was a peninsula, Rae had not himself completed a survey of the north coast of North America and had not found a passage. He had only completed his expedition's aim, "as far as practicable," a failure which the navy might now compound. For the very searches for the Franklin expedition, itself unable to report the passage it had found or would soon find to the west of Boothia, might now, by preoccupying Rae in other directions, keep him, paradoxically, away from the Boothia area. To reach Boothia's western shore, not quite achieved at the outset of Rae's career, would thus become eventually the long-delayed but last and chief aim in his exploration of the Canadian Arctic.

5

👑👑

Richard King and the Early Franklin Searches (1847–1849)

For months before John Rae's arrival in England in 1847 Richard King had been convinced that to the west of Boothia, or as he called it North Somerset, the Franklin party lay beset. That Rae's achievement might divert attention from this region explains in part, perhaps, King's caustic reaction to it. True to his pledge, Sir John Ross had already shown concern, by writing to the Admiralty in January and February of that year. Earlier than all save Ross, King wrote, on 10 June 1847, to Lord Grey at the Colonial Office: "One Hundred and twenty-six men are at this moment in imminent danger of perishing from famine. Sir John Franklin's Expedition to the North Pole in 1845 as far as we know has not been heard of since it sailed."[1]

Several times King compared the situation to that experienced by Sir John Ross on his second voyage. Because Franklin's route had "not . . . been sufficiently announced," King was in a position of difficulty; nevertheless, according to Sir John Barrow, Franklin's route was "by Barrow Strait and the Sea washing North Somerset on the one side and Banks and Wollaston Land on the other." Franklin must, therefore, have either sailed "southward along the Western land of North Somerset" or else "attempted . . . a short cut westward . . . and wrecked himself on Banks and Wollaston Land." Had he chosen the western land of North Somerset, one should certainly look there; but one should also look there if Franklin had chosen the second course. For, in that event, he would have run headlong into a danger King had already predicted, namely the ice that clung "to lands having an eastern aspect." If Banks and Wollaston Land were, for this reason, the resting place of *Erebus* and *Terror*, and the party had kept together, they would take to their boats and make for the ice-free western land of North Somerset, either to reach Barrow Strait in search of the northern whalers, or the Great Fish River in search of Eskimos, for provisions or "letter of conveyance" to the Copper Indians. "It is to the western land of North Somerset," wrote King, "that we must direct our attention." If he could keep his party together, Franklin would, in the manner of Sir John Ross, "rest where he was and daily look for assistance from home."[2]

According to King, there were only two ways to help Franklin: either to convey provisions to him, or convey him to the provisions. Only the latter, however, was practicable. One or more vessels should be dispatched in the summer of 1848 "with provisions to the Western Land of North Somerset by Barrow Strait." However, experience had shown the great superiority in arctic discovery of land journeys over sea ones, and the western land of North Somerset could "easily be reached by a party travelling overland from Canada." For that reason, rather than meet the "Provision Vessels" sent by way of Barrow Strait, it might be desirable that the lost party be led to Hudson's Bay Company depots on the Mackenzie River or on Great Slave Lake. Therefore a call should be made on the company "to use their best exertions to fill their northern depots with pemmican, dried meat and fish," also for the summer of 1848; and information of this should be conveyed by a small party provided with Indian guides and travelling (King implied) down the Back River. King volunteered his own services as leader of this small party, or he would go as subordinate to "any officer the Government" might appoint, provided the leader was of King's age and physical vigour. Finally, in King's view, there was the danger to Franklin of scurvy. Unless tidings of Franklin came by autumn 1847, Franklin's party would have to spend a third winter in the Arctic and, as Parry's second expedition had in its third winter, might experience serious cases of scurvy. Earl Grey, King trusted, would not allow a fourth wintering without permitting King to render the only likely succour, namely as "messenger" to Franklin as to "where provisions are stored for him."[3]

Several minutes were written on this letter of June 1847. James Stephen, permanent colonial under-secretary, said the matter was "very much out of my path" and presumed, if neither Hawes (the parliamentary under-secretary) nor Lord Grey was conversant with the subject, that the Royal Geographical Society or the Admiralty should be consulted. While noting that King did not even know Franklin's route, Hawes disavowed for himself any "opinion worthy of attention"; he advised that the Admiralty, or perhaps Sir John Pelly of the Hudson's Bay Company, be consulted. Lord Grey described himself as "totally unable to form an opinion" upon the matter and he too advised consultation with the Admiralty.[4] Admiralty opinion, indeed, soon came. On 17 June James Stephen received a note from M. A. Blackwood, senior clerk and head of the North American department of the Colonial Office:

> I have learned from Sir Edward Parry that Richard King ... is a person who omits no opportunity of directing public attention upon himself, so that it would be scarcely safe to follow his views upon this subject. ... The Admiralty and those persons who are qualified to form an opinion on the matter, do not entertain, at present ... any apprehension concerning the fate of ... Franklin and his party.

Hawes wrote that he himself had had a note from another source corroborating the tenor of Blackwood's minute, and a formal reference to the Admiralty, it was decided, was uncalled for. On 28 June King was sent a simple letter of acknowledgement without comment.[5]

The Admiralty did, however, decide that, if no news had come by late 1847, action should be taken. In November, in consequence, it planned for 1848 three projects, with Hudson's Bay Company help. The first was a search for Franklin by two vessels passing through Bering Strait, one of them *Plover*, a store-ship under Commander Moore of 226 tons with additional provisions for 138 men, over and above her own suggested crew of forty-five, in case she fell in with Franklin's party. From this ship boats would be detached so as to reach the Mackenzie River. The other vessel was the survey ship *Herald*, already in the Pacific under Captain Kellett. The second project was an expedition to Barrow Strait in two ships under Sir James Ross. After tracing the shores of Lancaster Sound, Barrow Strait, and Wellington Channel, it was to search, in 1848, the coast between Capes Clarence and Walker. Capt. E. J. Bird, second-in-command to Ross, was to winter in his vessel near Cape Rennell, while Ross in his own ship was to proceed to Melville Island or Banks Land, and winter there. During the following spring, Bird was to dispatch parties down the west coast of Boothia, possibly as far as Cape Nicholai (Cape Nicholas of today), and another party, if it was considered advisable, was to search the blank space to the southward of Prince Regent's Inlet. When the ice broke up in Barrow Strait in 1849, a steam launch of Bird's vessel was to proceed to Lancaster Sound to communicate with whaling ships, by which the Admiralty could forward further orders.[6]

Meanwhile a third expedition was to undertake a land search down the Mackenzie River, led by Sir John Richardson. With Rae as second-in-command, this party was to trace the arctic coast between the Mackenzie and Coppermine Rivers and the shores of Victoria and Wollaston Lands lying opposite Cape Krusenstern, for Richardson thought there was a channel to the northward between Wollaston and Victoria Lands. This, he felt, was the most direct route Franklin could have taken from Cape Walker to the continent; accordingly, if Franklin's ships were stopped and abandoned, members of his party would make either for Lancaster Sound to meet whalers, or else seek the Mackenzie by way of this channel, in order to attain relief at company posts. In the spring of 1849 Ross was to dispatch from his vessel at Melville Island one sled party which would proceed along the west coast of Banks Land to Cape Bathurst or Cape Parry and then ascend the Mackenzie to company posts, and another which would search the east coast of Banks Land towards the estuary of the Coppermine, join Richardson and assist him, or return home.[7]

The three projects, that by Bering Strait, that of Ross in his two vessels, and that of Richardson, were not disconnected enterprises. Each was expected to contribute its allotted share towards a single plan. It was a plan, however, with which Richard King voiced strong disagreement, when he wrote again to Lord Grey in November and December 1847. In his view the last ray of hope that the Franklin party could save itself had now vanished. At first he knew only of Richardson's proposed trip and complained that Richardson would be searching too far west; but later when he learned of the projected sea voyages, and more as well about Richardson's project, he argued that the plan was still inadequate. If Richardson failed to find the lost expedition between the Mackenzie and Coppermine Rivers, or on Wollaston Land, he was to search Victoria Land during the summer of 1849. But Victoria Land was as easy to reach from the Great Fish River as was the west coast of North Somerset, and by the time that Richardson got there "our lost countrymen will have ceased to exist."[8]

Besides, Victoria Land would not be the location of the missing party itself, since Franklin would make in boats for the west land of North Somerset which King now called the "Boundary of the Passage." This was the place where one was likely to find Franklin; but if Thomas Simpson in the prime of life could not reach this "Boundary" from Richardson's retreat (Great Bear Lake), was Richardson himself, at his age, likely to do so? Simpson was planning instead, when his death occurred, to use the Great Fish River, "the ice free and . . . high road" to the Boundary. So only Sir James Ross's project along the west coast of North Somerset offered hope of success. Yet Barrow Strait had been ice-bound in 1832, and might again be so in 1848. King, by contrast, would use a route (the Back River) already discovered, in which every step was sure. The search expeditions of Ross, Richardson, and King would provide "so many guarantees" that a full search would be "well done"; King's project would "fill up the blank" left by the Admiralty's plans, and satisfy the public that every rescue effort possible was under way. The Colonial Office, however, referred King in December to the answer they had already given to his letter of 25 November; in this they had, in turn, referred him for employment to the Admiralty.[9]

In his third and last letter to the Colonial Office King expressed sorrow at the most recent reply. Emphasizing that he was not soliciting employment but simply trying to "save the lives of 126 of our fellow creatures," he said that some change must have occurred if Grey's office was not the agency for his project, since it had sent out all polar land journeys; above all, King questioned the utility of his applying to the Admiralty. The Admiralty Board's "hostile feeling" toward his views on arctic discoveries had already resulted in the suppression of his name in a return to the House of Commons. King concluded: "For the sake of our suffering fellow countrymen, whose miseries and hardships I can perhaps above most men conceive and appreciate, I deeply regret your Lordship's determination. It is a hard thing that 126 men should perish when the means to save them are in your Lordship's power."[10]

Meanwhile King had had some notice in the press. In June 1847 *The Times* had (according to King) published the gist of his letter of the 10th of that month to Earl Grey. The surgeon, *The Times* said, had placed a heavy responsibility on Grey in claiming his project was the only one which would give the help Franklin had a right to expect. Commending King's excellence as a geographer, the *Nautical Standard* stated at about the same time that the surgeon was, "well known in ... arctic discovery, highly respected in his profession, and ... esteemed by scientific societies," and urged careful consideration of his plan. While the Franklin party should be sought by a "heavy arctic caravansary [*sic*]" under Richardson, the government should dispatch as well, at the mere cost of £10,000, an auxiliary party under King according to his own specifications. Let King's "little band of venturous *voyageurs* ... shout the glad *halloo* of coming help along the desert plains, and amid the mountain bergs of the icebound world of waters."[11]

Printing in November 1847 John Rae's official report of his trip, the *Athenaeum* argued that the successful coastal explorations of Thomas Simpson in the past and of Rae now, both "by the same simple means," contrasted with the current painful uncertainty connected with the large-scale sea expedition of Franklin. Not only did this antithesis give support to King's longstanding advocacy of polar land journeys by comparison with marine ones; Rae's successful journey had also supported King's emphasis that Boothia was peninsular. Formerly the *Athenaeum* had only given space for King to present his own views; now its support was active, and it insisted that his opinions were "entitled ... to serious attention." He should be heard on the subjects of Franklin's probable position and the best means of rescuing him. Another journal, the *Pictorial Times*, protested in December what it called "the gross unfairness" with which those in power treated King, "the most correct authority" on arctic geography, and the man best qualified to conduct a search for Franklin; it turned, it said, in disgust from the subject.[12]

Despite his reluctance, King did write to the Admiralty. In a letter of 16 February 1848[13] he repeated to the Lords Commissioners much of what he had already said to Lord Grey, but he wrote now with even greater urgency and quoted more directly from Barrow than he had in the past: "The old route of Parry through Lancaster Sound and Barrow Strait, as far as the last land on its southern shore, and thence in a direct line to Bhering Straits, is the route ordered to be pursued by Franklin."[14]

Assuming from this quotation that Franklin had been directed, not to Cape Walker as was actually the case, but rather to Banks Land, King spoke of Franklin being stopped (as Parry had been) between Banks Land and Melville Island. In that case he would sail south and west, "according as Banks Land trends for Victoria or Wollaston Lands," would likely be wrecked, and his party would make in "boats for the western land of North Somerset," providing it was not too distant. King should go, therefore, to this western land or else to the eastern part of Victoria Land. The Back River, King wrote, was the means to reach either location, but of the two his mind dwelt upon the latter, that is the west coast of Boothia. To get there he proposed to travel in one season from England to the mouth of the Back, a task normally taking two summers. His project, he wrote, would be "the boldest journey ... ever ... attempted in the northern regions of America," and was justifiable only by the extreme circumstances.[15]

King urged in his letter that, by contrast with his own, Richardson's plan was useless because, once again, he could not reach from the Mackenzie or Coppermine the western land of North Somerset; Simpson, King reiterated, had found he could do so only by the Back River. Further, a search by Bering Strait would assume that Franklin had accomplished a passage, whereas tracing the continuity of Banks Land with Victoria and Wollaston Lands (as Sir James Ross wished) assumed that Ross himself would accomplish a passage. Neither assumption was realistic. Barrow Strait had been blocked in 1832 and might be so again in 1848 and the Ross party might itself become lost. By contrast, a party of King's down the Back River would be conducted by someone who had been for two-thirds of its period acting commander of the Back River party of 1833–35. If King's plan was thrown aside, all would depend upon Ross's party, that is to say, upon "a single throw in the face of almost certain failure."[16]

By now, as already indicated, King's views had received publicity and Franklin had been absent, without word, for a considerable period. The Admiralty asked Parry and Ross to comment on King's letter. Parry, who had been a chief bar in preventing the Colonial Office from taking King seriously eight months earlier, was now in some ways favourably impressed. On 23 February he agreed that Franklin might have been stopped where King had suggested, and might have attempted "to fall back on the western coast of North Somerset," wherever, he added, that might be. Parry considered, however, that the means by which King proposed to get there were "extremely hazardous and uncertain," while "the energy, skill and intelligence" of Sir James Ross would, with Ross's ships, boats, or travelling parties, find it "a matter of no difficult enterprise" to achieve that same coast.[17]

It was Ross himself who was the most determined opponent of King's scheme and the warmest proponent of his own.[18] King's understanding of Franklin's course, he wrote on the last day of February, was directly contrary to Franklin's instructions. Assuming, nevertheless, that Franklin had sailed where King envisaged, his party would reach a point of land which was distanced only 280 and 420 miles respectively from the Coppermine and Mackenzie Rivers, both of them streams easily attainable, that afforded an advance of provisions, and that were relatively easy of access to England. On the other hand, the same position was 360 miles and 500 miles respectively from the west coast of North Somerset and the mouth of the Great Fish River, at neither of which could Franklin hope to get a single day's provisions for so large a party as his. Knowing well the impossibility of ascending the Great Fish River or obtaining food on the barren grounds, Sir John would make neither for North Somerset nor this river. There was, indeed, no conceivable position for the naval expedition from which it would head for the Back, or at which a party down the Back would reach it.

King, Ross continued, could not possibly reach Great Slave Lake before the first week in June of that year (1848). Could Indians then hunt in sufficient numbers for the crews of the two ships, and where? How long would Franklin be in getting to King, and on what would his party subsist as they marched? In other words, even if he reached Franklin, what use would King be? He would rather himself need relief than be able to provide it. If in 1835 the expert Back, "in 43 days of the best part of the summer," could advance only about sixty miles north of the Back estuary, how could King, with his small experience, imperfect knowledge of navigation, and relative lack of supplies, accomplish so very much in a single season? Moreover, while ice could occasionally cause delay or even a complete stoppage in Baffin Bay, it was not true that Barrow Strait had been ice-bound in 1832. Ross had never known it to be so in seven seasons of his own experience, or heard of it being so in thirty years. On the contrary, it was by steam launches, sent out from vessels which Ross himself would command on a voyage to Barrow Strait and beyond, that the western land of North Somerset and all its inlets could be "thoroughly examined." Small, powered craft could cope with that thin crust of ice which covered the sea before winter's full onset, enabling Ross's projected party to travel later in the season and along much more coastline than could ships or boats propelled by oars.[19]

King did not see at this time the letters of Parry and Ross. Shortly after they were written he again addressed the Admiralty. He had given his plan, he wrote on 3 March 1848, the most mature consideration, and would be only too pleased to explain it at the Admiralty in person. If his expedition was to go, it would have to leave by 15 March, and he would have to resign a number of offices and appointments. It seems possible King himself carried his brief letter to the Admiralty, or had a courier do so: on the day it was written the lords commissioners wrote in reply that they had no intention of changing their plans or asking for the surgeon's help. The final letter by King on arctic matters at this time was to Lady Franklin. She had promised prizes of £1,000 to the complement of any ship finding the Franklin party, making extraordinary exertions to do so, or conveying the Franklin party to England. On 29 March King told Lady Franklin she had been "very ill-advised." If, he wrote, prizes of the same amount had been authorized six months earlier for expeditions, instead, down the Back and Coppermine, the whole coastline from the latter to the west coast of North Somerset could have been searched in the summer of 1848. Even now, similar prizes might ensure that a large part of the coastline would be searched in the summer of 1849, a year in advance of Richardson's exploration and at about the same time that Ross's expedition, "a forlorn hope," would be en route.[20]

Richard Cyriax has made a study of King's proposal to the Admiralty in 1848 and of Sir James Ross's reaction to it.[21] He feels that, while an expedition down the Back River at this time would probably not have saved lives, it would doubtless have found traces of the Franklin party and directed the search to the proper quarter. Cyriax concedes, therefore, that it is "beyond question extremely unfortunate" that the "momentous decision" was made at the very beginning of the Franklin search not to go down the Back River. Nevertheless, he judges King's analysis to have been fortuitous rather than discerning, and calls into question the surgeon's plan. King, he avers, had an entirely erroneous opinion of the route Franklin was ordered to follow; no one at home knew for certain where the west coast of North Somerset lay; and, most important of all, how could Franklin, in the absence of any knowledge on his part of incoming help by the Back River, be expected to decide to retreat along it? If, indeed, King's opinions "are examined solely in the light of what was then known or could be reasonably inferred, it becomes apparent that he arrived at the right conclusion from extremely questionable premises."[22]

In contrast, Cyriax has a high regard for the opinions of Sir James Ross. Ross, he says, was the sole "Arctic" who had been at both the northwest and southwest corners of the quadrilateral across which Franklin was instructed to sail, namely Cape Dundas on Melville Island and King William's Land; alone among "Arctics" he had quite correctly adjudged massive ice at both these extremes to be a part of the same frozen stream which moves from M'Clure Strait down M'Clintock Channel and Victoria Strait towards Queen Maud Gulf. Although, when expert opinion had been canvassed in preparing Franklin's instructions, Ross himself had expressed only a slight misgiving concerning this stream, nevertheless Cyriax emphasizes that Ross had indeed discerned it and now accurately assessed it as the cause of Franklin's detention. In fact, Ross's views, compared with those of King, were "amply justified by the evidence then available" and came "very much nearer to the truth than those expressed by any of his [Ross's] contemporaries."[23]

However, Cyriax has neglected an important point. He has studied Ross's views from the early 1830s but has failed to do the same for King's. He does not refer to King's chart of 1845 and is not fully aware that in the period 1833–48 King had developed premises and a point of view leading him on a number of important matters to different conclusions from those of the Admiralty. Alone, he had argued the existence of Queen Maud Gulf and Cape Britannia and, with one other, Sir John Ross, the peninsularity of North Somerset. These features had by now been established, but in 1836 when King had made proposals which entailed them, he had been disregarded. He had accurately assessed as well the insularity of King William's Land and had developed a theory that, while ice clings to lands of eastern aspects, those of western aspects are ice-free. He had largely assessed the position, not just the nature, of Boothia or North Somerset; as a result, from 1835 he had viewed its western shore as probably the locale of the last link in a Northwest Passage and from 1845 had, with full justification, become convinced of this. King had predicted, accurately, the failure of Sir George Back at Repulse Bay in 1836. In contrast to Sir James Ross and other naval "Arctics," he had foreseen that Wollaston and Victoria Lands were one, and that the quadrilateral across which Franklin was instructed to sail was primarily filled with land.

Moreover, King viewed this composite land mass as having a particular contour that, first, sloped at its northern side towards the west coast of North Somerset and, secondly, had ice clinging to its eastern side, two assessments that entered into his opinion as to where the Franklin party had been stopped and would likely retreat, namely, North Somerset's west coast. Detention by ice was also a factor in King's thoughts. Indeed, whereas Sir James Ross had only hinted in 1845 at the possibility of this happening to Franklin in the quadrilateral, King had emphatically forecast it. In all, he had pictured the Franklin expedition as coming to the west coast of North Somerset either in search of a passage or in an attempt to escape from the Arctic, and what had in fact happened was a combination of both possibilities. Furthermore, only King had designated scurvy as a cause for unease about the expedition, and (discerning a third winter in the Arctic as crucial in this regard) he had felt, as Ross did not, the urgency of 1848 as a deadline for rescue.

Again, Cyriax has asked how Franklin could know that help would come by the Back River, and for this reason decide to retreat to it. This fails to take into account the possibility, already mentioned, that the party might march for the Back River precisely because an expedition had been sent down it in 1833 to seek the senior Ross. Certainly, at home, Richard King and Sir John Ross suspected that the Ross experience was being repeated, a point the Franklin party itself may well by now have felt was obvious. Certainly, also, King himself had left the way open for aid to come through either alternative of the Ross precedent. Rescue of the Franklin expedition might occur, as King envisaged it, either by whaler or other vessel through Barrow Strait (as, fortuitously, it had in the case of Sir John Ross) or by a party down the Back River, as had been deliberately provided for in 1833–35.

Furthermore, in assessing relative merit in the plans of Ross and King, one should take into account the physical condition of the two men. In the Arctic the ultimate mode of conveyance was the human physique and the ultimate motive power travel by foot, means which would come into play both in travel by the Back River to the west coast of Boothia and in sledding from ships to and along the same coast. Coming from ships, Ross's party was supposed to survey this coast, in Parry's words, "with ease." Yet in fact Sir James was now forty-eight, had retired from polar travel in 1844, and had since had, in March 1847, foot trouble which had placed him in bed for a week and thereafter under the necessity of walking for a time with a stick. Richard King, by contrast, was at thirty-eight a full decade younger than Ross, had only three years before been described as physically fine, and was accustomed in this period (as already stated) to shoot barefooted.[24]

Again, by contrast with Ross's proposed journey into a new region, King's would be secondary or follow-up discovery, and therefore faster than before, a point which is confirmed by the fact that Anderson's trip in 1855 was quicker than that of Back in 1834 down Back's own river, even though Anderson had not been down the river before (as King had), and was not (as King was close to being in 1848) in the prime of life.[25] As regards two further points made by Ross, it was not King's intention to feed Franklin's party but to be a "messenger" concerning where food was available. His aim was to direct the Franklin party to supplies, in whose provision the company was supposed to cooperate, by bringing food into its own posts and by hunting, there being, as King emphasized, a good deal of animal life along the Back River itself. Secondly, in reference to the lack of progress by Back at the mouth of the Back River, a reader of King's *Narrative* would know that, in King's view, this was prime evidence not of difficult travelling but of Back's lack of enterprise, of unnecessary trouble with Eskimos, and of a lack of the proper party and craft.

To sum up, King did have the handicap of not knowing at this time the Admiralty's instructions to Franklin, and had misinterpreted them. On the other hand, by adhering to his own views (more accurate upon a number of matters than those of the Admiralty), he had also been spared a number of the Admiralty's mistakes. He should be judged by his own conclusions, as worked out by himself from known facts, not by the charts and premisses of the Admiralty, as regards, in Cyriax's words, "what was known and what could reasonably be inferred." On this basis his opinions were, at least as much as those of Ross, "amply justified by the evidence then available." Clearly there was an element of chance attached to King's project for finding Franklin at this time. Yet there was a similar element attached to all the Franklin searches and King's "form" and "track record" made him by now a favourite in any Franklin or arctic "sweepstakes." Indeed, as one writer has put it, "The number of accuracies King exhibits stretches the chain of co-incidence to the breaking point."[26]

What one can do is concede to King—or to a Hudson's Bay Company traveller such as Rae—concurrent company help in preparing a wintering at Great Slave Lake and in hunting along the Back. Carrying perhaps a Halkett boat (as Richardson did to the Arctic in 1848 and Anderson in 1855), a party on the Back would have had a task in one way considerably simpler than many suspected. Meeting members of the Franklin party, possibly as far south as Montreal Island but more probably somewhere to the north of it, the rescue party's task would have entailed the care, at most, of a party much reduced in numbers by death. Yet the ability of this remnant to cope, even with King's or Rae's aid and encouragement, would have been small. Possibly, as Sir Clements Markham feels, some members of the naval expedition would have been spared, and a different kind of dénouement enacted for the Franklin expedition than that which actually occurred. At least, as already indicated, a trip such as King proposed, if undertaken in 1848, could have eliminated the need for most of the searches, and hence would have had, in all likelihood, a large impact upon the course of arctic exploration thereafter.[27] Had King made his trip we might also have today a fuller account than we do of what actually happened to the Franklin expedition.

One is tempted, therefore, to conclude that King's plan was rejected in 1847 and 1848 not so much because of inherent difficulties as of, first, overassessment of the physical problems of travel on the Back River and, secondly, underassessment of the difficulties Franklin would have in getting to the west. Thirdly, there seems to have been at work a potent dislike of King himself. His very accuracies appear to have worked against him, irritating the Admiralty and driving its consideration away from the locale that King emphasized.[28] He was also unpopular with the Hudson's Bay Company. Yet the chief apology for King rests not upon judging, as Cyriax does, his wish to use the Back River in 1848, but upon seeing his project in a longer perspective. King had repeatedly in the preceding dozen years put forward his project to use the Back River. Had it been acted upon up to or during 1845, it is arguable that the subsequent emergency would not have arisen. As it was, King had assessed the date of the emergency itself, named its locale, and stated the central causes of the crisis: besetment, scurvy, and starvation.

There is a concluding factor to be considered. Granted that King's plan of 1847–48 remains unproved as a rescue operation, to what extent were his cautions against other, concurrent plans justified? In those plans there was a duplication and intensification of a good many aspects of the Franklin trip itself. However, there was, from King's point of view, one advance. Earlier there had been only a modicum of cooperation between company and navy; now its degree was considerably intensified. Yet the expedition of Richardson, with the company explorer Rae as second-in-command, involved the Mackenzie and Coppermine rivers, not the Back, and a too-hopeful westward emphasis was present also in the project of *Enterprise*, Sir James Ross's particular vessel, and in the commissioning of *Plover* to go to Bering Strait. In short, the expeditions were over-optimistic in two ways, as regards, first, the hoped-for distant progress by the Franklin party and, secondly, the assumed ease by which rescuers could reach such an advanced location. The navy was searching for Franklin with the same emphasis on a very extensive area as that by which it had lost him in the first place.

With the risk of repeated error, Ross chose two vessels to approximate the size of *Erebus* and *Terror*. Because no naval vessels equipped for arctic service were available, he wrote that inquiry should be made "at Hull or in the River" regarding whalers of between 400 and 500 tons, "well and faithfully built," not more than five years old, and ready to sail by the end of April 1848. There were thus acquired *Enterprise* and *Investigator*, barque-rigged and of 470 and 422 tons respectively. Purchased and specially fitted out by Wigram and Green of Blackwell, early in 1848 the vessels were equipped at Woolwich with, like Franklin's ships, three years' provisions. The crews of his two vessels Ross likewise chose with an eye upon *Erebus* and *Terror*; the former had complements of sixty-nine and sixty-eight; the latter of seventy and sixty-nine. Also in conscious repetition, there were furnished for *Enterprise* and *Investigator*, as there had been for *Erebus* and *Terror*, nine boats each, ranging from pinnaces to dinghies. Both expeditions were provided with one extra craft, making a total of nineteen under each commander.[29]

Ross's vessels were of teak and, as *Enterprise* was to enter farther into the Arctic than *Investigator*, her bow had "upwards of seven feet of solid thickness of timber" and a cutwater "quite sharp in order to cut through the ice." For wintering each vessel had a roof upon deck, between the masts. The Silvester stove, as it had been for Franklin's, was a part of the equipment of Ross's vessels. Enhancing a bent established by Franklin, the Ross party was the most comfortably equipped yet to go to the Arctic. All officers had individual cabins, individually heated; while temperatures would drop "to $-52°$F., yet the stoves kept the temperature on the lower decks between 55° and 60°F.," making a difference of over 100 degrees between outside and inside temperatures.[30]

Yet one dissimilarity did exist between the Ross and Franklin expeditions: the absence of steam in Ross's ships, making the pursuers potentially less swift than the pursued. On the other hand, during preparations Ross showed a keen interest in steam launches. Each ship was given a steam-powered pinnace, designed mainly, it was now said, to keep up communication between *Enterprise* and *Investigator*, although earlier Ross had said that an aim was to range North Somerset's shores in quest of Franklin. Each launch had a mean draught of fifteen inches, a beam of six, and a length of fifty-three and a half feet, and was fitted with screw propeller and rotary engine, placed amidships, of five horsepower, designed to enable it to reach an estimated speed of six knots.[31]

In the actual event, not only was Baffin Bay extremely difficult to cross in 1848, but Barrow Strait was blocked by ice from Cornwallis Island to Port Leopold, making westward progress impossible. Ross writes that the steam machinery was useful in landing winter provisions at Port Leopold; Lieut. F. L. M'Clintock reports that on 15 September, after what he considered a useful trial, the steam machinery was taken out of the pinnace of *Enterprise* and not used again.[32] Steam did not contribute to coastal discovery and by the time winter set in, Ross's party had accomplished far less than Franklin's at the close of its first season. Moreover, Barrow Strait was blocked again in the summer of 1849 across roughly the same line as in 1848. As a result, *Enterprise* could not proceed westward as intended, and it was not by a party under Bird from *Investigator*, as had also been intended, but by one from *Enterprise* under Ross that, in the spring and early summer of 1849, the western coast of North Somerset was investigated by sled, at the same time as other parties went to the north shore of Barrow Strait and Fury Beach.

As regards Ross's sled journey down the west coast of North Somerset, there are differing views. Cyriax commends it as the longest trip by sled so far performed by the Royal Navy, save for one by Parry not in the Canadian Arctic.[33] When judged, however, either by company standards or achievement of its purpose it was a failure. Ross's men did not have northern experience and not being landsmen were in an alien environment. Ross himself was much older than John Rae; his party had not rehearsed sledding as Rae's had done early in 1847; and Ross got away a month later than Rae on his spring trip. Again, the Ross party used larger sleds than Rae's, carried heavier loads, had the wrong diet, made no use of dogs, used tents not snowhouses, had a larger number of personnel, and minutely surveyed the coast rather than explored it.[34] These are reasons why Ross in 1849 travelled well under half the distance of Rae on his journeys of 1847, at not much more than half Rae's daily rate. Rae's journeys in that year, one recalls, had totalled 1,284 English miles, accomplished at 22¼ and 21¼ miles a day, and the company explorer had discovered 655 statute miles of coastline Ross, by comparison, travelled 500 English miles in forty days, that is an average of 12½ miles a day, and he found about 150 miles of new coastline. Besides, Ross sledged only to a point (72° 38′ N.) which was far north of Bellot Strait, hardly within 150 miles of King William Island or Cape Nicholas, and over 200 miles from the place where Franklin's vessels had been abandoned. Again, while Rae had finished his first journey in excellent shape and his second "perfectly well and fit for more hard work," five of the Ross sledge crews were, upon return to their ship, "put on the sick list and in a few days the whole twelve were laid up with one ailment and another. Sir James Ross also had to lie by with sore feet."[35]

Moreover, *Enterprise* and *Investigator*, not freed until 28 August 1849, thereafter became fast in the pack when trying to get west in Barrow Strait, drifted into Baffin Bay, were released, and returned to England, but not before Ross, like Franklin before him, was searched for by still another expedition, that of the *North Star*, which cost the government upwards of £15,000.[36] Arctic exploration had become an exercise in elaborate multiplicity, a search for those searching for those who had found the Northwest Passage.

There was also the Richardson expedition, with Rae as its second-in-command. Rae himself was highly critical of the sappers, miners, and sailors of the party as northern travellers; he considered them the "most awkward, lazy, and careless set I ever had anything to do with," and felt that even the sailors of the party were indifferent boatmen. Richardson, who had previously found that naval men were not good at marching, now discovered that the members of all three groups, sappers and miners as well as the few seamen, easily became lost; one man was found walking contentedly towards the moon, low on the horizon, under the impression it was the bivouac fire of his companions. Hindered in this way and, in Rae's view, by a lack of vigour in the 60-year-old Richardson himself, the party was by August on the arctic coast and discovered in September a river, named after Rae, which entered the Arctic near the Coppermine. Obviously the party was searching too far westward to find the Franklin expedition; subsequently, on the overland journey to winter quarters at Fort Confidence, it was unable to take its boats up the Coppermine River.[37]

Thus in the succeeding summer, instead of the planned quest by two or three boats which could "aid each other among the ice," only one remained for employment, and this precipitated a direct choice. Forced to reduce the expedition to a single boat party, Richardson had to decide between generations, and between company men and methods, on the one hand, and the armed services' men and methods, on the other. In making the choice he had, he said, "no hesitation in deciding in favour of Mr. Rae" as leader for the summer of 1849, and felt as well that it would save expense without cramping the search to withdraw the European party and employ volunteers from the country. Accordingly, in May 1849 Richardson left for the south while Rae proceeded down the Coppermine, whose mouth he reached in July. Although he was able to trace westward the river named after him, in an attempt to find a short route for boats from Great Bear Lake, he was prevented by ice from crossing as planned to Victoria Island, and returned to Fort Confidence and then, by order, to Fort Simpson. Thus ended, he says, a voyage without results so far as its object was concerned.[38]

Failure, whether under Rae, Richardson, or Ross, had not been assignable to human factors only. Two seasons in succession as cold and backward as those of 1848 and 1849 were, according to Rae, seldom to be found. Franklin had made advances far into the Arctic during two especially open seasons, while two especially cold ones had thereafter greatly hindered and even confused the would-be rescuers. The Ross expedition had, as stated, brought word home of some 150 miles of new coastline and had discovered Peel Sound; it had furthered the career of R. J. L. M'Clure, brought forward the new figure M'Clintock, and given a basis for improvement in techniques. Yet Ross and M'Clintock had been left with the impression that Franklin could not have sailed through the very sound which they themselves had discovered, an erroneous conclusion which diverted the Franklin searches.[39]

The navy, in short, had now suffered another great arctic failure. While Ross "showed his usual animation," his career thereafter was not productive and Lady Franklin now spoke of Ross "in very severe terms." Richard King wrote that Ross had "wrecked himself at once and for ever." The *Nautical Standard* pointed out that Ross's vessels had drawn "more water than the field of ice" near the shore, exposing them to peril and unfitting them for coastal navigation. Yet he himself, it added, had approved these vessels, rather than choosing four small ones. The paper also said that Ross had left unexplored "about 140 miles of . . . country" on the west shore of Boothia "where . . . Franklin was the most likely to be found." Besides, why in 1848 had Ross reached Lancaster Sound three weeks later than the whalers?[40] M'Clintock, for his part, wrote that the Ross experience "afforded a very salutary and well-merited rebuke" to those who would attempt a Northwest Passage. His "imagination pictured," he said, "the hyperborean giant as being wearied by . . . repeated attempts to invade his dominion"; yet feeling "kindly disposed to those who are instrumental in carrying out such designs, he gently enclosed us in his icy grasp, carried us in perfect safety to the limit of his dominions; and . . . liberated us in a providential manner!" Surely, M'Clintock concluded, Ross's voyage "ought to be the last Polar expedition."[41] Where the navy had once believed that arctic discovery was easy, that service now showed, in M'Clintock, a tendency to believe it was impossible.

A related tendency showed itself in Parry. In a letter to John Barrow, a son of Sir John Barrow and now himself an Admiralty official, Parry labelled the article in the *Nautical Standard*, "that most atrocious, abusive and ignorant article," yet he also admitted great puzzlement to Lady Franklin at the negative turn of events. The puzzlement he "solved," however, by simply diverting attention from the area to which a good deal of evidence had pointed. Since Ross had not got far along North Somerset's west coast, why should Franklin have succeeded in doing so? There had been no success in the east, and the alternative was "a bold push" from Bering Strait and a reliance on help from the Russians, and perhaps from Rae, in the far west.[42] Parry's attitude seemed to be to search where there was open sea, not in a region which the navy (despite Parry's own earlier use of such words as "no difficult enterprise" and "with ease") had now found to be difficult.

Once again, much had occurred in accordance with King's views. Barrow Strait, as King had feared might happen and Ross said never happened, had been blocked by ice, not once but twice. The Ross party had itself become an object of search, as King had also feared. The central North American Arctic was now proving a more ice- and land-dominated area than naval men had pictured it to be. The sled travel of Ross along North Somerset's west coast had demonstrated that the navy did not yet have the same speed in coastal travel as the company. Further, Ross had used larger rather than smaller vessels, an approach contrary to that of King and a cause perhaps of failure. Again, although King had uttered no specific warning in this regard, Ross's confidence in steam launches as a means of coastal discovery had so far proved misplaced. Neither steam nor sail nor foot power had served Ross. Even had his expedition penetrated further south, it would have been one year later than the year of King's concern and of actual need. Not only was Ross's expedition a failure, as Cyriax concedes.[43] So also were the expeditions of Richardson and Rae, since, as King had warned, these leaders were searching too far westward.

6

Ω Ω Ω Ω Ω Ω Ω Ω Ω Ω Ω Ω Ω Ω Ω Ω Ω Ω Ω Ω Ω Ω Ω Ω Ω Ω Ω Ω Ω Ω Ω Ω Ω Ω Ω Ω Ω Ω Ω Ω Ω Ω Ω Ω Ω Ω Ω Ω Ω Ω Ω Ω

Discovery by Accident and Intent (1850–1852)

A basic theme in music may be repeated in a higher octave more insistently than before. In the search for Franklin between 1850 and 1854 features earlier apparent in arctic exploration grew even more marked. The Admiralty showed an increasing tendency to agree with M'Clintock's statement of 1849 against polar travel, but its aversion took time to develop. Besides, public opinion, voiced especially by and for Lady Franklin, was now more insistent than ever that Franklin be found. So, despite a growing reluctance, the navy continued to search and a paradoxical situation emerged. Unsure of where to look, the Admiralty "ran riot and despatched a whole fleet to the Arctic."[1] Exhibiting a surveying emphasis more intensely than before, it sent out two vessels in 1850 through Bering Strait and six by way of Baffin Bay. Yet there was one area to which the Admiralty did not direct its attention. Most naval leaders failed to recognize, forgot, or did not think it important, that Sir James Ross had not reached the west coast of Boothia in 1848–49 and that that region still remained unsearched. Instead, they left any quest in that direction to private effort and emphasized, for their own part, an open polar sea, and what they felt were other peculiar features in the north which had enabled Franklin to get as far west as Bering Strait. That is, there was a shift of emphasis from the coastal route to the Straits of Barrow, M'Clure, and Prince of Wales, as if (to pursue the musical metaphor) to a higher octave. With encouragement from the hydrographer of the navy, one officer went so far as to suggest that the lost party had travelled as far north and west as Siberia.

In short, the navy favoured, even more than before, a deep sea approach. There was also a renewed emphasis upon size. The standard sleds and sled parties were enlarged, and the variety of sizes of sleds increased, developments which showed the tendency towards massiveness and detailed surveying rather than light probes. The navy also increasingly stressed steam and other aspects of European technology, and rather than seeking to get word, first, of the location of the lost party, persisted in its purpose of simultaneous discovery, rescue, and transport of the Franklin expedition. In these circumstances the earlier pattern of loss was likely to recur, and for the Admiralty, as the search moved ever further afield, there would be a decreasing, rather than increasing, hope of finding the missing navigators. More and more sceptical of the possibilities of the Arctic, at the close of the period it abandoned the search.

In the same period (1850–54), characteristics already exhibited by the Hudson's Bay Company likewise became more pronounced. While the company sponsored a voyage in 1850–51 by Sir John Ross through Baffin Bay, its own expeditions were still under the single leader John Rae, and they continued also to be smaller and more indigenous in emphasis than those of the navy, and to be coastal rather than deep sea. The company searched, on the whole, closer to the actual scene of the disaster than did most naval expeditions, but it still looked, as it cooperated with the navy, by way of the Mackenzie and Coppermine, not the Back River. Nor did the activities of Lady Franklin lead to successful discovery in this period. At first she did sponsor searches in the direction of the west coast of Boothia, especially in sending out (1851–52) William Kennedy, who had a marked capacity for indigenous travel. Yet her emphasis, too, was deep sea, and she dispatched Kennedy by way of Prince Regent Inlet, not the Back River. Only Richard King continued to keep his eye upon the west coast of Boothia, and the Back as a means to reach it. He stressed that Sir James Ross had not in fact searched what King considered the crucial area to which Ross had been sent. Echoing language he had already used, King told the secretary of the Admiralty early in 1850 that all that had happened since 1848 tended to draw "attention closer and closer to the West Land of North Somerset as the position of Sir John Franklin, and to the Great Fish River as the high road to reach it." King also predicted that use of routes other than this one would lead, not to discovery of Franklin, but rather to a survey of the arctic coast and discovery of a passage.[2] By comparison, that is, with the company and still more the navy, his emphasis continued to be upon inland, sparse, and indigenous travel.

The very name "barrens" still seemed a warning against the Back River and the country through which it flowed. Naval personnel, the company,

Lady Franklin, and even William Kennedy were repelled by the region. There was also a new factor. Sir James Ross, it was now said, had wished in 1849 to revisit the north magnetic pole, the site of his triumph of 1834, not to find Franklin, but simply for prestige; and since the pole was to the west of Boothia, naval men were now reluctant, it was further said, to lay themselves open to a similar charge by heading in the same direction.[3] At the same time, King's own advocacy still seemed a cause of repulsion from the region rather than attraction to it. His plan was dismissed by the Admiralty in February 1850 on the grounds that enough expeditions had already been sent out and that King's project was the same as the one he had previously advocated.[4] Thoroughly thwarted, King lapsed into a period of silence on arctic matters which lasted almost four years.

Yet in this period there emerged another figure having some similarities to King. Born in Devon in 1826, Bedford Trevelyan Clapperton Pim, RN, was, at nineteen, a midshipman and veteran of four years on the China Station when he joined the *Herald* surveying expedition of 1845 under Capt. Henry Kellett. As that party shuttled on the west coast of the Americas between the tropics and the Arctic, Pim acquired a taste for exploratory travel in both zones and for ethnology, including an interest in Eskimos. In 1849 he was with *Herald* as she sailed a hundred miles north of Point Barrow "out of all published charts" and through what appeared impenetrable ice to the vicinity of Herald and Wrangel Islands. Returning with *Herald* to the mainland, he was part of a six-boat expedition which, accompanied by numerous Eskimos in their kayaks as guides, explored the Buckland River. In a report which formed a basis for a later project he wrote that *Herald* had traced the barrier of ice from the shores of America to those of Asia; gained the furthest north and west of any ship known; discovered islands and perhaps a continent; and searched the whole shore of North America from Norton Sound to Dease Inlet. "If," he said, "Franklin or any of the lost expedition were there, we would have found them."[5]

Pim transferred at this time to *Plover* so as to remain in the Arctic. He wrote of Eskimos as moving in their winter garb in an element "for which nature had admirably adapted them." In Kotzebue Sound, where *Plover* was wintering, Pim and two other officers went to live for ten days in the Eskimos' semi-underground dwellings, known as yourts, constructed of driftwood, and generally roofed with earth or turf; the officers also visited other Eskimo villages. Rumours had been heard of white men dressed as sailors, and Pim hoped that by going to the Russian fort of St. Michael on Norton Sound he might get more definite information. After repeated solicitations he was allowed to start from *Plover* on 11 March 1850. With a party consisting at most of himself, a Russian interpreter, and an Eskimo

guide, and on occasion of himself alone, and journeying eventually without a sledge but with snowshoes and inferior Eskimo dogs, Pim reached St.
Michael on 6 April, twenty-six days after leaving *Plover*. There he saw a
written account of what he felt might be the story of two boat crews from
Franklin's expedition. Pim himself would later claim, on the basis of his
returning with this account, the prize which the Admiralty offered for
bringing initial news of the Franklin party. Others have said the story Pim
was investigating concerned a boat party which Pim's own ships *Herald*
and *Plover* had dispatched to the Mackenzie River; Rae believed it arose
from a pillaging and starving of Hudson's Bay Company personnel some
years before. Pim experienced great difficulty in getting back to *Plover*.
When he did so, after an absence of nearly two months, Commander
Moore considered that the evidence which Pim had investigated was too
vague to act upon.[6]

Pim was not necessarily a good arctic traveller: he had his detractors in
this regard. Yet he had had by now the experience of an early start and of
travel by dog, sledge, and snowshoes. He had learnt something of Eskimos
and their means of survival, seen the ravages of scurvy, dealt with the
Russians in their sector of the Arctic, and been as far north and west as any
explorer from the English-speaking world. Of a "lone wolf" stamp, he was
an oddity among naval personnel in liking to travel by himself and in the
degree of his interest in indigenous peoples. Some of his experiences had
placed him very far from Richard King as an arctic explorer, but others,
and his travel characteristics and personality, brought him close to King.
Pim went back to *Herald* when she returned from the tropics for the 1850
arctic season. At midnight on 1 August off Cape Lisburne *Herald*'s commander Kellett shook the hand of Robert John Le Mesurier M'Clure of
Investigator before M'Clure entered the Arctic.[7] Neither Kellett nor
M'Clure could guess the circumstances of their next meeting, nor the part
that Pim would play in it.

In January 1850 there sailed from England *Enterprise* and *Investigator*
(Sir James Ross's vessels of 1848–49) with orders to search for Franklin
north and east from Cape Bathurst via Bering Strait. Despite explicit
instructions that they stay together, the two vessels were in fact ill-matched
in open sea and *Enterprise*, under Capt. Richard Collinson, early left
behind "Old Iron Bows," as *Investigator*, under Capt. M'Clure, was called
by her own crew. This discrepancy was accentuated at the Straits of Magel-
lan when the steam vessel *Gorgon* was used to advance the two vessels,
successively, into the Pacific; after *Enterprise* had been successfully
taken there a cable towing *Investigator* towards the same goal parted in a

gale, so that an even greater distance was placed between the consorts. When *Investigator* finally reached the Sandwich Islands, *Enterprise* had already left and, in what seemed to *Investigator*'s crew a justified riposte, M'Clure skilfully took his vessel by a short cut through the dangerous waters of the Aleutians, to reach Bering Strait many days, and to enter the Arctic a whole year, ahead of Collinson.[8]

The separation of *Enterprise* and *Investigator* may in fact have turned out for the best. The two vessels might not have navigated where M'Clure went alone, or the M'Clure party have found enough game to fend off, in its case, the same disease of scurvy that struck the Franklin party down in its third winter. Even had a joint expedition found a passage, it is still possible it would have proved too large to be aided by the rescue party which brought home M'Clure and his men from their single vessel; instead there might have been starvation and breakdown for rescuers and rescued alike. Meanwhile, also acting on his own, Collinson himself made an outstanding arctic voyage, although one which followed at many points in the wake of discoveries by M'Clure and Rae.

More important than the difference in sailing capacities between the consorts was a divergence between their commanders. Collinson (1811–83), officially in command of the expedition as well as of *Enterprise*, and one of the most able of arctic explorers, was also, it has been said, one of the most magnanimous. M'Clure (1807–73), in command simply of *Investigator*, had a character as contradictory as the mixed nature—that of open sea, land, and ice—of the Arctic he explored. Of great charm of manner, selfless and warm-hearted on occasion, he was also, on other occasions, an unnecessarily harsh commander, unsure of himself with his junior officers, and an author of ruthless orders. He showed bravery in the Arctic but also, it has been claimed, failure of nerve.[9]

Separation of one vessel from the other was a vital difference between the M'Clure expedition and that of Franklin, but similarities between the two expeditions and their respective commanders were many. Oddly, loss of rule over an island appears to have been a driving incentive in the case of M'Clure no less than in that of Franklin. Born a posthumous child, M'Clure was in effect orphaned when he was taken at the age of four from his native Wexford to become the adoptive heir of the governor of Alderney (whose name, Le Mesurier, he bore). He was, however, at the age of twelve abruptly disinherited, both of the governorship and the near-princely fortune attached to it. At sixteen he disclaimed the military profession of his father and adoptive father; running away from an army cadetship at Sandhurst College, he entered the navy instead.[10] It is not surprising that he showed insecurity in the Arctic where the twists and

turns of fate and of his own behaviour in the years 1850–54 recall his
unsettled youth. Like Franklin he was trying not so much to establish as to
re-establish himself. Again, behind intense ambition there lay, in the case
of both Franklin and M'Clure, an emulation of Nelson yet the lack of a
basic ingredient for its fulfilment: war and opportunity for advancement.

Franklin had served at Trafalgar; had treated polar service as a substitute for war after 1815; and had led on his final foray a party dubbed
"Nelsons of discovery." M'Clure had served initially in Nelson's old ship
Victory; had launched himself in 1836 upon an arctic career in circumstances that hint at emulation of Nelson; and had enacted, on the Canada
station in the 1830s, a form of placing a blind eye to the telescope: by
burning a fort and taking a notorious freebooter, while violating United
States territory to do so. Yet M'Clure, like Franklin, had had to cope with
peacetime conditions. As he sailed from England in the 1850s he had
already had a "long and severe probation in every grade," had not
advanced beyond the rank of captain, and was low in the commanders'
lists. At forty-three, he was, like Franklin when he sailed, past the best age
for exploration and, as in the case of Franklin, this lent a note of urgency.
M'Clure had vowed before leaving England that on this voyage he would
win his post rank, find Franklin, or make the passage.[11] He did not find
Franklin but he represented, in his determination to achieve success, a
return of Franklin.

Perhaps awareness of Nelson on the quarterdeck had its counterpart on
the lower deck where there was, quite literally, a "Nelson of discovery."
Possibly James H. Nelson, able seaman, had been influenced by his name
to go into the navy, or arctic service in particular, suggestions which gain
weight from the fact he was the keeper of a diary recording, through the
eyes of an ordinary rating, the first discovery and transit of a Northwest
Passage. Thanks to Nelson, we have some sense of the feeling aboard
Investigator when on 30 July 1850 that vessel spoke *Plover* at Kotzebue
Sound. By then, he says, *Investigator*'s whole crew felt Collinson had been
determined to enter the ice first, "caring very little" about *Investigator*.
The tables, Nelson notes with satisfaction, were "completely turned in our
favour" by the rapid trip from the Sandwich Islands through the Aleutians, so that now "Madame Enterprise" would have to experience the
same disappointment as *Investigator* already had. Kellett in *Herald* tried
to persuade M'Clure to await Collinson but, only a grade above M'Clure in
rank, he hesitated to make this an order. M'Clure, for his part, said that
Collinson might already have gone into the Arctic in fog. Twice challenged
by M'Clure to give a direct order of prevention, Kellett refrained from this
and, unhindered, *Investigator* went forward on 1 August.[12]

Whether or not there was a Nelson touch in M'Clure's semi-insubordination, there was no mistaking a Franklin touch in the way he proceeded. When Franklin had approached the polar sea in 1845, he had been reluctant to shorten canvas even in a high gale. When M'Clure on the night of the parting with Kellett encountered a "tongue" or isthmus of ice, he did so with a strong northeast wind blowing, and "under every stitch of canvas he could carry." He "coolly ordered" *Investigator* to be steered directly for what seemed an impenetrable barrier. The vessel struck, James Nelson writes, "the granite-like mass with such force as to bring her for a moment to almost a standstill ... causing the masts to shake in such a manner as to threaten their safety. However, the victory was ours for the ice split and parted, allowing us a free passage into the open water beyond."[13]

After she entered the ice *Investigator*'s crow's-nest frequently enabled her to avoid damage and to take directions through the ice most favourable to her progress eastward. First introduced by whaling vessels to spot their prey, the "nest," Nelson reports, was a "framework, composed of wooden hoops ... covered with stout canvas" that was movable and capable of being "placed in such a manner as to shelter the occupant ... from the pelting sleet storms" which at that time and place were "very prevalent." It was no sinecure to occupy the nest, Nelson adds, for there the cold was felt intensely through lack of exercise. Partly by this device M'Clure, like Franklin in 1845, made remarkable progress in 1850 before he was finally frozen in; indeed, Sir Edward Parry was to remark that it was "the most magnificent piece of navigation ever performed in a single season."[14] After a cruise eastward of five weeks M'Clure was able to strike northward and enter his discovery, Prince of Wales Strait. Having been sailed north to within twenty-five miles of Melville Sound, *Investigator* then drifted back again. Frozen in on 30 September, the vessel was, in this condition, blown around the Princess Royal Islands on her broadside until eventually, in October, she was worked back into an almost horizontal position.

M'Clure was now barely 100 miles to the southwest of Parry's furthest point on Melville Island. After his party had first made discoveries on Banks and Victoria Islands (in regions it called, respectively, Baring's and King Albert Land), a special project was launched. The M'Clure party had concluded that Prince of Wales Strait must enter Melville Sound. Beset, yet ordered to seek Melville Island, M'Clure was bent upon proving the final link in a passage before the arctic night set in. On the Queen's birthday, 1847, the Gore party of Franklin had set out, presumably to complete a passage. Perhaps with like sentiment, on Trafalgar day, 21 October, M'Clure and a small group set out on the same quest further north. The sled party this time consisted of M'Clure himself, Court, and five men, with provisions requisite for seven persons for fourteen days packed on a sledge. Then occurred a frequent feature of arctic travel: the false start. Court returned from the main M'Clure party on the same day, 21 October, with a damaged sled and word that five men for one sled were too few. He needed a new sled and on 22 October set out with a larger one, a tent, a day's provisions, and a fatigue party; this group reached M'Clure at 2 p.m., an exchange of sleds was made, and the fatigue party started to return.[15]

Although only as a member of the fatigue party, Nelson had now been introduced to sled travel. This is allowed by all, he writes, "to be the very hardest of all work," requiring "great power of endurance." Imagine yourself, he says,

> harnessed as it were by a broad canvas belt, to a sledge laden with necessaries, for a long journey, weighing from 12 to 14 hundred-weight and compelled for 12 hours out of 24 to drag the aforesaid sledge o'er icy hills and dales—then to pitch the tent—at times becoming nearly frozen in the operation,—and with the aid of a spirit apparatus provided for the purpose, warm if possible,—for it is by no means certain,—the allowance of food allotted for each meal, this accomplished, to kick your way into a huge blanket bag, and taking your knapsack for a pillow, endeavour to obtain an hour's sleep; the frost landing in festoon[s] o'er the skin covering, and quickly decorating the head of an individual that inadvertantly becomes exposed.

Extreme monotony, inducing melancholy and homesickness, also occurs on sled travel, Nelson concludes.[16]

For the main party, travel was made difficult by broken ice and water oozing up to the surface of the frozen sea, so that, as Hudson's Bay Company parties had often experienced, hauling was very sticky. Naval men seemed unaware that company travellers often ate pemmican cold, accepting thirst as a hazard of this; and John Rae has wondered why naval parties melted snow for water, instead of ice which produces much more water for the same quantity of heat. The M'Clure party was short of fuel with which to melt the snow and also heat the pemmican. Consuming during a total of ten days only 18 lb. of the fur traders' food and suffering a great deal from thirst, the men lost considerable weight, while the total sledge weight was increased by 100 lb., "from the accumulation of ice on the blankets, tents, coverings, &c., caused by the vapour from ... [the men's] bodies being rapidly converted into frost." Nevertheless, despite these difficulties, the expedition reached Point Russell on 26 October; before it lay what it knew must be Viscount Melville Sound. For the second time a passage had been found, on this occasion with a feeling of exaltation and pride. It was, the surgeon of the M'Clure expedition said, "the greatest Maritime Discovery of the Age," elevating the United Kingdom in marine matters "still further ... above all the nations of the earth." A cairn was built and the party made the return trip of about 110 miles at a daily average of eleven miles, reaching *Investigator* on 31 October.[17] M'Clure had performed for his expedition the task which his messmate in *Terror* in 1836–37, Graham Gore, had very likely completed for Franklin's four years earlier. But the difference between seeing a passage, as Franklin's men and now M'Clure had done, and discovering one by bringing the actual news home to Britain was very great: the loss of Franklin had proved this and the jeopardy of M'Clure's party was shortly to underline it.

M'Clure has been criticized for not making by sled from *Investigator* in Prince of Wales Strait to Winter Harbour in the spring of 1851. As already stated, he had been instructed to reach Melville Island, and in that same season there was approaching from the east an expedition under Horatio Austin with the object of searching by Lancaster Sound beyond the achievements of Ross and reaching that same island. Had M'Clure sledded to Winter Harbour and left a message there, this communication would, if picked up by the sledge party under Lieut. F. L. M'Clintock from Austin's expedition at Winter Harbour, have been the first to cross the passage; by giving news of M'Clure to the expedition from the east it would have led, no doubt, to his rescue. M'Clure, however, was bent upon bringing his vessel through a passage, and he did not send a sledge to Winter Harbour. Instead, unable to proceed in *Investigator* up Prince of Wales Strait, he carried out an extremely hazardous journey round the west side of Banks Island. He had already used gunpowder to free his vessel in the strait; he now used it as well on this perilous trip. Locked in on one occasion between two masses of ice and forced to drift along helplessly, he employed a charge of 150 lb. *Investigator* was thus freed when detention for five more minutes would have crushed her "like a nut in the nut-crackers."[18]

Having arrived with great skill on the northern side of Banks Land and within striking distance by sled of Melville Island, M'Clure, it has been suggested, showed failure of nerve in not attempting to sail *Investigator* herself to Melville Island.[19] In any event he was now once again close to Parry's furthest west, this time by potential approach through M'Clure Strait; he had virtually proved a second northern passage. On 24 September 1851 he went into the Bay of Mercy on the north coast of Banks Land, and there *Investigator* wintered and became, like *Erebus* and *Terror* in Franklin's second winter, permanently beset. Like Franklin, M'Clure had made substantial progress in his second season and, like Franklin, had failed in his haste to leave at a strategic point (in his case at Winter Harbour) a message concerning that progress. Yet, just as Franklin had been fatally baffled by barriers in the eastern half of a coastal passage, so now was M'Clure baffled by barriers in the western half of a more northerly passage. Would his expedition suffer the same fate as Franklin's? The difference lay precisely in the fact that M'Clure's voyage was a repetition. Now there were vessels in the Arctic searching for Franklin, a variation upon a theme which meant that, though it was like Franklin's at so many stages, M'Clure's expedition would have a happier ending than Franklin's.

The Austin expedition which sailed from England for Lancaster Sound in the spring of 1850 had the object, as mentioned above, of searching by the sound beyond the Ross survey of 1848–49. On the one hand, the expedition could apply lessons learned from the Ross voyage and, on the other, it was a precursor of Kellett's expedition of 1852–54. Lieut., later Comdr., Francis Leopold M'Clintock (1819–1907) was a member of all three expeditions and therefore forms, in his own person, a connecting chain. The *Assistance* and *Resolute*, commanded, respectively, by Captains Horatio Austin and Erasmus Ommaney, were purchased by the navy, were of the same class, and were specially strengthened for the expedition. *Resolute* was twelve or fourteen years old, of about 430 tons, and built of teak. *Pioneer* and *Intrepid*, the latter under Lieut. Sherard Osborn and the former under Lieut. Cator, were the sister vessels which acted as steam tenders to *Assistance* and *Resolute*. *Intrepid*, which M'Clintock would command two years later under Kellett, was purchased by the Admiralty on 1 April 1850. Acquired and fitted at an estimated cost to the navy of £5,000, she was a steam-propelled three-masted schooner of carvel build, square stern, and two decks and a break; she weighed about 228 tons, was nearly 23 feet broad, and was of an approximate depth and length of 14½ feet and 144 feet respectively. *Intrepid* had two low-pressure engines of 30 h.p. each, manufactured by Boulton and Watt and Company. In preparation for the Arctic, *Pioneer*'s deck was "covered with diagonal planking, with a layer of felt between the old and new decks" and in *Intrepid* there was a "mode of doubling and otherwise strengthening the Hull" and an installation of "Silvester's Warming apparatus," together with accompanying pipes.[20]

Yet for all its use of the new technology of steam, the Austin expedition did not proceed further west in its vessels than Griffith Island, where it wintered in 1850–51, and the only Franklin find which it made was that of Captain Ommaney who discovered in August 1850 Franklin's encampment at Beechey Island. That location, however, was by now only at the threshold of the Arctic; it was like a polar Gibraltar not only in appearance[21] but also in its situation, forming as it did an entry and crossroads from which one could go northward up Wellington Channel, westward toward Viscount Melville Sound, south and west down Peel Sound, or south and east down Prince Regent Inlet. Whether or not the searchers realized this, Ommaney's find gave no assurance of Franklin's direction after he left the island. M'Clintock, for his part, came to a wrong conclusion. Eager to participate in the searches yet strongly of the opinion that Franklin had got far west by either a coastal or a Wellington Channel route, he asked permission to look for the lost explorer at Melville Island. On a sled trip he used men who were, with one exception, in their twenties, started a month earlier than James Clark Ross had in 1849, provisioned for forty days each way instead of thirty or fewer, and used fatigue parties to extend his exploits. On 15 April 1851 he set out with a party totalling seven in all and a sledge named *Perseverance* which had as its motto, "Persevere to the End." His aim was to explore around southwestern Melville Island to Liddon Gulf. For this the constant weights aboard the sled were 417 lb.; the provisions and packages for seven men for forty-one days weighed 822½ lb., making total weights of 1,239½ lb. and a weight to be hauled by each man of 206½ lb. Melville Island was more than 300 miles away and the party, it was planned, would cover 900 miles, taking advantage by hunting of what was thought to be "an unlimited supply of venison stocks."[22]

There were difficulties. The first check was that of frostbite. Soon after the party had started out, the temperature fell to −40°F. Ten of the thirty-five men who, at the outset, were accompanying the party in four other sledges were rendered unfit for service and were sent back to the ships. The party, as was so often the case in arctic travel, slept by day and travelled by night to avoid, during the day, a snow glare that was "more than human eyes [could] endure." As on the Austin expedition generally, so on this particular journey the party often used sail, especially beyond Cape Dundas. M'Clintock says: "our tent 'floor cloth' [was] set as a sail upon the sledge," while the tent poles served "as mast and yard." In this manner, "we travelled into Liddon's Gulf, in a very thick fog, before a fresh, fair wind with the addition of a large kite, which not only gave us a friendly pull, but served to guide us wherever the land was obscured from view." Another difficulty occurred when the party encountered "a violent gale with very thick snow drift" in the vicinity of Winter Harbour on 21 May. It was impossible, M'Clintock asserts, to "face it; and having ascertained" that there were no ships, tents, or human beings in Winter Harbour, he "determined to defer . . . closer scrutiny" of the harbour until his return from the west.[23]

After passing Cape Dundas, leaving Parry's farthest point behind them, the expedition experienced its highest temperature: 52°F. at noon outside and 74°F. in the tent. While M'Clintock remarks that, "Much of this heat was owing to reflection . . . for the slightest wind felt cool," the experience demonstrated that the advance of spring did not necessarily dispel discomfort from arctic travel. On the homeward journey Winter Harbour was reached, by land, on 5 June. Here the Parry Sandstone stood out as a solitary and prominent landmark, ten feet high, twenty-eight feet long, and seven or eight feet broad; at it Parry's cairn was opened and his message of 1820 found. Winter Harbour had now, in Parry's own description, become "classic ground"; Richard King dubbed the Sandstone "the Post Office of the North Pole"; and at it M'Clintock now left a message which would prove to be the first communication actually to cross the Northwest Passage. The party was subsisting at this time upon the region itself, namely, upon musk-ox beef consumed in enormous quantities with a little biscuit only, and without any pepper or salt. Nor did the travellers lack for fuel, for coal was found in plenty.[24]

The return to the ships from Winter Harbour was accomplished between 6 June and 4 July. M'Clintock had not found Franklin but the Austin party had proved, at least, that Franklin had not sailed along Barrow Strait, and M'Clintock had discovered 160 miles of coastline. The outbound journey had taken forty-four days and the homebound one, with the weight of the sled-load decreasing by 20 lb. a day, thirty-six days, making eighty in all. The estimated distance travelled was 770.5 miles; the actual distance from the ship in a direct line, 300 miles; and the mean distance travelled daily was 10.4 miles for, although a great total distance had been traversed, the expedition's rate of progress had been slow: an average of about a mile an hour when on the trail. In this regard Rae was critical of the naval custom of stopping for luncheon, on which M'Clintock party had occupied forty-five hours or almost two days in all. Yet the men dragging the naval sleds had been, in constrast with those of Rae's parties, doing the work of draft animals, so perhaps a luncheon stop for them was absolutely necessary.[25] One of the few recommendations for change of equipment which M'Clintock did make upon his return to *Assistance* was that in the future, in the "gutta percha trough or boat," the gutta percha itself, which had a tendency "to split when roughly handled in cold weather," be replaced by oiled or painted canvas. He advocated particularly a very careful selection henceforth of the men employed upon sled trips and a considerable *increase* in their numbers. Austin's voyage had also brought attention to preserved (or dehydrated) potatoes which were widely used by the navy and by Rae, and which at the close of this voyage received a collective attestation of approval from Austin's officers. Finally, M'Clintock's sled journey had by no means been the only one from Austin's expedition at this time. On 15 April when M'Clintock had set out, twenty-one sledges in all had been dispatched for *Assistance* and *Resolute*.[26]

Yet there was criticism of the Austin expedition, at home and in the Arctic, both now and later. Not only had it found no sign of Franklin westward along Barrow Strait; Austin's vessels had not come anywhere near enough to Melville Island to furnish either direct support or provisions to the M'Clure party. Even in the task of communication there was a defect: M'Clintock had failed to leave at Winter Harbour word of the Beechey Island finds. John Rae was also to regret that Austin had not sent a sledge party into the quadrilateral southwest of Cape Walker. Another omission was that Austin only named and did not penetrate Peel Sound. In this the influence of the James Clark Ross expedition of 1848–49 was apparent. There was a further complaint that Austin's steam vessels had acted in no greater capacity than that of steam tugs. What, it was asked, could not steam do were the tenders allowed to travel on their own?[27] This was really a reference to Captain Penny, the whaler commander who in *Lady Franklin* and *Sophia* had been sent by the Admiralty to examine Jones Sound and Wellington Channel at about the same time (1850–51) that the Austin expedition was also in the Arctic.

Penny had voyaged in the polar seas since his twelfth year, commanded a whaler for sixteen years, and never had to make a claim upon an insurance company. On questions of arctic navigation, whaling officers were wont to ask, "What does Penny think of it?" Sent to the Arctic in 1851, Penny was unable to enter Jones Sound owing to ice and he wintered in 1850–51 on the far side of Wellington Channel from Beechey Island, not very distant from Austin. In 1851 two members of Penny's expedition, Goodsir and Marshall, went to the north coast of Cornwallis Island and, in a shallow cove on the western shore of Wellington Channel, found a piece of charred wood which probably belonged to the Franklin party, although it has also been said that "its origin remains doubtful." Secondly, Penny himself picked up a piece of English elm at Maury Channel which was probably from the lost ships. Discovering open water in Queen's Channel through the use of a sleigh, he returned there and completed a survey by boat. He achieved Cape Becher, and from it saw in the distance the final northward bend of the strait now called Penny Strait. Returning by 25 July to home base at Assistance Harbour on the southern shore of Cornwallis Island, he wanted to borrow one of Austin's steam tenders to continue the search in Wellington Channel.[28] Austin, wishing to sail eastward and reach northern waters by way of Jones Sound, refused Penny's request. As Penny put it, Austin would not himself go up Wellington Channel to amplify Penny's explorations, nor would he lend Penny one of his steam tenders so that Penny could go there. Once again, it appears, the navy played a dog-in-the-manger role. Thwarted, Penny sailed for home, later to be followed by Austin.

It was to a puzzled and resentful nation that the two men did return. In one quarter there was criticism that was reminiscent of an earlier censure. The journal which had especially supported Richard King and the Hudson's Bay Company in 1847 vis-à-vis the navy was now critical of the navy in relation to whalers. The fact of the case, the *Athenaeum* argued, was that in 1850–51 it was the whaling expedition which had done the major work in finding evidence of the early track of Franklin. While Penny, a commander without a commission, had personally explored a great deal, Austin had, "under shelter of a commission, baffled further results and remained snug in his ship during all the time when the sledding expeditions were out." Yet Austin, it complained, now received a lucrative Admiralty appointment, while the same Admiralty, obviously not wishing further expeditions of a mixed whaling and naval character, simply informed Penny, when he applied, that there would be no further need for his services. In any event, one consequence of the Penny expedition and controversy surrounding it was that the public was now conscious of Wellington Channel and what had been left undone there. As a result, there was a tendency for men to look northward, even when news of finds on the southern coast of Victoria Land was brought to England early in 1852. This was a misdirection, however, which might have been avoided had Penny had his way in searching Wellington Channel by steam tender.[29]

By now the search had become extremely complicated, as its very extensiveness over a wide area and its growing length in time carried hazards of their own in rumour and diverted effort. In this same period there had been sent out three private searches under, respectively, Sir John Ross and Commander Forsyth from Britain, and Lieutenant DeHaven from the United States. Yet, as Richard King pointed out, "Commander Forsyth and Lieutenant DeHaven were altogether unsuccessful; they failed in establishing even a wintering, and merely made the voyage to the Polar Sea and back. Sir John Ross secured his wintering and that is all." By September 1851 Penny, Austin, Ross, and DeHaven were back, and still the Franklin party had not been found. Not only had there been a geographical "escalation" as regards the searches. When the twenty-one sledges had been dispatched from *Assistance* and *Resolute* in April 1851 they had borne "appropriate names, flags, and mottoes, emblematic of the chivalrous notion of their service."[30] Escalation of a sentimental or romantic kind, in keeping with the spirit of the time, had also entered into the Franklin searches.

It was the whaler Penny, not the navy, who had brought home evidence that Franklin had sailed northward from Beechey Island. Another man connected with commerce rather than the navy, John Rae, found evidence in the same season (1851) that Franklin had sailed southward of Beechey Island as well, that is towards the North American mainland. In addition to having problems in relation to the Hydrographic Office, Rae had also been prevented from making his trip, as planned, in 1850 because of the needs of a naval boat party. This was an expedition under Lieut. W. J. S. Pullen, RN, which, Rae felt, had by no means fulfilled its expectations. Coming up the Mackenzie River from *Plover* and *Herald*, Pullen had wintered at Fort Simpson in 1849–50 and been instructed to search in 1850 from the mouth of the Mackenzie to Victoria Island. He had travelled, however, no further east in that season than Cape Bathurst. Rae noted Pullen's easy optimism before the event and disillusionment after it, and was confident that he himself possessed a more realistic understanding of the Arctic and mode of travelling it. Yet, as he contemplated the competition which he expected from naval men in the succeeding season, Rae was also fearful that his own physical strength had declined.[31] More aware now than formerly of the game of prestige as servicemen played it, his gambit was to try to win the Founder's Gold Medal of the Royal Geographical Society for 1851. Certainly in 1850–51 he could be his own man again, undeterred by the navy, and, despite his preliminary diffidence as regards his physique, his élan and strategy in these years are reminiscent of his first voyage. His instructions were to find the Franklin party or traces of it by continuing to search and delineate the topography of Wollaston and Victoria Lands. He was to find out if these bodies were separated by an ocean arm. Told to choose the approach he "believed most advantageous," he selected "without hesitation" that by Great Bear Lake and the Coppermine River, despite certain difficulties which this route imposed.[32] As in 1847 he planned to explore along two separate arms of a vast Y, with a single base at Kendall River Provision Station near the junction of the Kendall and Coppermine Rivers. Rae's wintering, however, was to be at Fort Confidence at one of the heads of Great Bear Lake. His means of reaching the lake was the Mackenzie River.

Some of the difficulties which Fort Confidence entailed were new to Rae. He brought only a week or two of rations beyond those required for the forthcoming explorations; Indian hunters had not been forewarned of his coming; boats for the expedition had to be built at the winter base, despite an absence of wood there; and, finally, Rae found there was not sufficient snow at the fort to renew his capacity for or train his men in igloo-building. Eight men were sent to look for wood for boat-building; two prepared nets for the fishery; and Rae himself reconnoitred a boat route to the Coppermine River. At about the same time he looked for and, by one means or another, found Indians who would supply his party with food; from them he secured fish in diminishing numbers and an irregular supply of venison. Otherwise, there was only a little barley or meal in addition to meat, which without bread or vegetables, Rae said, left something necessary out of the diet. The lowest temperature for the winter was −72°F. January was unusually cold and in that month, ink being frozen, Rae had to use a pencil to keep his journal. He practised for his forthcoming travels, munching frozen pemmican and drinking as little water as possible.[33]

Boats had to be seaworthy and yet suitable for transport to the Coppermine River and navigation down it. Wood that was knotty but sound and very tough was found on the Dease River. Rae made for the carpenter, Kirkness, a drawing in great detail and there was turned off the stocks on 2 November a craft of bent birch and clinker build with "great rake at stem and stern post." Two feet shorter than that of Dease and Simpson, the boat had a twenty-two-foot keel, a beam of six feet three inches, and a height amidships of two feet three inches. The second boat was finished in January. Rigging for both vessels consisted of two lug sails, cut, roped, and fitted by Rae himself. Caulking and pitching were left until April so as to allow the planks to thaw and shrink as much as possible. Equipped with oars and eight rowlocks each, either boat could be lifted by two persons with ease and carried by four without inconvenience. After heavy seas washed over them in an arctic storm that summer, twisting them in every direction, Rae would commend them as his "slight built but fine little craft." Though he had asked York Factory for a "MacIntosh air boat," Rae did not take a Halkett boat with him in 1851; later he wrote that, as the years passed, Halkett boats became larger and therefore (he implied) of less use to him.[34] Another means of transport was dogs. Just as Rae had concluded that the Indian flat-bottomed or toboggan type of sled was superior for the Arctic to Eskimo sleds with high runners, so he now chose Indian dogs as well. For his requirements, he wrote, were "great powers of endurance combined with moderate strength" and he found that, though smaller, Indian dogs were "much more hardy in every respect" than Eskimo dogs and required "less provisions"; the ones he obtained performed, he said, superbly in such preparatory tasks as hauling, in the spring, over a ton of pemmican and flour to Kendall River. For the spring expedition itself, the party would carry "not a pound of weight uselessly." Avoiding the naval practice of losing warmth (as Rae claimed) by sleeping separately, his party now, as in 1847, had a single bed. Weighing 22 lb., it consisted of a blanket and deerskin robe, and "two hairy deer skins" to place between the men and the snow. Rae had "travelling breeks," socks, and a flannel shirt "besides my every day suit"; he carried "a pocket comb ... tooth brush, towel and a bit of coarsest yellow soap" as his whole "toilet apparatus," and was in the habit of having his mitts (not gloves) hung round the neck. There was nothing to which he had not turned his own hand in preparation for the spring and summer season.[35]

Departure on the spring exploration was delayed by an unseasonable thaw in mid-April, which bared the ground of snow, by the difficulty of getting provisions from the Indians, and by starving Indians themselves, whom the party had to aid. Leaving base on 25 April, Rae took with him on his actual travelling party only John Beads and Peter Linklater, English-rather than French-speaking half-breeds from Red River, "as fine fellows as one could wish to travel with," he felt, although his opinion of Beads would change somewhat on a later expedition. Having a total lading not exceeding 560 lb., the party had pemmican, flour, and fuel sufficient for thirty-five days from the date of leaving the mouth of the Coppermine. Rae believed still in a division between Victoria and Wollaston Lands, and hoped, if he encountered no "very great obstacle," to "examine about 300 miles of new coast or sea." On this occasion there was a false start. Wood, Rae points out, runs smoothly on snow that is in its natural state. But because of the thaw and a subsequent freeze-up, the wooden runners of the sleighs required protection against the hard sharp surface of the snow, so that a man had to be sent back to pick up hoop iron for the runners, which caused a further delay of at least a day. On 27 April the party reached the Kendall River Depot and on 30 April Rae set out with Beads and Linklater, two sledges drawn by five dogs, a small sledge drawn by himself, and a fatigue party of three men and two dogs which accompanied Rae until 2 May when the expedition reached the coast.[36] By noon of that day it was at Richardson Bay, about five miles west of the mouth of the Coppermine.

Travel had been very hard on the dogs, as the sharp crust of the snow cut their feet, even though they were provided with shoes. Once on sea ice, however, the party found the surface not unfavourable for travel. Journeying by night because he had already had a slight attack of snow-blindness, Rae advanced rapidly and before midnight on 5 May had crossed Dolphin and Union Strait to reach Wollaston Land. Turning eastward to trace new coastline there, Rae discovered that it was difficult to find one's way past small bays and islets in hazy weather, and so struck overland, leaving the shore to be traced on his return, when the land would be more discernible after, as he hoped, a thaw. Although detained for a night near Wilbank Bay, by 9 May Rae had proved the nonexistence of the expected strait between Wollaston and Victoria Lands; for now, travelling eastward, he had reached without finding a break in the coastline the same land-mark, Cape Louis Philippe, which Simpson had reached when, returning from Castor and Pollux Bay in 1839, he had travelled westward along Victoria Island's coast before crossing over to the mainland. However, the fact that Wollaston and Victoria Lands were one, as Rae had demonstrated, posed a problem. Should he now go northward overland in search of a sea coast, or turn westward again "in hopes of finding that some of the spaces of Wollaston Land left blank in the charts, might prove to be a strait"? He chose the latter alternative. For northward the ridges of land lay across the direct line of route, were mostly clear of snow, and would become clearer still. Travelling in that direction with sledges and dogs could become in warm weather completely impracticable. Rae turned back on the night of 10 May with a storm at his back. The gale blew away loose snow from the party's outbound track, so that Rae could follow this even in "drift ... so thick that we could not see 10 yards ahead." Otherwise only constant, and time-consuming, compass readings would have kept the party on course.[37]

Since travelling down the Coppermine River, Rae had hauled his own sledge, a drag weight of 90 or 95 lb., and then of 70 lb., which lessened the load for the dogs and gave Rae flexibility as leader. Amounting to a "satel-lite" sledge (a type referred to later), it carried bedding for Rae, instru-ments, a gun, and a good supply of pemmican, as well as tools for building a snowhouse. Self-sufficient, Rae was thus able to "examine bays, rivers, inlets and other localities on the route when requisite," while the other two members of the party made "a straight course in the direction pointed out to them." Progressing westward, Rae passed his point of first arrival on what he had now shown to be Victoria Island; continuing along what was new coastline he reached and named Dickens Point, in the vicinity of Douglas Island. On 17 May he deposited his own sled at a location about seven miles from Cache Point, and by 22 May met Eskimos in lodges near what he named Cape Hamilton. From them he purchased seals' flesh and fat for the dogs. The time for his return had "now arrived," Rae wrote later; as he actually turned back on 24 May (once again the Queen's birth-day), one feels that he may have had this date in mind for some time as that for his furthest advance on the spring journey. On the night of 23–24 May, with no other encumbrance than a "small piece of pemmican for

1. **Steam machinery from Sir John Ross's H.M.S. *Victory*, Victoria Harbour, 1957**
    Canadian Forces photo

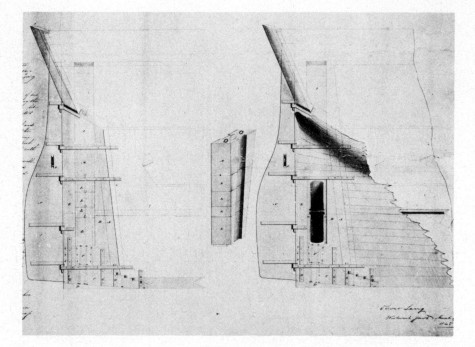

2.   Plans for installation of a screw propeller, H.M.S. *Erebus*, 1845

3. H.M.S. *Erebus*

4. Inflatable india rubber boat (the Halkett boat), Rae expedition, 1846–47

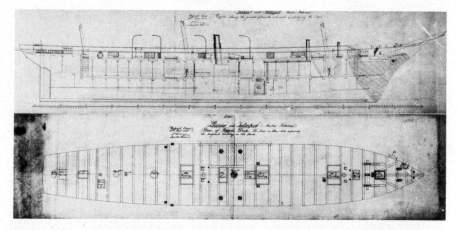

5. Profile and plan of upper deck, steam vessels *Pioneer* and *Intrepid*, 1851

6. H.M.S. *Assistance* and steam vessel *Pioneer*, Queen's Channel, 16 August 1852
Courtesy of the British Library

a terrible life as we recently experienced; there
should lurk in the heart's inmost recesses
misgivings as to whether they were not Going
"Home" to meet an untimely end among the
bleak polar wastes over which they were
about to journey? — when lo' a confused
murmuring of voices is heard — then the
words "Deer are crossing the Bay— I see them
through the haze", — another moment— "Esquimaux
are coming toward the ship"— then the
reality.— It was a Sledge party from
Her Majesty's Barque Resolute!
This most unlooked for and joyful meeting
happens in consequence of Lieut. Mecham
of the Resolute-(Commanded by Capt. Henry
Kellett C. B. late of "Herald") parted with
on our entering the ice off Cape Lisburne)
having visited the Parry Sandstone at
Winter Harbour,— on his return from searching
after Sir John Franklin in the fall of
1852, and found on it the record deposited
by Captain McClure in April last.—

7. Extract from the diary of A.B. James H. Nelson, 5 April 1853 (see p. 133)

H. M. S.hips *Erebus and Terror*
{ Wintered in the Ice in

28 of May 1847 { Lat. 70° 5' N. Long. 98° 23' W

Having wintered in 1846—7 at Beechey Island
in Lat 74° 43' 28" N. Long 91° 39' 15" W after having
ascended Wellington Channel to Lat 77°, and returned
by the West side of Cornwallis Island.

_____ Commander.

Sir John Franklin commanding the Expedition.
All well

WHOEVER finds this paper is requested to forward it to the Secretary of
the Admiralty, London, *with a note of the time and place at which it was
found* or, if more convenient, to deliver it for that purpose to the British
Consul at the nearest Port.

QUINCONQUE trouvera ce papier est prié d'y marquer le tems et lieu ou
il l'aura trouvé, et de le faire parvenir au plutot au Secretaire de l'Amirauté
Britannique à Londres.

CUALQUIERA que hallare este Papel, se le suplica de enviarlo al Secretario
del Almirantazgo, en Londres con una nota del tiempo y del lugar en
donde se halló.

EEN ieder die dit Papier mogt vinden, wordt hiermede verzogt, om het
zelve, ten spoedigste, te willen zenden aan den Heer Minister van de
Marine der Nederlanden in 's Gravenhage, of wel aan den Secretaris der
Britsche Admiraliteit, te London, en daar by te voegen eene Nota
inhoudende de tyd en de plaats alwaar dit Papier is gevonden geworden.

FINDEREN af dette Papiir ombedes, naar Leilighed gives, at sende
samme til Admiralitets Secretairen i London, eller nærmeste Embedsmand
i Danmark, Norge, eller Sverrig. Tiden og Stœdit hvor dette er fundet
önskes venskabeligt paategnet.

WER diesen Zettel findet, wird hier-durch ersucht denselben an den
Secretair des Admiralitets in London einzusenden, mit gefälliger angabe
an welchen ort und zu welcher zeit er gefundet worden ist.

Party consisting of 2 Officers and 6 Men
left the Ships on Monday 24th May 1847

Gm Gore Lieut
Chas F Des Voeux Mate

8. Document found at Point Victory in 1859 (see Appendix 3)

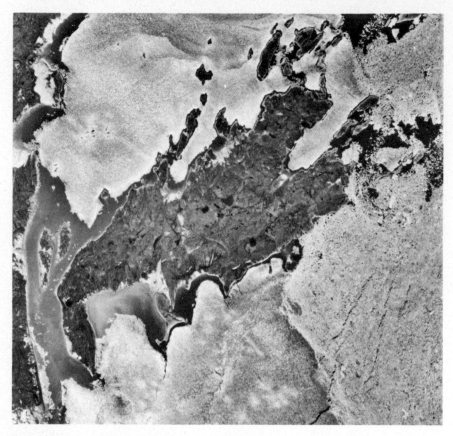

9. Aerial view of Montréal Island

Photo by Surveys and Mapping Branch, Department of Energy, Mines and Resources

10. View from the King cache on Montreal Island

I am totally unable to form an opinion on this subject. The best course will probably be to request the advice of the Admiralty. — G. 14/

Mr. Stephen. Perhaps the following information may be of service in deciding as to the value of this letter. I have learned from Sir Edward Parry first that the writer of this letter is a person who omits no opportunity of directing public attention upon himself, and that it would be scarcely safe to follow his views upon this subject. 2ly that the Admiralty and those persons who are qualified to form an opinion on the matter do not entertain, at present at all events, any apprehension concerning the fate of Sir J. Franklin and his party, and thirdly that according to previous concertment an expedition under Dr. Richardson is about to start immediately over land for the purpose of meeting Sir J. Franklin. Whether that expedition follows the route proposed by Dr. King I am not able to say. AB. 17 June /47.

11. Colonial Office minutes on letter of Dr. Richard King, June 1847 (see pp. 72–73)

C.O. 323/232, Public Record Office

12. John Rae's sketch of Fort Confidence, Winter 1850–51, showing boats used in his voyage of 1851

13.   Sled party with the J. C. Ross expedition, Somerset Island, 1849

14. George Back

15. John Rae

16. Robert M'Clure

17. F. L. M'Clintock

lunch," and "a gun telescope and compass," Rae made a ten-hour trek with one of the men to note his furthest landmark, Cape Back, named after Sir George Back.[38]

As was his custom, Rae investigated on his return trip coastline left in doubt on the outbound one, tracing by "a circuit route round" all doubtful bays, while, once again, "the men and dogs followed the straight" route. On 30 May the cache of 17 May was reached and on the night of that same day the party crossed to the mainland; by the morning of 4 June it was encamped near the mouth of the Coppermine, two miles from where on 2 May the spring journey proper had commenced. By this time water on the ice precluded sled travel and the last part of the spring trip was "by far the most disagreeable." As the party made its way along the estuary of the Coppermine River and the river itself, through "every hollow and valley" there flowed "a stream more or less large," sometimes forcing a detour of three or more miles to find a ford. On 10 June Rae and his companions arrived at the Kendall River Provision Station, from which he planned to begin his summer boat trip.[39]

The company explorer calculated that in thirty-three days his travel party had used 54 lb. of flour and 128 lb. of pemmican, or nearly 2 lb. of flour and pemmican a day for each member. During the same time it had also used, taken as a whole, 1¼ lb. of tea, 2 lb. of chocolate, and 10 lb. of sugar. Cooking on the spring trip had been by driftwood as well as grease. On the last leg the dogs had provided a sufficient diet for themselves by killing the lemmings that were migrating northward, very numerous, fat, and large. Not only had these small animals kept the dogs fed; for the men they had proved "very fine when roasted before the fire or between two stones." On the return leg lemmings, geese, and partridges had formed the party's principal food, although a large musk bull had also been shot. Its flesh, Rae wrote, was almost equal to that of four or five deer and helped to satisfy "a prodigious appetite" which the party had on its arrival back at Kendall River. Rae felt that the food of his parties was more antiscorbutic than that of the naval parties.[40]

The snowhouse, a mainstay of Rae's travel methods, had served him well on his spring trip, providing snugness in temperatures as low as −22°F. As the Eskimos did, Rae camped on low ground where the snow was best for building. At the start Beads, the snowhouse builder, had taken more than an hour and a half to construct the night's shelter but had improved on this with time. Not only was an igloo warmer than a tent. In the latter vapours from the men's breath and warm tea and food would adhere to the walls and then, after freezing, fall to the men's bedding, giving it a "sheet iron consistence," as both tent and bedding daily became a greater burden to haul. By contrast, these troublesome vapours would in snowhouses simply freeze to the walls, becoming part of them. The snowhouse was impenetrable to the wind; required no canvas and poles to haul; and, once erected on an outbound trip, stood ready for use on the return one.[41]

Because he was travelling on foot, Rae had achieved at Wilbank Bay a more accurate placing of the coast than Simpson had in boats. Collinson, coming by ship, would shortly judge Bell Island, in the vicinity of Lady Richardson Bay, to be a cape; Rae, perhaps once again because he was on foot, had already discerned that it is in fact insular. Many years later he was to be complimented for his exactness on this trip. He had also shown a sense of return, in cautioning McKenzie, his second-in-command, on the procedure to follow in this regard if Rae himself did not come back from his spring trip and again near Cape Back, where he had travelled more and more lightly as he had approached the cape. However, although at Wilbank Bay he had disproved, as in 1847, the existence of a strait, at Cape Back he had been unable to investigate thoroughly Prince Albert Sound and had wrongly continued to call it a strait. Here, nevertheless, he had clearly seen at his furthest point the shore on the north side of the sound which Lieutenant Haswell from *Investigator* had reached only ten days before. The extremes of the two travellers had been only forty miles apart.[42] As in 1847, in relation to the Franklin party, so in 1851 Rae had been within hailing distance of the finders of a passage who were themselves in great danger.

If one records his trip as occupying thirty-four days, from the coast at the mouth of the Coppermine on 2 May to a return there on 4 June, for a distance of 685 miles, Rae had averaged just over twenty miles a day. If one takes into account, as Rae himself did later, the distance he had covered between Great Bear Lake and the mouth of the Coppermine River, he had travelled 1,080 miles in thirty-nine travelling days, and had thus averaged nearly twenty-eight miles a day. He had travelled at twice or even something approaching three times the speed of M'Clintock on his 1851 trip. Tired and in a hurry, and certainly anxious to have news of this achievement reach the Royal Geographical Society as well as his employers, Rae wrote upon his arrival at the Kendall River Station, without waiting to sleep, one of the liveliest of all his letters. The measures, moreover, which he took to ensure that a copy of the letter reached the society turned out to be effective; it was received before the end of December.[43]

On 13 June, three days after Rae's return to the Kendall Station, the boats from Fort Confidence arrived there under McKenzie. On his second trip of the season Rae's course was eastward and then northward along the coast of Victoria Land, much past the easternmost extent of his spring trip. Now Rae had with him not two men but a party consisting of a dozen in all. There were four main methods of advancing the boats: by sail, oars, pulling, and poling. Rae had felt that from Cape Krusenstern a passage would be found along the shore of Victoria Island. However, he now judged there was ice in that direction and for this reason sailed along the mainland coast, though progress was slow and difficult. Cape Alexander was reached on 24 July, two days earlier than Dease and Simpson had arrived there in 1839. Yet Rae had to wait until 27 July for the ice to break up before crossing to Victoria Island, when for a time progress was more rapid. At the outset no one other than Rae had known how to tack when plying to windward, and so he had to teach other members of the party this skill. Now Rae would take a bearing when he saw a straight piece of coast before him and would lie down, having given orders to be wakened if anything unusual was seen. There were, he said, always two or three pairs of keen eyes in each boat on the lookout for anything connected with the Franklin search. Naming features as he went, on 1 August Rae passed Sturt and Macready points as the party neared the southeast corner of Victoria Island, and on 2 August with an ebb tide strongly in their favour, the boats made a 100-mile run in twenty-four hours. The expedition not only rounded the corner of the island, Kean Point, where there is flood water, but reached Taylor Island far beyond.[44]

Succeeding progress was, however, relatively slower and recourse to poling and rowing became especially necessary. On 7 August, for example, oars were used for seven hours to travel some twenty miles. Quite often driftwood was used for fuel. Rae praised the compass he had with him, yet there was a region, towards his furthest point, when it was "perfectly useless, being acted upon," he suspected, "by the large quantities of pyrites that were strewn along the beach." On 12 August, with little prospect of a change in the wind that would enable advance by boat, Rae made preparations for a journey on foot. Deer had previously been shot for food; now the deerskin so obtained was used as footwear, for Rae and the three men he had brought with him found themselves on ground so rough that moccasins were worn through. When the party went inland, walking was still rough and the travellers had to make long detours to avoid lakes that intersected the country. On the morning of 13 August Rae called a halt, and chose the two least injured of his men to go forward. The other man and Rae, suffering badly, remained behind and Rae himself took observations. For the first time he was not personally making his own furthest advance. In the evening the men returned, lame, having walked three to four miles beyond their point of disappearance from Rae's own view; from their furthest they estimated they had seen another seven or eight miles northward to a feature to which Rae gave the name Pelly Point.[45]

Retreating to the boats and the rest of his party Rae then ran south, for safety's sake. His real aim was to get further north by boat, or else to cross to Point Franklin, first reached by Sir James Ross in 1834, on King William's Land, not much more than forty miles. Rae gave the name Victoria Strait to the body of water which separated him from that land; but although he was such a short distance from Franklin Point, and a comparable one from the location of Franklin's ships in 1848, he was nevertheless cut off from these by the stream of ice from Winter Harbour in which the Franklin expedition had become embayed; and this ice cut him off also from Eskimos who might know of the Franklin party. Rae remained until 19 August near the east shore of Victoria Island, trying to get either east or north; but in the end the ice defeated him, and now new ice was forming. This, Rae found when he turned back on that date, sometimes cut the boats and also caused water to freeze on the oars.[46]

At Parker Bay just beyond the southeast corner of Victoria Island on his return voyage Rae made the only actual finds relating to Franklin of either leg of his 1851 travels, and the most significant finds yet made by any party. At 3:30 p.m. on 21 August there was discovered a piece of wood and shortly afterwards a second piece. "Both pieces of wood were 'touching the beach' and had apparently been washed up by the flood tide only a short time before they were found." The first of the two was of pinewood and appeared to be the butt end of a small flagstaff. The second, found about half a mile from the first, was of oak and seemed to be a stanchion. That the flagstaff had come from one of Her Majesty's vessels was certain both by a marking on it and by a red thread in a line attached to it. Of the finds Rae himself wrote immediately in his rough notes, "They may be portions of one of Sir John Franklin's ships!" Today it is "virtually beyond doubt" that they were.[47]

The rest of the journey back to the mouth of the Coppermine was a quick but rough one. From Back Point onwards, the party encountered no more ice.[48] At Bloody Fall, well up the Coppermine, one of the boats was left, while the other, after being strengthened, was eventually taken by Rae as far as Lake Athabasca, where ice precluded further navigation for that year. From Fort Chipewyan Rae made his way, after the freeze-up, to the Red River Settlement and thence to St. Paul, Detroit, and New York, where he arrived on 8 March, and from which he set sail shortly thereafter for England.

Rae's relationship with the indigenous peoples, Indians and Eskimos, had played an important part in his journeys. There was a tendency for service personnel to think that they were superior to Eskimos in the art of survival in the Arctic. The truth, Rae's travels indicated, was that Europeans could survive in the Arctic by considering themselves not superior in this art but learners. Rae wrote of "My Friends, The Esquimaux," drawing a sympathetic picture of them as he remarked upon their customary truthfulness, their neatness and cleanliness, their capacity to observe, their eye for science, and the excellence of Eskimo women as cartographers. He had argued that, while friendly relations should be established with them, this was nevertheless "not easy to do, as they are very shy and timid." Eskimo ingenuity and practical sense made Rae feel himself very much a learner. Yet he knew Indian methods as well as those of the Eskimo, and had brought northward with him Indian dogs as well as sleds. Rae had brought south to the Indians an Eskimo device: at Fort Confidence in April 1851 he had made a small spear in the Eskimo manner and taught the starving Indians there how to fish for "herrings" in the manner of the more northern natives.[49]

To make finds is the first great requirement in exploration; to ensure that word of them gets home is the second. In August Rae had judged with a fine eye how late he could stay out, and had made certain he kept clear of the ice. But besides knowing how to return with his finds, he was aware now of the third factor in exploration: that of gaining recognition at home for what he had discovered. Rae on his boat trip had gone from the Coppermine to the east end of Victoria Land and back, 1,390 miles. He had travelled in all in the 1851 season, on the spring and summer trips, 2,470 miles; and he had found a total of 630 miles of new coastline. John Arrowsmith, the cartographer, gave to the Royal Geographical Society his opinion that Rae's explorations had been "*the discoveries of the year 1851*."[50] This commendation improved Rae's chances of receiving an award from the society. He had sought as well the support of Sir George Back, the society's vice-president. Perhaps he realized that Back had had a negative effect upon the arctic work and influence of Richard King. At any rate, Rae had been careful to avoid, in his own case, such a result. He had given to the most distant feature he saw on 24 May 1851 the name of Cape Back, and where his discoveries commenced on his summer boat trip, he had been careful to preserve upon the map the vice-president's name, at Back Point, even though this required (because of a mistake by Thomas Simpson) a transfer of the name from one feature to another. These attentions were the opposite of harmful. Back was also, like Arrowsmith, one of the voices counselling recognition of Rae; he wrote that the company explorer deserved recognition for his work in 1846–47, and for his work with Richardson, as well as for his travels in 1851. Traditionally, the annual meeting of the Royal Geographical Society was on the Queen's birthday. Exactly one year after Cape Back received its name, on 24 May 1852, in the absence of Rae himself who was away with his family in Stromness, Sir George Back received on behalf of the coastal explorer the Founder's Gold Medal of the society.[51] Rae's travels in 1851 had in themselves been worthy of reward, but this time, by keeping on good terms with Back, Rae had buttressed his claim to attention with a show of psychology.

Rae had gained personal recognition but another kind did not accrue. He had brought to England in late March 1852 the two pieces of wood which, we know today, were from Franklin's vessels, and which came from a point further along his track than any other evidence so far carried home; properly identified, the finds would give an approximate location for the Franklin party. Even Rae, however, had become diffident about them; from Detroit he had written that his search for Franklin had been fruitless. Responsibility for identification rested not with Rae but with the navy; yet it already had plans under way for a more northern trip than this evidence entailed. It launched an investigation and showed the items to Sir James Ross, who felt that they were so familiar that they must have belonged to a vessel in which he had served; besides, they came from an area close to that which Ross himself had named in 1848 as the likely location of the lost party.[52] Since that time, however, he himself had failed to get to Boothia, and had become convinced, erroneously, that Peel Sound was impassable, an opinion which seemed confirmed now by Lieut. W. H. Browne of the Austin expedition, who had come to the same conclusion on a spring sled journey along the east coast of Prince of Wales Island in 1851. Franklin, Ross now believed, had not sailed southward from Barrow Strait towards the mainland.

On the other hand, since 1834 Ross had had, in the search for a passage, a bent of his own towards the far North. It was he who had counselled incorporation in Franklin's orders of the instruction to sail in certain circumstances up Wellington Channel; and that channel had now been shown to have, in fact, much open water. Given Ross's present convictions — his northward emphasis and his confidence that he knew Rae's items — it is not surprising that he disregarded as a source for the finds his own vessels *Erebus* and *Terror* of his antarctic expedition of 1839–43, and instead suggested *Fury* in which, nearly three decades before, in 1824–25, Ross had sailed under Parry into Prince Regent Inlet. This interpretation fitted in with the finds of the Penny expedition in Wellington and Maury Channels in 1851 that were Franklin party artifacts, or probably so; and it was an interpretation which appeared to be strengthened by the fact that by the spring of 1852 word had reached England of Bellot Strait, newly found by the expedition (1851–52) which had been sent under William Kennedy to investigate Boothia by sea. This channel, it was suggested, might indeed have conveyed Rae's artifacts from *Fury*, wrecked in Prince Regent Inlet in 1825, to Victoria Strait where Rae had found them.[53] From such a viewpoint Rae's finds were not considered to have come from *Erebus* or *Terror* at all, and there was no need for the navy to divert any of its attention towards the mainland.

Yet there was evidence that ran counter to Ross's interpretation. Captain Austin had also served, like Ross, in *Fury* in 1824–25; and he did not think that the stanchion which Rae had found had come from that vessel. Besides, there were now appearing in public print for the first time letters by Captain Fitzjames of the Franklin party, written home by him in 1845, and revealing in Franklin a personal predilection towards not a northern but a coastal passage. Long held back in secret (a critic would later claim), these letters denuded of its chief support (he would also argue) the naval wish to look northward. Finally, and perhaps most important, among all of those who had served in *Erebus* or *Terror*, the navy restricted its canvass as regards Rae's finds to Sir James Ross alone.[54] Indeed, its advisers on other arctic matters as well as this one, appeared to have a penchant for open and deep sea navigation, optimistically assumed to exist in the far North. The navy seemed, that is, prone to investigate less fully factors which had to do with the coastal aspect of Franklin's instructions than it did those relating to the far northern and deep-sea aspect. In any event, presented with its own artifacts, it failed in the manner outlined above to recognize them and to gain an approximate location for the lost party. Penny's finds to the north, rather than those of Rae at Parker Bay, continued to be influential and, judged by results, discovery of Franklin remained as far away as ever.

Indeed, so complicated had the search become and so misdirected to the north, that the only way now in which to find the Franklin party was, paradoxically, to give up the search. Rae himself was, at thirty-eight, like an athlete who is just past his physical prime but has acquired great compensatory skills and knowledge. He chose, with company support, to travel now without reference to the Franklin search. He would make one more trip to the Arctic, this time with his original intentions of 1846–47: to complete discovery of North America's mainland coast and to reach the magnetic pole.[55] It had been the peninsularity of Boothia and the search for Franklin which had prevented these intentions being carried out. Now Rae seemed free to accomplish them and, on his own initiative, he proposed to the Hudson's Bay Company a plan for an expedition which was accepted by them. Yet frustration and the unexpected were still to pursue him. He was unaware that in 1851 he had found what everyone, including himself, was looking for. On his final trip he would find what he had ceased to look for: the locale itself of the Franklin party, although discovery of the last unexplored part of the mainland coast would still elude him.

Meanwhile the M'Clure party lay beset in the west in danger of repeating the Franklin experience.

7

The First Discovery of a Northwest Passage (1852–1854)

On the same day that John Rae was awarded a medal, *Investigator*, beset in Mercy Bay, saluted Her Majesty with a 21-gun salute. Of the vessel's guns James Nelson wrote:

> Oh did we not wish their boom could be heard by the dear Lady our Sovereign! The truth is, our present condition,—so isolated and so particularly void of variety,—tends to a constant yearning after home, and however much we may endeavour to shake off the habit of 'thinking' (which, unless powerfully sustained by *hope* is very apt to produce a sort of melancholy)....I find the all-engrossing talk is home,—the vows to be faithfully carried out when 'home' is reached;—air built castles! scattered and destroyed by a few days consecutive frost in Autumn—.[1]

The winter and spring of 1851–52 had been depressing for *Investigator*'s complement. On a clear day one could see from a mountain at Mercy Bay Cape Hay on Melville Island;[2] and beyond that the party was within striking distance of Winter Harbour and completion of a passage. This proximity in the second winter and the appearance of scurvy in the spring were further parallels with Franklin's expedition. Gore had left the Franklin vessels with one other officer and six men on 24 May 1847, probably to complete a passage. M'Clure set out with a similar purpose, also with one other officer and six men, but six weeks earlier in the season, on 11 April 1852, prior to the firing of the guns. His progress was less than expected and the party was placed on a two-thirds allowance. Unable on these provisions to accomplish a daily twelve-hour stint, it travelled six hours and slept six hours, a good system, the surgeon Armstrong says, for men who were debilitated; however, this obviously required preparations for camping and de-camping twice each day, detracting from travelling or sleeping time. The group became more optimistic when one of its members reconnoitred ahead and saw to the north plain flat ice of the previous year. Otherwise the party would have turned back to the ship, but, on the strength of this news, it pressed forward. On so fine a thread did rescue of the M'Clure expedition and discovery and transit of a passage depend. On 28 April, the eighteenth day of its journey, the sled party came to the Parry Sandstone.[3]

Investigator's crew had been sure that one or more ships would be found at Melville Island; they found, instead, only M'Clintock's message which told of the "Mary Yacht" of Sir John Ross and of provisions at Cape Spencer near Beechey Island but gave no other assistance or information. At the Sandstone M'Clure left a message and map showing his discoveries and *Investigator*'s location. With a good deal of self-abnegation, the leader stated that under certain circumstances his vessel should not be searched for; any ship, he wrote, that entered the polar pack would inevitably be crushed. The return of M'Clure's party to *Investigator* on flat ice of one year was much faster than the outgoing trip, occupying as it did ten days, so that the group reached *Investigator* on 9 May. It had "made, to a certain extent, the Northwest Passage." Four or five years behind the Franklin party thus far, M'Clure had placed himself in a good position, by the message deposited at Winter Harbour, to be the first to complete a passage.[4]

The M'Clure party was now convinced that it was entirely on its own. If the Queen's birthday had proved depressing, the summer did also. The Investigators found that they were entrapped in a bay whose waters did not always melt in the spring. The average temperature in May 1852 was 8° colder than in the same month of 1851. M'Clure attributed the scurvy which showed itself to the heavy labour of ballasting and watering in which the men were now engaged; they would return to full health, he felt, when this was done. Nelson, for his part, criticized his commander. Snow-blindness has been described in our own day as "an affliction that turns the whole world crimson and makes the victim feel as if his eyeballs are being scoured with burning grit." Taking towards the end of May "a long journey inland," Nelson lost by this ailment "the sight of both eyes for a week" and was in intense pain. Yet M'Clure declared this was "entirely in consequence of carelessness," and that he would "make 'Abstainers' of us all if we are not more careful." The rum allowance at that time was in any event, Nelson emphasized, only "¼ of a gill per day!" Nevertheless he wrote, "my patience! as if the being snow blind was from choice." As soon as his sight was restored he intended to make himself "a pair of spectacles," using as his pattern "a representation in the Penny Magazine, of 'Horses blinkers' worn while turning a mill."[5] He thus unconsciously illustrated the fact that on naval sled trips seamen performed the task of draft animals.

M'Clure was very optimistic in thinking the scurvy aboard ship would disappear. It did not and protest against conditions became more overt. On 5 October Stephen Court, second master, wrote: "This morning the whole of the Petty Officers came on the Quarter Deck by the Ships Company's request, to represent the hardships of living upon the present small allowance of provisions. They were spoken to at the Divisions by the Captain and shown the impossibility of increasing it under the present circumstances, after which they went quietly to their work banking the ship up."[6]

Already *Investigator*'s daily allowance was halved, so that in the third winter the allowance consisted of ⅔ lb. of bread, ½ lb. of meat, 2½ oz. of vegetables, ⅔ or ¼ oz. of tea, 1¼ oz. of sugar, 4 oz. of lemon juice, 1 oz. of pickles, and ¹⁄₁₆ pint of rum.[7] With the growth of winter hunger, the difficulties of hunting, cold, and sickness all increased. Nelson dreamt of food. Hungry men, the surgeon said, were supposed to talk of "the luxuries of other climes," and aboard *Investigator* at that time this was indeed true. There was Silvester heating in *Investigator*, and even the use of a red-hot ball suspended in the air. Yet January's mean temperature was −44°F., 17°F. colder than for the same month in 1852, and there were lows in January 1853 of −65°F. and −67°F., greater cold than had been experienced by any former naval expedition, although Rae had experienced colder weather when wintering at Great Bear Lake in 1850–51. The low temperatures, together with an insufficiency of firing and food, made the decks clammy and cold and caused sickness among the men. Exercise was regular on all days. M'Clure, nearly forty-six, felt the cold more than others. The captain "never flinches an hour but carries out in his own person the law laid down [of exercise on deck]. He cannot stand the cold so well as we. To him it is a constant trouble as the least exposure subjects him to severe frost bite."[8]

At the same time as the first general appearance of scurvy, the party started to encounter muskoxen which, it was believed, were difficult to shoot. There had been several hunting adventures. One member, Woon, had only just saved himself by firing his ramrod as ammunition. Another,

Anderson, had been almost frozen to death; only by the action of Woon was he saved. A third man had resisted a potentially fatal temptation to fall asleep when lost one night. Now, on two occasions, guns exploded when fired. Nelson is praised for continuing to hunt, when the other men had abandoned the practice and only the officers continued it.[9] The heads, hearts, and livers "were the hunters perquisites, as were also the necks of the animals"; but these had to be given "some statutory limit," because "old sportsmen got into the way of cutting off the head and neck well down between the shoulders."

> Foxes and hares were eaten almost indiscriminately, even the few wolves shot being devoured by stealth. When out shooting the men would often eat the hearts and livers raw, rather than wait till their return to have them cooked.
> Several of the officers did this also but did not let it be publicly known.[10]

Yet it was found that those who only took sufficient exercise for health were in the long run better off, since those who hunted suffered greatly from hunger on the day following their activity. Indeed, "exposure and exercise in a severe temperature" were "so exhausting as to require an unusual amount of food." On the other hand, perhaps hunting helps to account for the fact that, although scurvy was widespread, there was no actual loss of life until the very eve of rescue, as compared with the epidemic loss of life aboard *Erebus* and *Terror* during the Franklin expedition's third winter. This does not mean that the hunters were efficient. The Kellett expedition (the party from the Atlantic destined to rescue the crew of *Investigator*) caught nearly three times as much usable meat, 25,878 lbs. as compared with 9,000, in two-fifths the time, by and for a crew half again as large as M'Clure's party.[11] John Rae, who criticizes the nervous attitude of the M'Clure party towards the wolves around their vessel, is also critical of the party's capacity to hunt. Of this he writes:

> The fact is, that if the description given of the quantity of game seen at Mercy Bay is true, two moderately good hunters could have killed sufficient deer and hares to have procured ½ a ration each for every man on the ship, provided always that the bunglers were not permitted to frighten the animals away. It seems fish of a good size were seen in lakes; but we are not told of any attempts to catch them in nets.[12]

Such skills displayed earlier might have prevented the debilitation which now affected the hunting itself. By December dysentry and many other illnesses filled the sick-bay and hammocks. Attending in praise-worthy manner to the incapacitated, the surgeon found it pitiable to see the wreck to which a man would be reduced after a few hours' illness as scurvy "seldom failed to supervene." The party by the following spring was

> a sight not easily forgotten. They [the Investigators] were almost all excessively reduced in body and seemed impoverished in intellect also; they stared about with a vacant expression and constant broad grin—poor fellows! They were certainly weakened in mind and had themselves noticed during their last winter that many men had become forgetful, and had their memories greatly impaired.

The officers maintained decorum and discipline in the gunroom as the situation grew more desperate. The expedition saved up for Christmas and suffered sickness in consequence, from too full meals; nevertheless, the ushering in of the new year was merry.[13]

Yet, as winter progressed, starvation, cold, and sickness brought increasing gloom and depression. The second-in-command speaks of a lowering of morale in the third winter: "The spirits of the men began to flag; they felt themselves abandoned, and evils comparatively light before pressed heavily upon them. The long unceasing night, the constant gnawing of hunger, and the dread that was stealing over them for the future, conspired to make that winter long and dreary."[14]

"Early in February," Nelson writes, "a most dense fog visited us ... with cold so piercing as to be almost intolerable. Gales of wind were frequent." On 1 March 1853 the ship's company was examined by the surgeon and some of the men told off for leaving *Investigator* in the following month. On 2 March M'Clure gave details of his plan. Unlike the Franklin party, M'Clure's expedition was to attempt to send only six men, together with an officer and the interpreter (Miertsching), out by an inland river (the Mackenzie); it would dispatch its twenty-three most ill members to the North Somerset region, to be picked up there, it was hoped, by whalers or to use the yacht *Mary* left there by Sir John Ross; the third group of thirty-four would stay with the vessel to attempt to extricate her. Armstrong and his assistant surgeon (Piers) protested that none of the men were equipped to travel at all. Those who were to travel had mixed feelings.

Isolated and alone [Nelson writes] ... enduring one continual round
of monotonous existence and just about to separate—perhaps never
to meet again ... it is not surprising that beneath the external appearance of pleasure at the prospect of a speedy release from such a terrible life as we recently experienced; there should lurk ... misgivings
as to whether they were not leaving 'home' to meet an untimely end
among the bleak polar wastes over which they were about to journey.[15]

On 4 March provisions were taken up from the hold and the carpenters
were engaged in sledge-making. The armourers were at work upon the
construction of kettles in the first half of the month and in the second half
upon the cleaning of arms and the preparation of gear for the travelling
parties. On 15 March the exact allowance was listed for the thirty-one who
were going to the Mackenzie River and North Somerset. On 5 April there
occurred the first death in the M'Clure party and the gloom of the expedition on the evening of this day was great. M'Clure assembled his men and
addressed them from the quarterdeck, showing a capacity for leadership at
a time of crisis. Appealing to the men's pride in the service of which they
were a part, he pointed to a cloud with a silver lining and likened the
present situation to this, as one of hope even amidst gloom.[16] The next day,
as a grave for the dead man was dug, M'Clure's speech was vindicated
much more directly than he expected.

After the midnight parting of Kellett and M'Clure at Bering Strait on 1
August 1850, Bedford Pim sailed with Kellett for England. Arrived there
by way of Honolulu and Cape Town, in June 1851, and promoted to lieutenant at twenty-five, he was soon involved in another arctic project. As
already stated, Pim had been part of Kellett's trip further north and west
than any other expedition, when Kellett's party had discovered, it was
conjectured, an arctic continent or at any rate an archipelago off the
Alaskan and Siberian mainland coast. Pim had dealt with the Russians in
their sector of the Arctic, lived with native peoples, and shown, unlike
other naval officers, a wish to travel alone or almost so. The influence of
this background is apparent in a project which he now brought forward, to
look for Franklin in Siberia.

In a plan submitted in November 1851 to the Royal Geographical
Society Pim reasoned that Franklin had reached the Russian Arctic by way
of a relatively open polar sea.[17] For this the young lieutenant found support in Wrangel's *Narrative*, Sabine's analysis of isothermal lines, Penny's
discovery of an ice-free sea north of Wellington Channel, and, finally, a
gratifying coincidence of his own opinion and that of the chief hydro-

grapher, Sir Francis Beaufort, who sat upon the council of the society which assessed and approved Pim's plan. Pim based his proposal upon the supposition that Franklin, after passing through Wellington Channel, had become embayed in frozen masses of ice and islands at the meridian of Bering Strait. At the mercy of winds and currents, he would have been driven to the coast of either the new or the old world. Richardson, Kellett, Pullen, and Rae had shown that it was not upon the latter. Siberia therefore was now the location to search. Travelling to the edge of Russian settlement, a four months' journey, Pim would "traverse the wilds of the Tchuktchi race, and from their shores ... pass over channels of water in India-rubber or skin canoes, to tracts inhabited by the most northern Esquimaux, and there endeavour to learn [Franklin's fate]."[18]

Pim, in short, was under "the mystic influences of the north,"[19] but in this he simply carried to a further extreme, with a more youthful and lone wolf zeal, a tendency of many others in the search for Franklin. It was easy to trace Pim's route "upon the map ... across the ... solitudes of Northern Siberia," the Russian chancellor, Count Nesselrode, wrote in comment when Pim arrived in St. Petersburg. But he noted that Pim's plan involved a traverse of immense deserts buried under eternal snows, with no means of transport through unexplored regions where there lived tribes completely savage, over which Russia exerted very limited control. Wrangel's expedition, much smaller than that of Pim, covering a third of the distance Pim planned to cover, had still required 600 dogs for fifty sledge teams, each needing fifty to seventy herring a day. Pim would need 1,200 to 1,500 dogs, and provisions in proportion; he would ruin the population of the region through which he passed; and his search would be "directed ... at random, towards an unknown point" in an "immense space." His party, wrote Pim in rebuttal, would be considerably *smaller* than that of Wrangel: probably just Pim and an interpreter, for experience showed that the smaller the party the greater the chance of success. Pim's route would be the same as, not different from, that of Wrangel and could not be much longer even if Pim reached the desired latitude, from which he then planned to go forward by sea and islands. For he wished first of all, he said, to investigate an island 160 miles from the coast, of which Wrangel had received accounts and which English geographers believed to extend from the Parry Islands to those discovered by Kellett. His project would thereafter complement the work of four British ships that were about to proceed to Wellington Channel in the track of Franklin. Pim, as indicated, wished to explore from Asia across ice and land in order to meet this party. He was anxious that native peoples should not suffer and would entrust himself to them alone.[20]

In reply, Admiral Matyischkin, who had accompanied Wrangel to Siberia, said there was no evidence of a range of islands 160 miles from the continent, or that north of such islands there was an open sea. The Russian government would be "charmed" if Pim could succeed without its aid, and it would study further means for obtaining information of any vessels driven upon the Siberian coast; but it would not supply help to Pim. Yet support by the Royal Geographical Society, upon which Pim relied in part to carry out his plan, had been predicated upon Russian help and it "would be ... little short of madness" for Pim to proceed without it, said the British minister at St. Petersburg.[21] Pim returned home from the Russian capital early in 1852.

It can be seen that, on the slender evidence of Herald and Wrangel Islands, there had now arisen a converse to the Wrangel fallacy of 1845. When Franklin sailed, argument by analogy had held that North America's Arctic was as island-free as Russia's. Now, because of Herald and Wrangel Islands and a painful new awareness of an archipelago in the North American Arctic, in Pim and others there had arisen the opposite surmise, that there was, by analogy to these islands off North America, a large land mass off the shores of Siberia, or even in the Beaufort Sea. Yet the Russians, from direct knowledge of Siberia and its environs, had now dismissed this idea, and any idea as well that it was easy to cross their vast territories. Knowing the size of the Franklin party and accustomed themselves to a very massive mode of transport, they may have thought that Pim was only the advance agent of some huge expedition, and feared a violation of Russian territorial sovereignty. Oblivious of the notion of a small, light party, they seemed to be uncomprehending or incredulous in face of the possibility that Pim did indeed represent an emphasis opposite to that of Franklin.

Pim's project, and promises of future cooperation by Russia as an alternative to it, indicate how the Franklin searches had expanded to an international plane. Behind the feeling that Franklin had reached Siberia there lay another development. Sir Roderick Murchison, president of the Royal Geographical Society, had seen something of Franklin in 1845 and was therefore in a position to know of the latter's emphasis upon a coastal passage.[22] Yet he now expressed the opinion that Franklin had been resolved "to penetrate, if possible ... into an open polar sea," a view which, he said, was "mainly founded upon the character" of "the inflexible Franklin." Pim, for his part, had already spoken of Franklin as "a man, combining bravery unmatched with a perseverance, skill and science rarely to be met with."[23] Franklin was growing to the stature of a legend.

Steam was a factor at this time in making the search still more elaborate and off-course. For some time there had been a wish to use it by way of

Bering Strait. In November 1851 Kellett had said that steam would have made it easy to reach the land he had seen from the neighbourhood of Herald Island. In Bering Strait a vessel with steam might enable an explorer "to work round ... through lanes of water between Siberia and ... Northern packs of ice," and so "*meet* Franklin" as the vessel proceeded towards "an open polar sea." Comdr. Rochefort Maguire added his support. Like Pim he had served in *Herald* and when given command of *Plover* on the Pacific side of the Arctic he did all he could to acquire "an efficient aid in steam," to help naval vessels already there, and to examine more thoroughly the sea in that direction for traces of Franklin. Like Kellett he argued that steam would also enable the search from the Pacific to be extended in the direction of Sir Edward Belcher's parties from the Atlantic.[24] Penny, as well, spoke in favour of steam. Use of it and of the screw in particular, "elicited hopes which in olden times might have been considered visionary." Not only should a small screw steamer be sent to Maguire to search for *Enterprise* and *Investigator*; along the American shore, from Spitzbergen to New Siberia and the Asian shore, a large sea must exist, stretching even to the Pole. Here was a route clearly demonstrated. Entering the Arctic from the Asian shore, explorers could carry on an extensive search in the arctic basin from June to September.[25] Steam, in short, in alliance with the idea of an open polar sea (now confirmed, it seemed, by open water in Wellington Channel) was a further stimulus to a perennial arctic optimism; it was helping to lead the quest for Franklin ever further astray.

Upon his return to England from St. Petersburg Pim volunteered to join his former commander, Kellett, in what was soon to become a separate wing of the new Belcher project to search for Franklin by Wellington Channel. At the conclusion of Austin's operation there had been established a parliamentary committee which, among other matters, looked into the subject of arctic equipment, and to it M'Clintock and others had reported.[26] One of the committee's recommendations was that the navy use larger sled parties, composed of ten men. There was also an investigation as to where to look for Franklin. This involved consultation with what has popularly been called the Arctic Council, which did not meet as one but was, rather, a number of eminent "Arctics" who were asked to advise in the search. The great weight of opinion in the council was in favour of looking for Franklin north and west up Wellington Channel. It was, as we have seen, Penny's finds to the north, not Rae's at Parker Bay, which had an effect, and other factors also appeared to point northward. There was even advanced a new reason for not going southward. Boothia, it was now claimed, was a barren region by contrast with a North where there was new evidence of abundant life.[27] The needle of opinion had swung so definitely to northern rather than southern possibilities that even evidence to the contrary had a tendency to be neglected.

Possibly Richard King is an illustration of this. Fitzjames's letters and especially Rae's finds might have been used by him as a vindication of his long-held views, and as a support for a campaign once again to search near the continental mainland. Instead, King was silent. Experience may simply have convinced him that speaking out brought no results. Alternatively, he may now have come to believe, as had so many others, that Franklin had gone up Wellington Channel. Three years later, however, he gave no hint that this had been his view. By 1855 Boothia was known as the approximate locale of the Franklin disaster but Wellington Channel had not yet been revealed as a region to which Franklin had also sailed. It was hard, King said in that year, to see how in 1852 the Admiralty could possibly have erred, in that "Captain Austen's [sic] thorough but fruitless exploration from Barrow Strait to Melville Island ... had *closed the search* in that direction," while Sir James Ross "had *left open the search* in the direction of the Great Fish River." On the contrary, the Admiralty, King said, "were determined to go wrong." Why, King would also ask in 1855, had Sir John Ross, Austin, Penny, M'Cormick, and King himself not been called before the Arctic Council in 1852 and why, on the other hand, had Sir James Ross and Back been called, "seeing that they were both committed over and over again to very grave errors"? Parry, King complained, had argued in 1847 that the only reasonable plan was to push supplies to the northern coast of America by Hudson's Bay Company methods, whereas by 1852 he was of the opinion that after the first winter Franklin had gone up Wellington Channel.[28]

It is true that Rae's finds had arrived in England only in early March 1852 and that the Belcher expedition sailed from the Thames at the end of May. Yet, although it did not change its plans because of Rae's discoveries, the navy did alter them on reasonably short notice for a humanitarian reason. Family intervention in order to save life was now an established feature of the arctic story. Sir John Ross in 1833 and Sir John Franklin since 1847 had evoked by their respective disappearances the activities of relatives. M'Clure's second-in-command was Lieutenant Cresswell, whose father was a friend of Parry. The M'Clure expedition, the senior Cresswell now pointed out, might face a third winter in the Arctic. The Admiralty acknowledged the force of the suggestion that a part of the Belcher expedition should go westward along Barrow Strait to look for M'Clure, not northward up Wellington Channel to look for Franklin.[29] Kellett was chosen to lead *Resolute*, with *Intrepid* as steam tender, in the new direction, while

Belcher himself was to lead *Assistance*, with *Pioneer* as
along the original Wellington Channel route. Thus the co..
tion had the same four vessels as Austin in 1850–51.

Sir Edward Belcher (1799–1877), one of two native British No..
Americans who led exploring parties to the Arctic in this period (the other
was William Kennedy), was born in Halifax, of a long New England and
Nova Scotia background. A veteran of the War of 1812, he had proved
himself in the waters of the South Pacific an able hydrographer. Indeed,
his capacity as a surveyor and failure as an explorer are evidence that the
two activities are not necessarily the same thing. Moreover, there is wide
agreement that he was not a leader of men, and at fifty-three he was old for
exploring. Once again, in this case upon the expedition and choice of its
leader, King made an acerbic comment. Belcher, he wrote in 1855, was "an
officer advanced in years, who had spent a whole life proving himself to be
the very last man fitted for so honourable a service."[30] Under Kellett there
was to sail, as well as Pim in *Resolute*, F. L. M'Clintock, who was now
given his first command, that of *Intrepid*. It has been emphasized that
King, Rae, and Pim were in varying degrees individualists or "loners." By
training and temperament M'Clintock fitted more easily into group endeavour. Used to having shipmates from the age of twelve, he was a team
personality, as indicated by his reaction, referred to below, to a trip he
would shortly make with one man only. In him loyalty was a very marked
trait, and this is apparent in his relations with Sir James Clark Ross and
Lady Franklin. Trained by the exigencies of his profession in many skills,
he had a more complex approach than that of Rae. He had, for example, a
schooling in steam. There was a further contrast with Rae. The North
American Arctic was very nearly the end-all and the be-all of Rae's career,
whereas it was only one phase (granted the most famous) in that of
M'Clintock. M'Clintock belonged to the seven seas, Rae to only one of them
and its environs.

Intrepid and *Pioneer* had work done upon them at the Woolwich Yards
after their return in 1851 from the Austin expedition.[31] During that voyage
Intrepid's false keel had been "knocked off with the trifling exception of
twelve feet" in buffeting by ice in Baffin Bay. Now this was replaced, as
were *Intrepid*'s masts and yards. By contrast with *Pioneer* which required
much replacement of her planking and new boilers, *Intrepid*'s machinery
required scarcely any repairs. When the four vessels of the Belcher party
sailed in 1852, *Intrepid* had on board 250 tons of coal. Low in the water as
she left Stromness, she carried about four years' provisions.[32] After leaving
Cape Farewell the voyage of the whole party could be divided into two
periods: that through Baffin Bay and that after the party reached Lan-

caster Sound. In the first of these periods the use of steam and a relationship with the whaling fleet were central. The whaling vessels, M'Clintock writes, were a mere remnant of a once proud fleet, and the men who sailed them, he claimed, were possessed of a tenacity with regard to old ways worthy of the Chinese. Their health was in the hands of medical students of doubtful calibre so that "Jack" was eager to come to the navy for medical attention. In July there was what M'Clintock regarded as a most distasteful display of disorder when, after he had done much to assist the American whaler *McLellan*, this vessel was upended and crushed to pieces in the bay. Performing at this time a police function, the navy also gained from the wreck of *McLellan* provisions, firewood, and coal, and some of that vessel's crew used the epithet, "Ned Belcher the Pirate." On the other hand, whalermen had their own lore. They believed that a change of moon and an attendant change of weather would break up the ice, and this proved to be so.[33] They chose to use the north-about or north end of Baffin Bay rather than attempt to go through the heavy ice at the centre of the bay. When they did encounter ice they would deal with it by cutting it up into manageable pieces and floating these away. They would also cut docks in the ice in which their vessels sheltered, and the naval vessels sometimes used these. There, on one occasion, the navy encountered fourteen vessels and 200 or 250 whalermen, "looking very earnestly at the unusual appearance of steamers in their wide domain."[34]

Travelling by way of the north-about, the navy used steam to tow its own and other vessels, and for reconnaissance for leads through the ice. On occasion, *Intrepid* and *Pioneer* were lashed together, so as to tow side-by-side, making in this way some two and one-half knots. On other occasions the tenders towed in tandem. Another way to use steam was to "charge" at the ice, providing it was decaying and only two or three feet thick; otherwise to do this was like charging a stone wharf. By the close of July *Intrepid* had learned how to conduct her towing operation more efficiently and the vessels she was towing had learned how to avoid her when she was suddenly stopped by ice. M'Clintock had all-night sessions on the deck and in the crow'snest. Another method of travel was tracking or towing the vessels as one walked along the ice. As the expedition completed the north-about and made for the west side of Baffin Bay all were in good humour. Now for a time towing and related difficulties were at an end and the fires in the engine room were put out. By early August *Intrepid*'s stock of coals had been reduced from 250 to 154 tons, but she could now show her sailing form; with an improvement in trim, she proved "the Clipper of the Squadron."[35]

The Belcher expedition had some association with Eskimos as well as whalers. At Lievely (Godhavn on Disko Island) M'Clintock acquired seal-skin boots from an Eskimo woman who made them for him in rapid time, and also obtained eleven Eskimo dogs. In Melville Bay, further north along the Greenland coast, Kellett used gunpowder to blast ice and found that when this was light, up to three feet thick, small charges of four or five pounds were most effective. Floes were also cut by saws, mounted within triangles on the ice. Once a whaleboat was used to feel the way forward in fog, and later, off the Devon Island coast, smokeballs were tried as a method of indicating to one of the vessels another one's position. Securing water was a problem. On one occasion there was found by M'Clintock on an iceberg a clear pool of fresh water into which there flowed a streamlet whose bubbling was "like the voice of an old friend." But water from floes, though tasting good when picked up, could become salt in a few days; it was necessary to have the doctor inspect the water before it was brought on board. M'Clintock was pleased that the Kellett expedition reached Lancaster Sound on 4 August, earlier than any other expedition, including that of Parry in 1819, but not earlier than certain whalers, one of which had in the past arrived in Lancaster Sound as early as 15 June.[36]

After arrival at Beechey Island, *Intrepid* performed two reconnaissance functions, first a foray to test for open water up Wellington Channel and secondly a return along Devon Island to find Belcher's *Assistance* which had fallen behind. These tasks accomplished, *Intrepid* returned to Beechey Island where she took aboard some 41 tons of coal, so that she could now proceed westwards from the island with 178 tons on board. At Beechey Island there was also a further thorough search for a Franklin record and the two wings of the expedition prepared to separate. At parting in mid-August Belcher announced to the ships' companies assembled on the ice that while earlier expeditions had done all that was humanly possible to find Franklin, this one, he hoped, would achieve still more because of its "increased intellectual power." A document was signed enabling all to share in the pecuniary award any one might acquire by finding Franklin's ships or crew. M'Clintock was sure that in proceeding up Wellington Channel the Belcher squadron was on the right track to find Franklin. Yet the Kellett wing was elated now to be left on their own and heading westward to a country of relative plenty.[37]

On the first stage of the westward trip *Intrepid* was a chief factor in saving *Resolute*. Just before noon on 16 August, in attempting to go into Assistance Bay at Cornwallis Island, *Resolute* ran aground. *Intrepid* tried to tow her but her towing hawser fouled her screw, the tide fell rapidly, and *Resolute* became immovable. Tons of provisions were removed from the vessels, as planned, for a depot at this point, but *Resolute* was severely pushed around as a floe half a mile in diameter "crushed up against her side with such amazing force" that pieces of it were "heaped up nearly as high" as her deck. After an hour or two, however, the floe moved slowly out of the bay as the tide rose rapidly, and now *Intrepid* could anchor nearby in order both to heave and tow. For all this, it was not until midnight that *Intrepid* finally succeeded in pulling *Resolute* off. All felt grateful that, although *Resolute* had had "a most tremendous twisting," she had sustained no other injury than the loss of her false keel.[38]

Thereafter, for a time, progress was good; Lowther Island was reached and in its lee a landing made. Here, however, ice was an obstruction and *Intrepid*, with Kellett aboard, made a foray of seventy miles, northward to Bathurst Island and southward to Young Island. Hope for a future clearing lay, it was decided, to the north and northeast of Lowther Island, and from a hill on that island daily reports were now "as anxiously looked for as the Morning papers during parliamentary debates; and the movement of the ice as closely watched as ever was the French fleet."[39] Already a lack of power in the compasses posed a problem but a device was worked out to deal with this. The only alternative to a compass was knowing the true bearing of the sun, and this was

> calculated to every twenty minutes of apparent time, between the 70th and 80th degrees of North latitude. The month's true bearings were painted on a board and hung abaft the mizzen mast. A graduated brass circle, with eyepiece and sight-vane, was placed before the wheel, and with this instrument the angle between the sun and the ship's head was obtained. This, applied to the true bearing of the sun, gave the true course the ship was steering.[40]

At first the expedition gave up hope of reaching Winter Harbour. Then the ice broke and by early September the vessels were off the harbour, the first to reach it since Parry's *Hecla* and *Griper*. Steam had now been used as an aid in transport as far west as the longitude of Medicine Hat, not reached by steam on land until 1883. Unable, however, to stay at Winter Harbour, the expedition returned to Dealy Island some forty miles to the east. There at Skene Bay the Kellett party prepared for fall journeys that would set depots, and also for wintering. The journeys included two by M'Clintock and one by Lieutenant Mecham. The aim of M'Clintock's trips was to prepare for a sled expedition in the succeeding spring across Melville Island to the north, the area M'Clintock had chosen as the most propitious to a search. The first of his depot journeys was a twelve-day trip by two carts, with complements, respectively, of M'Clintock leading seven men, and his surgeon, Robert Scott, leading six men. M'Clintock's second trip occupied the period October 7–25 and consisted of two sledges drawn by ten men each, with as usual the sleeping equipment taking on extra weight so that for each man the burden of buffalo blanket and coverlet increased from 6½ to 10 lb. Years later M'Clintock would refer to the men as the "baggage animals" of sled travel. Now, however, there was uppermost a chivalric emphasis of a fashionable kind, already referred to as regards the Austin expedition. Dedicated ladies had prepared for M'Clintock's sleds, *Hero* and *Star of the North*, "very handsome and appropriate banners" like ensigns. "Unconsciously [M'Clintock wrote] they have created an age of Chivalry in favour of our long absent countrymen and thereby invested the grand object of the Expedition; we are made to feel as did the crusaders of old, and most ardently do we hope to do honor to the work of their fair hands."[41]

M'Clintock congratulated himself upon being the only traveller of the Kellett expedition to complete his fall journeys as planned.[42] Yet among autumn journeys, it was that of Lieutenant Mecham (1828–58) of *Resolute* which produced the most dramatic results. Mecham was only twenty-four years old and was destined the next year to make one of the longest arctic sled journeys on record. He had instructions now to advance a depot at Fife Harbour (a part of Winter Harbour) to Liddon Gulf, or as much further as the season permitted, preparatory to searching in the next year westward along the southern coast of Melville Island. The young officer had one sled *Discovery*, manned with ten men and provisioned for twenty-five days, and an auxiliary sled *Fearless*, manned with six men, provisioned for the same period, and led by mate George S. Nares, of future fame, then twenty-one. The party was supplied as well with a cart for land travel. Mecham's instructions were to deposit printed papers at his furthest and other prominent points, and to place a report of the Kellett expedition at Winter Harbour. Instructed to examine all cairns seen on the trip, he was to assess as well the ten-man party and sled. Would its strength prove equal to the increased weights it would have to carry, and would the few days' extra provisions it would bear warrant the increased number of men pulling it?[43]

Winter Harbour was only forty-one miles from the Kellett party at Dealy Island yet, commencing on September 22, the Mecham sled trip there and beyond was a difficult one. On 26 September the party reached both the depot at Fife Harbour and beyond this the head of Winter Harbour itself, where 160 lb. of pemmican and the cart (to be picked up on the return journey) were deposited. The dragging weight of each man after Winter Harbour was 225 lb. and, in all, it took eight days to cross from the head of Winter Harbour to Liddon Gulf, a distance of only twenty miles if measured without regard to the ravines. At Cape Hoppner on the southern shore of the gulf on 7 October, the sixteenth day out, the depot was deposited; a conspicuous cairn was erected and in it a document placed. On the return journey on 12 October Winter Harbour was reached for the second time and now the party examined, as it had not on the way out, the Sandstone Boulder. M'Clure's record and accompanying chart were found, and the chart to "the astonishment of us all unfolded the mystery of the North West Passage and solved all the problems with regard to Banks and Wollaston Lands." There was now, for the first time, a real likelihood that news of a passage would reach London and that the M'Clure party, otherwise in direst straits, would be rescued. Leaving behind Nares and the sledge *Fearless*, with orders to Nares to complete the expedition's instructions and return to the ship with all dispatch, Mecham with *Discovery* made for *Resolute* by forced marches of thirteen, seventeen, and eleven miles on the successive days of October 12 to 14, arriving with his stirring news aboard Kellett's vessel at 4 p.m. on the latter date. Two days later the Nares party reached *Resolute*, having been delayed for one night by a storm.[44]

Mecham had been away twenty-three days and had travelled 184 miles. His outward journey had been at an average rate, in miles made good per diem, of 4.2; his homebound trip for the same had been 9; and the average mileage made good per diem for the journey, taken as a whole, was 5.7. He complained only of the bad construction of two principal articles: the spirit lamps for cooking needed considerable repair and a better compass was needed for travelling in bad weather, one so fitted that it could be placed upon the ground. The sledges, Mecham reported, were much better in every respect than those of the old pattern; they were equal to the weights they had to carry save that in their uprights they appeared weak. A party should carry spare uprights of iron in case of accidents, to be inserted by means of a screw in the place of any broken one. Ten-man crews were very efficient, but an inconvenience did arise when sled parties of different sizes were working or provisioning together. The number of animals seen during the journey, especially muskoxen and reindeer, had surpassed all expectations. Three of the latter had been shot and had formed a valuable addition to the preserved meat, which when taken alone had proved unsatisfactory. The men had always performed their work with cheerfulness and goodwill and the reduction of one man from the crew of the *Fearless* had been amply made up by Nares himself who had never left the drag ropes while the sledges were loaded.[45]

It was decided that in spite of the news which Mecham had brought, the season was too advanced to attempt in that year to bring news of rescue to the M'Clure party, which might by now, in any event, have left Mercy Bay. Aboard *Resolute* and *Intrepid* in the winter of 1852–53 there was a different spirit than aboard *Investigator*. Kellett's expedition, well supplied with fresh meat killed during the fall, did not have to expend energy upon hunting, and other supplies were also ample. On Christmas day for the lower deck there were private stocks provided by the men themselves in addition to the ship's own stuffed pig. Venison was the *pièce de résistance* for the officers; the dogs were not forgotten, and the pups were so uncomfortably crammed that they could scarcely waddle. Indeed, very far from thinking constantly about food, as M'Clure's party tended to do, officers of *Intrepid*'s mess, M'Clintock complains, having plumbed each other's topics, were reduced to such conversational trivia as "how much bishops get paid." In addition, there was much entertainment. The crew staged, for example, on Guy Fawkes' day, 1852, in competition with the men of *Resolute*, a well-costumed procession on the ice, complete with a sailor impersonating the lord mayor of London in a cocked hat. The Intrepids staged farce and drama during the winter, and they supplied most of the musicians for the expedition's brass band.[46]

Officers were allowed by Kellett to take their pick of tasks for spring journeys. M'Clintock certainly thought that the Belcher expedition was following the track of Franklin and was therefore on the correct course, but for that very reason he entertained hopes that he himself might meet the lost navigator emerging towards the Pacific; so he had chosen to lead a party northwest of Melville Island to the northern shore of Prince Patrick Island. It was typical of Bedford Pim that he chose the task of reaching the M'Clure expedition. This was not only because Pim liked to travel early in the season, with dogs, and with a small party; his choice revealed what would prove a lifelong interest in a short commercial route to the East, which even now, against contrary evidence, Pim still believed existed in the Arctic. On 10 March, with the temperature at −51°F., accompanied by Dr. Domville and nine men, Pim led a party with one large man-hauled sled and one small dog-sled drawn by six dogs, on what was, by nearly a month, the earliest naval sled journey thus far. Pim can hardly have taken into account Mecham's autumn report upon sleds; for shortly after the start of his trip, his man-hauled sled, turned over by hummocks, had all its poppets broken off. Mate Richard Roche, one of the group accompanying Pim and Domville at the outset, was sent back to the vessels for a new sledge. Though Roche reached *Resolute*, he was then delayed at the vessel by a gale which blew for three days, a typical arctic blizzard which,

M'Clintock said, prevented one seeing objects that would be distinct in the thickest fog, and which covered one with fine penetrating material in a few seconds. As Roche finally set out with a new sled, men of Kellett's vessels could see from a nearby hill the Pim party encamped eight miles off; they saw Roche's party meet Pim's, and watched the two groups start out together under sail.[47]

By prearrangement, Roche returned to the Kellett vessels; after journeying with Pim for three days, he left him travelling rapidly over very smooth ice with a fair wind. Yet Pim's party suffered a further breakdown, this time fifteen miles beyond Cape Dundas and once again through a defect in Pim's man-hauled sled. This time the young lieutenant switched crews and equipment. He handed the damaged sled over to Dr. Domville, with orders to go back to Cape Dundas and there await him, while Pim himself proceeded across M'Clure Strait with the dog-sled and dogs of Domville, and with two men only. Once again Pim was journeying as he liked to do, with dogs and a light party, and this time with the assistance of coal, often found near his campsite. Fearful though he was that by delay he might miss the M'Clure party, Pim took nevertheless twenty-eight days in all to complete the journey from Dealy Island to Mercy Bay, 160 miles as the crow flies, an average of about six miles a day.[48]

At 10 a.m. on 5 April Pim arrived at the cliffs of Mercy Bay. At mid-morning on the following day, when the temperature stood at twelve below zero, he reached the sea ice and started to cross the Bay of Mercy. Hidden by hummocky ice from view or awareness of *Investigator*, he was proceeding to trace the coastline in search of a cairn when one of his men reported seeing something black up the bay. By telescope Pim made out a ship and altering course went in advance of his men. By 4 p.m. he could see people walking about and a cairn and staff on the beach before him; by 5 p.m., still unobserved, he was within a hundred yards of *Investigator*:

> two persons taking exercise on the ice discovered that I did not belong to their ship upon beckoning they quickly approached and proved to be Capt. McClure and Lt. Haswell, their surprise and I may add delight at the unexpected appearance of a stranger who seemed ... to drop from the clouds ... is needless ... to describe, one of the men at work near them conveyed the news on board and in an incredible short time their deck was crowded, every one that could crawl making his appearance, to see the stranger and hear the news. The scene which then presented itself can never be effaced from my memory nor can I impress any idea of the joy and gladness with which my arrival was hailed.[49]

Nelson, writing of the gloom aboard the vessel following the death there the day before, reports his own reaction:

> when lo! a confused murmuring of voices is heard—then the words "Deer are crossing the Bay—I see them through the haze;"—another moment—"Esquimaux are coming toward the ship"—then the reality—IT WAS A SLEDGE PARTY FROM HER MAJESTY'S BARQUE RESOLUTE! This most unlooked for and joyful meeting happens in consequence of Lieut. Mecham of the Resolute ... commanded by Captn. Henry Kellett C.B. late of 'Herald' ... having visited the Parry Sandstone at Winter Harbour ... in the fall of 1852, and ... of ... Lieut. Pim ... leaving the Resolute on the 10th. of March—being 28 days performing the journey from ship to ship.[50]

Not only was Pim a strange figure, "as black as Old Nick," from the smoke of cooking in his tent as he travelled. His meeting with M'Clure was made all the more complicated by the fact that M'Clure had last seen Kellett and *Herald* on the Pacific side of the Arctic, where Pim had also been. Now, having completed a circumnavigation of the globe and visited Russia in the interim, Pim was the first to see the M'Clure party when coming to it from the Atlantic. This was a fact which confused M'Clure at first, delaying for an instant the full import of Pim's appearance. It is M'Clure himself who has given classic expression to the effect of the arrival of Kellett's emissary upon M'Clure's party. Yet even he concludes by saying that he could "go on writing," but could "never convey the most faint idea of the scene."[51] Well, Nelson says,

> might Capt.n McClure call such a deliverance providential! ... I am confident a release ... was about as much expected, as the removal of the highest peak towering over the borders of Mercy Bay.
>
> It would be a mere waste of words, to attempt a description of the feelings which animated every heart on board the Investigator ... [with an] effect [that] could be traced on the cheek of many.[52]

Pim was shocked at the sight and diet of the complement of *Investigator*. Starvation as well as scurvy was a factor; for the condition of the men who had been put on extra diet for spring travel away from *Investigator* had shown already a distinct improvement. At home in England Armstrong had carefully selected men by physical criteria for the M'Clure voyage; and this probably helps account for their survival thus far. However, three deaths in a few days after Pim's arrival showed, Armstrong himself argues, the proximity of outright breakdown when Pim arrived.[53] Perhaps it indicated as well that, when men were already in a precarious state of health, the very excitement of good news might cause death.

Kellett had entrusted a letter to Pim which requested M'Clure to ascertain by medical examination whether his men were, unaided, fit for another winter in the Arctic. *Investigator*'s commander must have known that his men were not; the graphic quality of his own description of the unexpected turn of events indicates that he understood fully the import of his crew's situation, of Kellett's welcome presence at Dealy Island, and of Pim's arrival. Yet M'Clure wished to contest the point of fitness with Kellett, and to make sure that if his vessel was abandoned, this would be by Kellett's order, not his. Claiming that *Investigator* could be got out by her own crew and that there was need therefore (pending a final decision on the fate of the vessel) to preserve supplies for the voyage, M'Clure gave a ruthless order not to change the half-rations of *Investigator*. Bedford Pim, for his part, had a further task: to search for Collinson's *Enterprise* along the west coast of Victoria Island and down Prince of Wales Strait, and also to deposit records. Because, however, of his broken sled at Cape Dundas, he was now unable to complete this further assignment.[54] For these reasons on Friday, 9 April, Pim and M'Clure set out for *Resolute*. It was also agreed that Cresswell, Miertsching, and twenty-four of the feeblest of the crew were to leave as arranged on 15 April and follow M'Clure to Dealy Island. Of this party Armstrong writes: "Some were obliged to be carried on sledges, several were incapacitated from dragging, and all arrived [at Dealy Island] in a state of great exhaustion and debility—so much so that to lighten the sledges they threw away their spare clothing on the ice."[55]

Nelson himself was ordered to his hammock upon arrival at the Kellett vessels. *Intrepid* was hastily prepared to take in many of the survivors. On 19 May M'Clure returned to *Investigator* with doctors from Kellett's party. He found that the required quota of twenty of *Investigator*'s complement still aboard her would not volunteer to sail her further; nor did Kellett's doctors sanction continuation of *Investigator*'s voyage. On 3 June, therefore, the vessel was abandoned and the remainder of her complement, twenty-eight including Armstrong, set out to join the Kellett expedition. When they arrived there, so well had their shipmates who had gone ahead recovered that Armstrong could scarcely recognize them. Signs of weakness had vanished as the result of a liberal allowance of food, including muskox beef. At first the convalescents "became full faced and bloated, then fell off again, but subsequently regained their strength and a healthier appearance."[56] "Their only fault," Kellett said of his guests, "is that they eat."

In addition to Pim's party to *Investigator*, Kellett had sent out in the spring M'Clintock to Melville and Prince Patrick Islands, Mecham to other parts of these islands and to Eglinton Island, and Hamilton to Melville Island; and these leaders would perform journeys of, respectively, 1,400, 1,160 and 650 miles. Nevertheless, Kellett still managed, in spite of the absence of so many of his officers and men, to scrape together under his mate Roche a travelling crew to conduct Cresswell and the least fit Investigators to Beechey Island. There sail and steam took over as Cresswell set out for England in H.M.S. *Phoenix*, much the biggest auxiliary steam vessel in arctic waters in this period. At 5 a.m. on Friday, 7 October 1853, M'Clure's second-in-command knocked on the door of the London residence of John Barrow.[57] By the dispatches Cresswell bore and by his presence in London, he had completed the discovery and transit of a Northwest Passage. The late Sir John Barrow had said in 1844 that this task would take the Franklin party two months after leaving the Atlantic, alone and unaided. The task had in fact required eight years, approaches simultaneously from both the Atlantic and Pacific, and in all the presence in the Arctic of twenty expeditions.

A passage had been achieved, yet M'Clure and most of his men remained in the Arctic. Not until the next year did they too return to the United Kingdom, accomplishing thereby a transport operation for which Cresswell had performed the task of initial communication and "small party" transit. At first M'Clure was enormously hopeful of reaching England with his officers and men in the same year as Cresswell, and events gave some basis for this hope. In August there was a sudden break in the ice so that Kellett left Dealy Island in such haste as to abandon a boat there; indeed the sudden departure convinced *Resolute*'s sailing master that Franklin might have left Beechey Island for a like reason and in similar haste.[58] Yet, though freed temporarily and able to use the engines of *Intrepid* to some avail, the Kellett expedition made only some hundred and fifty miles to the eastward before becoming again icebound. At M'Clintock's request, Miertsching had captured a snowy owl which sat at the end of the commander's cabin table and became a symbol of the Kellett party's own detention. M'Clintock's comment is an example of his poetic touch and habit of observation. The "noble looking immense bird," he wrote,

> seems quite at home but quietly watches every movement ... ; both of us are detained against our will; but I am impatient and unreasonable whilst my captive with better sense sits opposite me,—the personification of tranquility, not one feather out of its place. He is a model for those who labor under a reverse of fortune. I never saw

such beautiful eyes. The pupil does not contract by candlelight, as it does when he looks up through the skylight.[59]

The winter of 1853–54 was a harsh one for *Resolute* and *Intrepid*, all the more so because of the extra men and officers aboard the vessels. Scurvy and even starvation might have resulted save for splendid hunting in the fall. Two further deaths occurred during the winter, not, however, of *Investigator*'s men; one of the casualties was Thomas Hood, who had served prominently in sledge travel with M'Clintock. As spring approached there came the celebrated order by Sir Edward Belcher to abandon ships. It was imprecisely worded at first, and officers of Kellett protested against it. M'Clintock was sent to reason with Belcher or, if this failed, to secure more precisely written instructions. Travelling 460 geographical miles with one man and dogs for fifteen days, that is at an average daily rate of thirty-one miles, M'Clintock remarked laconically of his foray that such rapid travel was harassing but dull work; as already noted, he preferred to be part of a team. He had found that Belcher and his vessels were in bleak condition, and that Sir Edward was bent upon abandonment despite strong representation.[60]

In the spring, *Investigator*'s complement left *Resolute* and *Intrepid*; and later, on Belcher's orders, Kellett's own officers and men deserted their vessels and made for Beechey Island. Arriving there on 23 April 1854, Nelson termed it a second Gibraltar; he was assigned to the depot ship *North Star* and soon took time out to observe the graves of Franklin's crewmen, feeling anew as he did so his own good fortune by contrast with that of the Franklin party. Nelson and his shipmates did in due course reach England, borne home by *Phoenix* and *North Star*. "No ice in sight!" he wrote triumphantly in large letters when past Holsteinborg in mid-September, the first such occasion in "4 years and 2 months." Three weeks later he expected soon to see the "white Cliffs of Old England" and on 8 October 1854 the vessel to which he was assigned arrived at Sheerness, bringing to an end a voyage of "4 years, 8 months and 20 days."[61] At Plymouth some of the Investigators had been assigned to their fifth ship of the voyage. Already M'Clure himself had landed in Ireland and on 28 September had reached London.

The 300-year old search for a Northwest Passage was now complete. It had been very much a cooperative effort starting from two oceans, in which the finding of a passage by the outbound expedition of M'Clure had been made into a full discovery through the meeting with Kellett's expedition, and a sharing thereafter in his homebound voyage. The key importance, in the whole story, of the meeting at Mercy Bay is demonstrated by comparing the emotions felt there with those experienced in regard to various other events in the story. The feelings associated with the other events, were, first, a strong emotion of national pride when M'Clure had sighted, at the extremity of Prince of Wales Strait in 1850, the last link in a northern passage. Secondly, there had been the feelings attendant upon M'Clure's sled trip to Winter Harbour in 1852; that foray had also found the last link in a northern passage (M'Clure Strait) and this time the link had been spanned as well as observed. Yet awareness of this achievement was accompanied by a feeling that completion had occurred only "after a fashion." For since there were no ships or other means of assistance at Winter Harbour, the task of just getting home now overshadowed all other considerations. Depression was therefore the prime feeling, and this had deepened in the winter of 1852–53 into a dread analogous to what had been, no doubt, the feeling among the Franklin party in the winter of 1847–48.

Yet Kellett's party to the east had had a counterpoised emotion. For its members, M'Clure's message at Winter Harbour had set up an intercommunication between the two expeditions, and given to Kellett and his followers a reasonable hope that the lost explorers and their news of the passages would reach England. Not, however, until the meeting at Mercy Bay had all three elements—rescue of M'Clure, conveyance of information, and transit of a passage—seemed sure, to rescued as well as rescuers. That is why there was then, at the bay, an apogee of jubilation and thereafter, in subsequent emotions, a quality of epilogue: in the feelings, for example, of Nelson when he had sighted for the first time an iceless sea and, finally, the cliffs of home. That the emotions experienced before and after Mercy Bay were less strong than those at the bay demonstrated that the meeting there had been central, and showed once again that in discovery one had to convey home news of finds as well as make them. What had been found, it was now said, were passages that formed a "geographical curiosity," and existed, for commercial purposes, "in vain"; they were considered to be frozen phantoms. Yet they were passages which had enough reality to inspire attempts at commercial use of them far into the twentieth century.[62]

Not only had the achievement been a cooperative one. It had also been one in which, at Melville Sound, Winter Harbour, Mercy Bay, and London, small advance parties had at crucial stages found or carried initial information preparatory to more massive transit and transport. Within the M'Clure–Kellett expeditions small parties had laid the basis for large-scale developments. The achievement had been carried through, moreover, by multiple techniques. There had been employed sail, steam, and dogs, and the discoveries had been accomplished, most of all, by walking, and by sled work in which there had occurred the man-killing labour and drudgery of "standing pulls." Only men trained in hauling at ropes, M'Clintock would say, could have accomplished the naval form of sledding; and he commented upon the noticeable incidence of ill-health and even of death among these men.[63] Of naval sled travel Kellett wrote:

> I have been a long time at sea, and seen varying trying services, but never have seen (for men) such labour, and such misery after. No amount of money is an equivalent ... Men require much more heart and stamina to undertake an extended travelling party than to go into action. The travellers have their enemy chilling them to the very heart, and paralyzing their very limbs; the others the very contrary. I should like to see the travelling men get an Arctic medal.[64]

In due course an arctic medal was awarded, fittingly to officers as well as men; for they had taken part in sled-pulling, and here too it is possible the strain showed. Lieutenant Mecham, for example, credited with one of the longest sledge journeys on record in this period, died of bronchitis at thirty a few years later.[65] Perhaps, indeed, the very availability of these men and officers had worked against the navy, enabling it to concentrate upon heavy parties whereas in other circumstances lighter travel means might have been devised.

The accomplishment had involved a proximity to death on the part of the Investigators, bringing them close to repeating the Franklin experience. Like Franklin, M'Clure had been urged on by a special personal incentive; now because of his arctic endeavour he was once again a figure in the world. So great, indeed, had been this incentive that M'Clure was blind to a matching collective motive for his accomplishment. M'Clintock said later that the motive of saving life was a much stronger one in bringing about arctic discovery than had been that of acquiring geographical information.[66] M'Clure did not allow due credit to sailors from the Atlantic who, exerting themselves to the point of suffering casualties, had made the rescue and completion of discovery possible. It was this attitude which deprived Kellett and his expedition of the recognition they deserved, a failure which occurred especially in the context of Parliament. Like the rest of the British nation, that body was ignorant as yet of Franklin's coastal passage, and for Parliament as for the nation as a whole M'Clure's information and his return stood out clearly as a set of "firsts"; in addition, the Crimean War was going badly, and the legislators felt the need for a national hero. A parliamentary committee justifiably decided that the operation of which M'Clure was a part was the first discovery of a passage; but, like M'Clure, it failed to appreciate the part Kellett had played in this, and Parliament's award went solely to M'Clure.[67]

Yet perhaps this failure was not attributable only to M'Clure and Parliament. There was a nation-wide fallacy involved. Victory at Trafalgar and the tradition of Nelson had had an influence. Discovery, it was felt, was something which one could accomplish while dying, in the manner in which Nelson's victory had been achieved. Yet Nelson had assured his own victory before he died, and the likening of exploration to battle has pitfalls. "Never turn your back to the enemy while you've a face to face him with," a family retainer had said to the twelve-year-old M'Clintock when taking him to join the navy—good advice for battle. But "never . . . go" to a place you can "not come back from," this same wise servant was soon to warn M'Clintock, as that explorer set out upon his successful discovery in *Fox*.[68] The two remarks, taken together, sum up succinctly what Parliament and the public had not grasped, that there was a difference between warfare and discovery. In the first case one should never turn one's back; by not doing so one could assure victory. In the other case, quite to the contrary, one should make absolutely certain that one could turn around and get home again, or there would be no discovery. Yet the aura of heroic death would shortly be carried over and applied, fallaciously, to Franklin, who had seemingly emulated Nelson, facing forward to the end, and yet who had in fact (unlike Nelson) accomplished only half his job before he died. Carrying the fallacy still further, Parliament would, in a very few years, write off M'Clure's operation entirely, unanimously reversing itself and awarding credit for initial discovery of a Northwest Passage to Franklin. Nor was it simply Parliament which went through this process. The Royal Geographical Society likewise did so. In 1854 it awarded M'Clure the Patron's Gold Medal for discovery of a passage; yet by the end of the decade its president, Sir Roderick Murchison, and the society itself, would lead the way in espousal of Franklin, not M'Clure, as deserving of the accolade of initial discoverer. Thus from attaining at first a position too high in arctic annals, M'Clure would shortly be relegated to a position too low. For a sober estimate of M'Clure's attainment one can go to Kellett, the man M'Clure had most slighted. *Investigator*'s commander, Kellett told the parliamentary committee, had exhibited perseverance "unparalleled . . . and I have seen a good deal of it."[69]

Finally, there had been an element of repetition in the arctic story as between King and Pim. In a number of ways the two men were different. Half a generation younger than the surgeon, Pim would leave the navy after serving with distinction and being wounded, both in the Crimean War and in a war in China. Reaching, on the inactive list, the rank of rear admiral, he would become a barrister specializing in Admiralty law, an entrepreneur who sought to complete a trade route to the Orient by building a railway across Nicaragua, and a member of Parliament. King, on the other hand, was a critic of the navy who derided or ignored commerce and was without a sense of the politic. Further, Pim was a world traveller who in his Russian venture had helped carry geographical eccentricity in the Franklin search to an extreme, while the surgeon was a man who, on the basis of only one trip to North America, had put his finger upon Franklin's actual position. These are differences, yet they indicate that both King and Pim were individualists. Each was unpopular with other "Arctics"; of Pim, for example, it was said that he quarrelled with every man he travelled with in *Resolute*, including the kindly Kellett.[70] Each showed an interest in indigenous peoples: King as a founding member, for example, of the Ethnological Society and Pim as a founding member of its successor, the Anthropological Society. Both stressed indigenous means of travel and, as a part of this, were vocal proponents of small parties. Above all, Pim had now in one four weeks' trip accomplished all that King had wanted to do in the Arctic over the course of twenty years. Since 1833 King's two polar ambitions had been to save life in the Arctic and to complete the discovery of a passage. Now Pim had done both these things in his single trip to Mercy Bay. Years before, the *Nautical Standard* had written, with naïve quaintness, that others might lead a "heavy arctic caravansary" in the search for Franklin, but that King should be allowed to take to the polar regions a small party that would "shout the glad *halloo* of coming help . . . amid the mountain bergs of the icebound world of waters."[71] Such a feat Bedford Pim had now accomplished, in terms not of a coastal passage and Franklin but of a northern passage and M'Clure. Not only had Pim done this in King's manner, by a light "arctic caravansary"; he had conformed as well to King's pattern in that he had brought rescue to M'Clure not by carrying heavy supplies to his party but rather by telling that party where food, supplies, and rescue were available. Pim might not rank in the first roll call of arctic explorers at this time. Certainly Markham and M'Clintock imply criticism of him as a traveller; and M'Clintock appears to have been physically capable of outdoing Pim in Pim's particular form of travel. Yet Pim had himself chosen the role of "lone wolf" and was fitted by personality to it, as M'Clintock was not. In the navy, M'Clintock said, voicing a typical naval feeling that contrasted with the feelings of Pim and King, "it had been found that by grouping the men together better work was done than when small sledges, with only one or two men, were used."[72]

In the light of the foregoing considerations it is not surprising that King and Pim were to form henceforth a close relationship. To King it seemed that the younger man was proof by example and experience of the efficacy of factors that King had stressed. The two men, as we shall see, would cooperate in suggesting a two-pronged project by which King was to go by a land party down the Back River to its mouth and Pim by a sea party through Baffin Bay to Boothia and the same locality, in a final search for Franklin. On one occasion Pim made over his life insurance to King; after the older man's death Pim was a friend to King's widow and a self-appointed guardian of King's reputation in arctic and related matters.[73]

Upon arrival at Beechey Island M'Clintock wrote that, of all the news which awaited the Kellett, M'Clure, and Belcher parties, two items stood out, that the location of Collinson's party was still unknown and that war had broken out with Russia. The long frustration of peace for the Royal Navy was over and its officers could participate in warfare, the navy's main purpose. "We are dreadfully confused in our wits," M'Clintock wrote in description of his own and his fellow officers' dilemma, as between the desire to search for Collinson and the desire to participate in the Crimean War. But two other important events had occurred. In March 1854 the Admiralty had officially abandoned the search for Franklin, giving him and his party up for lost.[74] Secondly, John Rae, who had also given up the search, had nevertheless encountered, by serendipity, Eskimos with undoubted Franklin relics and with news that the Franklin party had perished in the vicinity of a great river in the west. The very act of abandonment of the search had been a factor in bringing about initial success in it. The first uncontested find had now been made by Rae's coastal and light party means, pointing in the direction King had for so long stressed. More complete or follow-up exploration remained to be accomplished in the voyage by *Fox*, that is, by sea means in a heavy manner.

8

Epilogue and Conclusions

In October 1854 the British public received the initial news of the loss both of the Light Brigade and of the Franklin expedition. The long, trying years of peace for both the army and the navy, with peculiar results for each, were over. Yet the substitute for war which the Arctic had provided for the navy remained to haunt it. The location of the Collinson party was unknown and, most of all, the location and fate of the Franklin party remained undiscovered in a follow-up sense. It was in the period after 1854 that the navy officially credited Rae with succeeding where it had failed; that at long last by its own advice the Back River was used in the search for Franklin; that King and Pim, the men who had advocated, respectively, searching the closest to, and the furthest away from, the Back River, formed a joint plan for the search; that M'Clintock was forced into the position of reluctant rebel as he secured leave from the navy to do what it would not do, attempt to solve the Franklin question; and that, in follow-up discovery, Lady Franklin and the Royal Geographical Society under Sir Roderick Murchison played at last a successful role. Let us review this epilogue, commencing with its immediate antecedents.

Rae planned the route and destination of his last arctic trip of 1853–54 on his own initiative, without consulting Sir George Simpson. He attempted to use Chesterfield Inlet as a means of reaching the Back River and the west coast of Boothia so as to complete exploration of the northern North American shoreline.[1] Although in this attempt he discovered the Quoich River, he failed in his main aim of crossing from the inlet to the Back, and so went instead to his old wintering ground at Repulse Bay, from which he set out in the spring of 1854. Rae had thus been forced to use an alternative path, yet in either case Hudson Strait formed the basic route of approach, giving the enterprise a Hudson's Bay Company emphasis which was also apparent in the intention of completing discovery of the continental coastline. Rae demonstrated in 1854 the insularity of King William's Land by tracing Rae Strait, but he ran into unexpected difficulties which caused him to turn back to his base at Repulse Bay. It was as he was making this return journey that he met Eskimos of the Pelly Bay region who had substantial news and evidence of the Franklin party. From these Eskimos Rae obtained undoubted relics and the account, already referred to, of a numerous party of men who had perished at the mouth of a river to the west. It was now May and too late to go to the Back River in that season. Rae felt, as well, compelled to carry home as soon as possible the artifacts and the news of the Franklin expedition so as to ensure that the Admiralty had the opportunity to recall the Belcher expedition.[2]

This time, in contrast to the reception of his artifacts in 1852, the relics and the news which Rae took home were fully accepted. For this very reason he was now, in a full and practical sense, "initial discoverer" of the lost expedition. His means of discovery had been coastal, not deep sea or (since he had not used the Back River) inland. Further, he had not visited the locale of the disaster himself; rather, he had obtained his information by hearsay, from Eskimos who had themselves received it from other Eskimos, and he had obtained the relics in the same manner. Characteristically as regards initial discovery, that is, his finds were incomplete and preliminary. Nevertheless, the Admiralty, preoccupied with the Crimean War, was pleased to be quit of the Franklin searches, as Rae's finds, it was believed, largely enabled it to be.

There were, however, attitudes which differed from the Admiralty's among members of the Royal Geographical Society, including naval "Arctics" there. Sir Roderick Murchison was a civilian who was high in the counsels of the society: he had been its president when Franklin had sailed and during most of the searches for the lost navigators, and would become its president once again. Murchison now wrote to the society's council and members of "all [us] geographers who founded [our] hopes" upon a search far north; he wished very much to evoke gratitude to Rae for being the first to point the search with certainty in the right direction. Murchison's aim, however, was doubly difficult to achieve. For Rae had given an unfortunately brief explanation of the circumstances in which he had found his information and the relics, namely, when he was returning from the Boothia region, not going towards it; and secondly, Rae was involved now in a celebrated controversy over alleged cannibalism in the Franklin party. The two factors made the company explorer the subject of a good deal of public criticism. Asked to chair, on 12 November 1854, the first meeting of the society after Rae's arrival in England, but unable to attend owing to ill-health, Murchison wrote as well to the secretary of the society and to its current president, Lord Ellesmere. He had looked forward, he told the former, to presiding when his "esteemed friend Dr. Rae" was "brought upon the boards" and there were present other "fine fellows" from the Arctic. There would be need, he warned the latter, of a "good pilot" at the meeting, and he emphasized to the secretary that it would be important to support "poor Dr. Rae" for the positive things he had accomplished and "*all that... he has been the means of doing*," a task all the more necessary because, as he warned Ellesmere, "so many jostling seamen" would be present at the meeting. In his letter to the society itself, the erstwhile president emphasized again the contribution of Rae as the first to bring positive evidence of the fate of some, if not all, of the missing crews. "Unable in the present winter to verify by personal researches the amount of truth of the tale of the Esquimaux," Rae had adopted a line of conduct dictated "by good sense and right feeling." By his prompt return with relics from the party, "he sagaciously hoped to prevent researches in quarters too remote from the tract whence the relics came."[3]

Yet, aware of these points, Murchison also felt that this was a situation of transition, as between initial finds and demands for more elaborate ones, and between landsmen or coastal explorers and seamen eager to take up the quest. He had a sense, that is, that sea means and naval personnel might play a part in a powerful "follow-up" operation. The government, he suggested, might "send out some of the younger intrepid naval explorers," who, placed as they now were upon the right track, could aspire "to clear up the mystery" which had "so long hung over" Franklin's fate. In private he also wrote that Lady Franklin would not be satisfied until steps were taken to hunt out the ships themselves; the landsmen and Canadians, she felt, would never do in this last or maritime part of the search. Indeed, Lady Franklin felt "so strongly the desir[a]bleness of employing in the search competent, Arctic, Naval explorers now that we have a true clue for the purpose of tracking back the wanderers to the spot where they abandoned their ships, that in default of such effort" by the government, she was resolved to expend "the last remnant of fortune coming to her by her husband's will, in fitting out another expedition." Murchison himself shared her concern. "*Canadians and landsmen*," he wrote, would "never really take up the scent." For that reason, all geographers should use their influence to see that "Arctic *naval* explorers" would be employed in "the proper search now to be made."[4]

Murchison had thus discerned very clearly a sequence of events which, however, would take a good deal longer to occur than he anticipated. On 24

October, the day of Rae's arrival in England, Back received a note from the homecoming explorer and on the following day heard from Rae in person of his journey and meeting with the Eskimos. In response to the finds Rae, Sir George Back, Sir James Graham (once again first lord of the Admiralty), Sir Francis Beaufort, Captain Shepherd (deputy governor of the Hudson's Bay Company), and others discussed at the Admiralty in the following two days the sending out of two inland expeditions, to search, respectively, down the Mackenzie River for Collinson and the Back River for further information concerning the Franklin party. Sir Francis Beaufort (perhaps fearful the Admiralty would be criticized for ignoring King) called upon Back with "Dr. King's scurrilous pamphlets to Sir John Barrow — and some others."[5] Whether because it was so engrossed in the Crimean War, or was now very wary of the Arctic, or for both reasons, the Admiralty seemed to concede by these plans the efficacy of inland approaches in searching for sea parties. Before the plan to find Collinson could mature, however, news reached London, on 8 November, that the missing commander had been seen in Bering Strait returning from his arctic voyage.[6]

Public pressure existed, nevertheless, to find further evidence or bring help as regards the other and much more longstanding problem, that of the Franklin expedition. So use of the Back River to find information regarding Franklin went forward as the sole project. Yet this was the more dubious of the two proposals because, paradoxically, just when the Admiralty was at last willing to use the Back River, the full usefulness of that route in the search for Franklin had passed. Although Rae's finds, in pointing to the Back River estuary, had at last won from the navy a modicum of respect for Richard King's emphasis upon that river, those finds had at the same time outdated to a considerable extent the serviceability of the river, by making a follow-up discovery by sea the more practicable approach by which to secure further and more precise information. Yet the navy failed to appreciate this point, and instead withdrew from the search just when it was at last really in a position to help.

Thus it was that in July 1855 Chief Factor James Anderson went by canoe and Halkett boat down the Back River for the Hudson's Bay Company. Reaching Montreal Island at the end of the month, the party found a few relics but the unsoundness of the canoe, the lack of any interpreter through whom to speak to the Eskimos, and other problems, including that of an early season, made the results of the expedition less than they might have been; the party started back on 10 August.[7] King was bitter about the manner in which the expedition was conducted; in particular he felt that his cache at Montreal Island should have been searched because the

Franklin survivors might well have deposited journals or a message there. Of the expedition he wrote:

> They reach Point Ogle and Montreal Island. They find undoubted evidence of the truth of the Esquimaux accounts, and they are content with collecting a few relics to add to Dr. Rae's relics, and return. They never search King Cache of Montreal Island,—because they had no map,—because they had not read the narrative of Thomas Simpson,—because they had selected a crew who were utter strangers in the land.
>
> They do not ask of the Esquimaux the particulars of the Franklin tragedy—because they could not speak to them—because they had no interpreter. They did not mark the spot where forty of their countrymen met their death,—because they had not provided themselves with a simple monument of granite. They do not seek for the history, in writing, of their sad fate in the only spot it was likely to be found because they had never heard that such a spot had existence.

King said that the sea expedition of Sir George Back was known as "The ill-starred Voyage in the Terror"; this one would be known as "The Ill-conceived search for Franklin."[8] The company, indeed, does not seem to have put the same heart into this expedition as had gone into Rae's and Simpson's travels. Members of the Anderson party may even, unknown to Anderson, have seen on the arctic coast one of Franklin's vessels. Nevertheless, Rae himself felt that the expedition potentially embarrassed Sir George Back, for Anderson completed the trip more rapidly than had Back.[9]

King's second reaction in this period concerns the award which the Admiralty had promised for rescue of the Franklin party or discovery of information concerning it. It has been stressed above that Rae was the first discoverer of the fate of the party and the locale of the disaster. On the other hand, Richard King had long before pointed in the direction of the foot of the Back River and the west coast of Boothia as the place both for completion of a passage and for the finding of the Franklin party. Now, in 1855, he published his correspondence with the Admiralty and others on the expedition, under the title, *The Franklin Expedition from First to Last*, and won sympathy from some newspapers. When in January 1856 the Admiralty placed a notice in the *Gazette* that Rae had put in a claim for the reward of £10,000 and said that in three months the award would be adjudicated, King became one of the most vocal claimants for recognition.

Enumerating what he said were his accurate assessments concerning the area where the Franklin party had perished, the Northwest Passage, and "the conformation of the Polar regions," he firmly claimed a portion of the prize that had been offered to those who first ascertained the fate and locale of the lost navigators.[10]

While Rae was given the reward this was only done through the intervention of a political figure and against the advice of senior naval officers. The new hydrographer, Captain Washington, for example, wrote against rewarding Rae on the ground that he had neglected to bring back full information. Much less were naval personnel likely to espouse any claim by King. His case was referred to by a civilian at the Admiralty, ironically the son of Sir John Barrow. On 24 January 1856 the junior John Barrow wrote to Sir Robert Peel, himself son of the late prime minister and a junior lord of the Admiralty. Barrow said:

> It is impossible not to admit that Dr. King, in the year 1848, volunteered his services to proceed down the great Fish River, and to the very spot indicated by Dr. Rae where the relics of the lost Expedition have been found.
>
> The plan was at the time duly considered, and referred to Sir Edward Parry, and Sir James Ross—but they neither of them held out any encouragement to the undertaking.
>
> The last spot that any one but Dr. King (—and Lady Franklin—) considered it *likely* that traces would be found, happens most unfortunately to be the spot of all others that, if searched, might have led to the safety of some of the party, and is the only spot unsearched.[11]

Beneath this summary there was placed the word "Perhaps" which, apparently, was later crossed through, as though King's claim had been considered and negated. On the memorandum of Peel, who had the final voice in adjudicating the award, there were listed the names of claimants in a sequence and with numbers assigned to them which formed, it seems, an inverse scale of merit; thus Rae's name, labelled seventh, appeared last, and King's, labelled sixth, second-last. That is, King may well have been "runner-up" for the award. In any event, the selection of Rae lent weight to King's stress upon the efficacy of land and coastal rather than sea means in achieving initial arctic discovery.[12]

A third reaction of King in this period was an offer early in 1856 (after what he considered the failure of Anderson's party) once again to go down the Back River. His mind was still upon the King cache on Montreal Island at the foot of the river. "In all human probability [he wrote] a history of the Franklin Expedition still lies buried in my *cache* beneath the rocky shores of Montreal Island, and ... it is within the bounds of human probability that this record may be recovered."[13]

The Admiralty once again replied that it did not consider it advisable to send an expedition down the river. King, however, was now willing to use the other entry routes. Indeed, that was precisely what was now, in his view, required, as he formed a plan in association with Bedford Pim in order to finish the task of searching. On 8 December 1856 he and his young friend proposed "to make a combined effort ... by sea, through Barrow's Strait and down Peel's Sound; by land across the continent of America and down Great Fish River, meeting at the Magnetic Pole." On the sea expedition there would be used a small screw steamer. The starting-time of the land journey would be towards the end of February, that of the sea journey the end of June.[14] It was a combined plan which largely conformed to that of the Anderson party down the Back River and that of the M'Clintock *Fox* expedition, yet to sail. Yet the Anderson party had already completed its trip and the second part of the plan was to be forestalled by M'Clintock himself, who would find a message from the Franklin party close to the magnetic pole.

As already indicated, neither Lady Franklin nor a strong segment of influential public opinion was content to rest simply upon Rae's findings. They regarded them, rather, as a springboard for further endeavour. Yet with the ending of the Crimean War in 1856 it became apparent that upon the matter of the Arctic the navy continued to get matters exactly upside down. Having felt in 1845 that arctic travel was easy, it now felt that it was impossible. Too optimistic before about its capacity for initial discovery, it was now too pessimistic about its capacity for secondary discovery. Too unwilling before to use land means for the former, it was now unwilling to use sea means for the latter task. Lady Franklin claimed that, upon the prompting of Prince Albert, Sir Charles Wood, now the first lord of the Admiralty, had made certain promises of assistance to her. However, Sir Charles announced in the House of Commons early in 1857 that the Admiralty would not support another expedition in search of Franklin.[15]

In April Lady Franklin replied at length. The locale of the disaster had been pinpointed, narrowing the search down to a very diminished area which the Admiralty had amply recognized as certain to be the right locale by the reward to Dr. Rae. Now, too, Kellett's abandoned vessel *Resolute*, after drifting into Baffin Bay and being picked up and then refitted in the United States, had been returned to the Royal Navy in England. There was, Lady Franklin wrote, an obvious American interest in having this ship used for the purpose of searching for the Franklin expedition. If not *Resolute*, then Lady Franklin asked for use of one of the other five arctic vessels of the navy, available but unemployed, or at least a gunboat as tender to an expedition of her own. She had received assistance in the past under three administrations, in matters of dockyard help, crew, and officers, the supply of pemmican, and generous advances against her husband's pay, even to the extent on one occasion of £2,000. Though she did not mention him by name, she seemed already to have in mind M'Clintock as commander of the projected expedition.[16]

Yet, though Lord Palmerston as prime minister was for sending out an expedition, Sir Charles Wood was unalterably opposed. He commanded that Lady Franklin be informed that the Admiralty commissioners saw no reason for risking life in a project which, they felt, had no chance of saving life. If the best means possible, namely, a government expedition, was not available to her, then how much greater would be the risk entailed in a private one. They were aware of no promises requiring them to give her assistance and they wished to discourage such an enterprise.[17]

On the same date as that of Lady Franklin's letter, 4 April 1857, McClintock wrote to Sir James Ross asking for his counsel.[18] M'Clintock was "just havering" as regards serving as leader of Lady Franklin's private expedition. Unless the search was completed M'Clintock did not think that arctic men would ever receive the credit they deserved, and unless the present opportunity afforded by humanity and science was seized upon he did not think any future government would "reopen the Arctic Regions." All his inclinations were to accept, which he would do if he saw enough means put at his disposal to ensure as far as possible a successful outcome. How far, M'Clintock asked Ross, might he expect the countenance of the scientific bodies towards such an expedition as Lady Franklin planned, and to what extent ought he to obtain Admiralty sanction in leading such a project? He did not wish to be so impolite as to act contrary to their wishes. If the Admiralty was to withhold all assistance, M'Clintock could hardly undertake the expedition, even if it was possible to get away that season. He did not know much about private voyages and might form an erroneous opinion respecting them. What were the feelings and acts of the Admiralty towards Sir John Ross's expedition in 1829?

On 10 April M'Clintock again wrote to Sir James Ross. Lady Franklin proposed to send M'Clintock to Aberdeen to look at a steam yacht, and he felt that she would buy it. The navy had adamantly refused to aid her and M'Clintock wished to know if Sir James thought that it would be wrong in such circumstances to ask for a leave of absence for the purpose of commanding the proposed expedition. M'Clintock was thus forced into a position of nonconformity, in the sense of departing for a time from the navy, for the Admiralty lords, while still disapproving of a voyage, did eventually grant him an eighteen months' leave of absence.[19]

To the Admiralty's letter of refusal Lady Franklin replied on 21 April. She had indeed been promised help by Lord Wrottesley, president of the Royal Society, and Sir Charles Wood, especially if there was no government expedition. However, in the absence of any definite word of aid from the Admiralty, she had had to go ahead with arranging for a vessel of her own. There was plenty of public monetary assistance; a great deal had come in recently in aid of her scheme.[20] In fact, from her own point of view perhaps Lady Franklin was fortunate. She had obtained in M'Clintock a commander well trained in relatively large-scale travel, yet one who was freed from the still heavier approach which the navy itself would probably have espoused had it taken up this project. Again, there was a merchant marine as well as naval element in the party, and because he sailed for Lady Franklin rather than under the more centralizing control of the Admiralty, M'Clintock was able to operate with a flexibility he might not otherwise have had. Furthermore, Lady Franklin was probably fortunate in having only limited means; she was in a position to buy, for example, only a relatively small vessel. In other words, she had a good deal of the best of two worlds, as she planned, with considerable help from such figures as Sir Roderick Murchison, an expedition that was under the private sponsorship of herself and others.

Fox, the vessel in which M'Clintock sailed, had been built in 1855 by Messrs. Thompson, Hall and Company of Aberdeen as a yacht for Sir Richard Sutton, a member of the Royal Yacht Squadron. Purchased by Lady Franklin and praised highly for her performance in the Arctic by M'Clintock, *Fox* was 122.4 feet long, 23.9 feet broad, and had a depth of 12.9 feet. Compared with 340 and 370 tons, respectively, for *Erebus* and *Terror*, her gross tonnage was 177.4 and her weight per register 155.56 tons. She was thus about half the size of Franklin's vessels and her complement was twenty-six, or less than one-fifth of the combined complement of 138 for *Erebus* and *Terror*. Oak and larch had been used in *Fox*'s construction and, for the Arctic, elm was incorporated. *Fox* had horizontal trunk engines, a tubular boiler, and screws fitted for lifting. For her Arctic trip she took aboard at Aberdeen 100 tons of coal, for bunks amidships between one mast to the fore and two to the stern.[21]

As stated, Captain M'Clintock was naval-trained but privately sponsored, as Sir John Ross had been on his second voyage. Yet M'Clintock had advantages not enjoyed by Ross. He was not an innovative amateur in steam as Ross was; rather, he had acquired at Portsmouth in 1842 a first-class certificate in it. He seems to have studied steam formally again in 1855, and he had by now, of course, a thorough practical experience of it in the Arctic.[22] In sledding there had been a vast improvement among naval personnel since the days of Sir John Ross and in this development M'Clintock was by now a pre-eminent figure. He had covered, for example, on his trip in 1850–51, 770 miles in eighty days; and he had made a sledge trip of 1,400 miles on his spring trip in 1853 while with Kellett. He said he had learned thoroughly on these travels that lightness of burden was all.

Having sailed from Aberdeen on 30 June 1857, in August *Fox* was frozen in Melville Bay; drifting south, she was only released in Davis Strait in the following April. Returning north immediately, M'Clintock was at Beechey Island by 15 August 1858; stopped by ice in Peel Sound, he took *Fox* round to Bellot Strait in the same month but could not get beyond the western end of that strait. He had now experienced two major disappointments, and his reaction recalls his own comments upon his captive snowy owl on the Kellett expedition. He would never, M'Clintock's surgeon aboard *Fox* wrote later, "forget the two times when [M'Clintock's] soul was most tried, when we were beset in Melville Bay, and we were stopped by the ice in Bellot Strait. But M'Clintock at once accepted the inevitable, and adverse circumstances only strengthened the resolve to do his best."[23] M'Clintock, that is, had learned to live with the "hermetical sealing up" which had so frustrated Parry many years before, and of which he himself had written in negative mood at the close of his own first arctic trip.

Having wintered in 1858–59 at the eastern end of Bellot Strait, in the spring M'Clintock took to sledge travel. He has said that snow conditions where the navy operated in the Arctic were such as to preclude the Indian type of runnerless sled and even the igloo-building of company men. Now, however, in the Boothia–Somerset region he had entered an area where William Kennedy, a former company man with Labrador experience, had already been, on his journey in 1851–52 in *Prince Albert* for Lady Franklin. There Kennedy, even more deeply committed than Rae to indigenous methods of travel, had quickly decided to switch, for efficiency, from the Eskimo type of sledge with high runners to the Indian runnerless sled, and had made what was claimed at that time to be a record trip of 1,100 miles with dogs by this means. He had also found snow for snow huts, to the construction of which he had rapidly taken.[24] Furthermore, he had, as already stated, travelled all winter in this region, not waiting for spring.

In short, there was good evidence from Kennedy as well as from Rae that in this region (if not also to the north) the Indian means of sledding, the Eskimo method of housing, and the practice of winter travel were both possible and superior techniques. By contrast with Kennedy and Rae, however, M'Clintock did not switch to the flat-bottomed sled, nor did he know how to build igloos in the Eskimo manner; instead, he could construct for himself only a shelter whose walls were of snow but whose roof, a vital feature in a snowhouse, was canvas, a deficiency of a serious nature, negating much of the advantage of an actual igloo.[25] Certainly also, although M'Clintock did start on his first sled trip on 17 February, a large advance for the navy, he did not travel all winter long. In other words, to the end of the period to 1860 the navy continued to employ less indigenous methods of travel than did men of a company background. Despite his own stress upon lightness, M'Clintock was inherently of a follow-up stamp and used in fact means that were heavier than Rae's and Kennedy's.

But M'Clintock had, as Rae did not, a nearby deep-sea vessel as his base, and a crew twice the size of Rae's crews. He could mount a number of sled journeys as Rae could not, so as to fan out over a wide range of coast, sea, and land. He could follow up with relative thoroughness now that Rae had shown where to search. On 1 March 1859 by dog team he met natives near the north magnetic pole and obtained from them relics and information. On 2 April main parties set out: M'Clintock, by west Boothia and eastern King William Island (as it was now known to be) to Montreal Island and then west about King William Island itself; Capt. Allen Young of the merchant navy on a survey of the south coast of Prince of Wales Island; and Lieutenant Hobson also along the coast of King William Island. It was the last-named who found at Victory Point the only written record which we have of the Franklin party after it was last seen in July 1845. (See Appendix 3.) From that document, in part by implication, we know the outline of a story: of the attempted course by the party southwest from Cape Walker in 1845 and its actual course in that year up Wellington Channel, of the wintering at Beechey Island in 1845–46, and of besetment in 1846–48. We know also from the document of Franklin's death in 1847, of the severe outbreak of scurvy in the winter of 1847–48, of the finding of a last link in a passage either in 1847 or 1848, and of the final intention of the party to march in the spring of 1848 to "Back's Great Fish River." Through the evidence of skeletons, a boat, and other artifacts brought home by M'Clintock's expedition, it is known that the party, decimated and emaciated, travelled near and in the estuary of the Back, and then perished.

Because of *Fox* and her proximity as base, the M'Clintock party had more time at its furthest point than Rae had on his expedition and thus found a good many more artifacts and much more substantial information than Rae had been able to do; M'Clintock had also had time maturely to reflect upon the nature and implications of the evidence, in the locale where the evidence was found. Finally, the *Fox* expedition, by the fact of its vessel and of its numbers, was able actually to bring home a more substantial collection of relics than Rae had done. One can also make a comparison between M'Clintock and Anderson's expeditions. Anderson's had been a light trip, undertaken during wartime; it had reached the foot of Boothia and returned in one season—but had not found a great deal. M'Clintock's expedition, not mounted until after the Crimean War, swept out of Baffin Bay in first year and taking in all three seasons as compared with Anderson's one, had been able to accomplish a good deal more than Anderson's party.

Besides finding the most substantial information which we have of the lost Franklin party, M'Clintock's expedition had also made geographical discoveries. It had completed the work both of Franklin and of Rae. For M'Clintock accomplished, finally, the discovery of the west coast of Boothia and of a coastal passage. Most important of all, M'Clintock brought his information home, as the Franklin party had been unable to do. Released from the ice in August 1859 and sailing on the 15th of that month, M'Clintock bore the document, the relics, and the geographical information to London.[26] The *Fox* voyage was a brilliant achievement. Bringing to fruition much that had been learned and developed since 1818, it represented a fulfilment of combined sled and sea means of travel. The voyage redounded to the credit of the Royal Geographical Society which had had much to do with its dispatch and successful return. For all that, as regards both the Franklin party and geographical discovery, the *Fox* expedition had conducted a mopping-up operation. In respect to the Franklin party, it had depended upon initial finds of Rae; and M'Clintock had depended upon the geographical discoveries of Sir James Ross in Peel Sound, of Kennedy and Bellot at Bellot Strait, of Rae at Rae Strait, and of Back at the mouth of the Back River, many of these discoveries having been made by land or coastal means.

In the sequence of initial and follow-up discovery by which Rae and M'Clintock had made their finds, there was an irony apparent. Led by Rae, a coastal traveller, to the right spot, M'Clintock by his deep-sea means had paradoxically proved that over both men, Rae and M'Clintock, there was cast the shadow of a still earlier figure, the inland traveller Richard King— an explorer *in absentia*. For, in the first place, the very method of discovery of information concerning Franklin had demonstrated the validity of a point upon which King had been vocal: that reconnaissance should be conducted first from the land (as it turned out, by Rae) and, if justified by the findings from the land, that there should then be secondary discovery by a follow-up sea party (as it turned out, by M'Clintock). The method of discovery, that is, had validated the reasoning which had led King to predict the loss of Franklin. Secondly, the information itself was a specific justification of King. In the document found at Victory Point a decade after its composition, M'Clintock had brought to the world news regarding the Franklin party which showed that events had happened to a very considerable extent in the area, the year, the season, and in the manner that King had named and had wished, from 1847 forwards, to verify. Finally, M'Clintock's geographical discoveries had also verified, as King had wished to do years before, that the last link in a fully coastal passage was on Boothia's western shore.

It may thus be seen that the primarily deep-sea methods of M'Clintock entering the Arctic by Baffin Bay, following upon the primarily coastal methods of Rae entering the Arctic by way of Hudson Bay, had proved that King, the most inland man of all, had a claim in one sense paramount even to that of Rae, namely, that of a peculiar kind of foreknowledge—a prescience, as early even as 1840, of a Northwest Passage, and, as early as 1847 and 1848, of the location of the Franklin party, although his awareness had gone unrecognized, much as Rae's finds of 1851 had also gone unrecognized.

A pattern seems to have appeared as the quest for a Northwest Passage and then for Franklin was pursued. There had been great and seemingly inexplicable disaster and failure, through unawareness that priorities existed and had become inverted. There had been disruption because a man who was himself a potential "first discoverer" had not been called upon, either for action or for advice. As a result, even though a coastal passage had once been much nearer to completion than a northern one, full discovery of it had been delayed for a quarter-century, by which time the more northern passage had been found. As a further result, the Franklin party had both perished and been lost, and had remained lost for the best part of a decade. Indeed, so long had been the period when the party's location was unknown that by the time of the *Fox* voyage only a few traces of it remained. The Franklin locality had been found and searched, on the whole in a thorough manner, but ten years late. By then it was unlikely that the fullest survey by a heavy party could have been as efficacious as a much earlier foray by lighter, more rapid, and more inland means. Furthermore, to the last an ignorance concerning, or an animus against, Richard King persisted. On the trip by M'Clintock, as on that by Anderson, Montreal Island was visited but the King cache there was not investigated, and it may not have been even to this day. Thus the use of too elaborate means, too early, had resulted not only in the loss of Franklin. The failure to use light means early enough in the search for him had, in like manner, led to the loss of all hope of saving the party, and in the later searches to extreme slowness as well, probably to the detriment of what we know of the party's fate. The elaborate and methodical approach of the navy was not only a slow way to explore; it is likely that it also led to irreparable loss.

As we have seen, the differing personalities of King, Rae, and M'Clintock represented, respectively, inland, coastal, and deep-sea approaches, as well as abilities variously adapted to initial and final discovery. King, we have seen, was an individualist; his writing style has been criticized as both irregular and too sparse. Rae, we know, was also a "loner." Of his style it has been written, "Rae's writing is very plain, but it improves with each reading because of its economy, intellectual clarity, and sympathy with nature and men." M'Clintock, by contrast, did not really relish travelling alone. His style has been described by the same critic: "M'Clintock's outstanding characteristic . . . was straightforward intelligence interested in everything. Nothing seems to escape his attention—men, dogs, wild life, the weather, the ice, the ship—all are set down in unencumbered quick marching prose."[27] This does not take account of the touches of humour, poetry, and the romantic which are also apparent in M'Clintock's writings. He had a greater variety than the two other men and, judged on the widest basis, a more complex nature. These facts bespeak a difference of type in each case.

One of the reasons for the strange situation was the milieu in which it occurred. A characteristic for which the eighteenth century was noted had to a considerable degree survived into the succeeding one. In the earlier century men had confidently shown over-optimism with regard to the quest for a Northwest Passage; there had been a "persistent contrast" between "sanguine theories" and "frustrating experience."[28] In the nineteenth century, as the search moved to the Arctic, the contrast had continued, although in a modified form. A reason was that the strategically oriented Admiralty and commercially oriented Hudson's Bay Company had allowed aims hopeful as regards their own respective purposes to becloud their judgments. Representing by contrast a humanitarian agency, Lady Franklin had had in some ways a greater realism than the Admiralty or the Hudson's Bay Company. She long maintained that Boothia was the right direction in which to search for Franklin, and had sent two expeditions that way in *Prince Albert*, under Forsyth and Kennedy respectively. They had failed, however, to get far enough south, and thereafter even Lady Franklin had forgotten the Boothia area until Rae's finds redirected her attention there. In any event, having a naval connection, she had favoured a deep-sea approach; besides, not liking King personally, she had written of his project for a Back River trip that it was merely "a birch bark canoe expedition."

King, by contrast, appears as a figure who derived a discerning and quite accurate analysis from an absence of distracting incentives even more marked than in the case of Lady Franklin. He stressed the northwest rivers and lakes route which now lacked independent commercial importance yet was still a rapid and relatively all-seasonal means of communication with the Northwest. He also stressed its least commercially valuable extension, the Back River, which though physically difficult was the most direct final extension of the northwest route to the central North American Arctic. A proponent of the scientific approach, he had also understood the barrens better than others, and one of his main incentives had been the humane one of rescue or discovery of evidence of the Franklin party, yet without a deep-sea emphasis. It was in this way that King had moved, more than others, outside either a commercial or a naval context. The most inland of all rivers to the Arctic and therefore the one of least intrinsic interest to the navy, the Back also failed to appeal, during the Franklin search, to the Hudson's Bay Company, for it flowed through a country misunderstood as "barren" rather than treeless and was strongly felt to lack commercial navigability; it seemed stripped of economic as well as naval importance. The Great Fish River was simply an explorer's river, the right route in King's outlook for initial discovery of a final link in a Northwest Passage in the Boothia area, and later for initial discovery of the Franklin party. Not on the whole of primary use for other matters, it was very precisely located for these purposes. Failure to use it had possibly caused delay in finding a Northwest Passage and still greater delay when, the original neglect leading to further trouble, the Franklin searches got under way. At the very least the Back River had proved for Richard King an effective heuristic device. By thinking in terms of it he had come to some remarkably accurate conclusions.

Thus strategy and commerce, although they had made possible and had aided discovery by putting parties in the field, had also acted as a deterrent to realistic use of them. Yet, despite his advantages in this respect, King had been barred or had barred himself from all agencies, the economic one of the fur trade, the strategic one of the navy, and later the humanitarian agency of Lady Franklin herself. His detachment from their incentives had given accuracy to his views, but his isolation had stood in the way of an effective use of that accuracy. Besides, two inverse phenomena had exacerbated each other. King may very well have helped drive the navy away from the Back River which it or its officers already misunderstood; the navy, for its part, had helped drive King into isolation and make him still more acerbic. It was in this context that he had been the most realistic spokesman at the Admiralty and the Colonial Office and before the public upon a Northwest Passage and Franklin. He had written of unwelcome facts as opposed to "sanguine theories" and "ill-founded optimism." Others were hardly aware of King, yet he represented both a stark awakening from a 300-year-old dream, and at the same time a potentially effective strategy to cope with the situation that did exist.

As contemporaries did not fully recognize Richard King, so posterity has failed fully to understand him. Markham observes that he had been reduced to a footnote in the arctic story.[29] Cyriax not only calls M'Clintock the real discoverer of the fate of Franklin, slighting Rae in this regard, but finds King lucky in his conclusions without examining him in his totality. Others have also tended to judge King as showing "brilliant guesswork," rather than realism and a dawning scientific spirit. For the stronger the case for King, the greater the necessity to downgrade a good deal of the adulation bestowed upon Franklin and to judge that certain tasks of exploration could have been performed more expeditiously, with less risk of disaster and less "heroics." Humboldt's description of stages in the popular view of a discovery is relevant here. The first stage is a conviction that the thing discovered does not exist, and the last is an attribution, when the discovery has been verified, of credit for it to someone other than the initial discoverer.[30] By 1854 and still more by 1860 King's map of 1845 had been proved essentially correct in its emphasis upon an archipelago in the Arctic where the navy had thought there was mainly ocean, and in many other details. (See Maps 7 and 14.) He had accurately predicted disaster or failure for Back in *Terror* in 1836; for Franklin in 1845; for James Clark Ross in 1848; and, in the absence of his own approach, success in the 1850s in a survey of the North American coast and discovery of a passage, but failure in the search for Franklin. He had sensed also the element of elaboration which had occurred.

Earlier King's views had gone unnoticed. Now that they were confirmed he was largely forgotten. Like other antibodies in relation to a fever he perished in the process of bringing the fever down. He wrote again upon the Franklin expedition and its aftermath in a revised version of his earlier work, which quoted newspaper articles commending his prescience.[31] He received some recognition and sympathy but his eccentricities continued to be a handicap. It is true that Montreal Island remained unsearched, even by M'Clintock's party, for the King cache or any message left at the cache. Yet it is also true that the explorer C. F. Hall was to conclude in the 1860s that none of the Franklin party ever did reach Montreal Island.[32] In any event while others, as King had said many years before, were "showered with honours and emoluments" for their Arctic service he alone among "Arctics" was "unhonoured and unrewarded." After failing in vigour for three years, he died in obscurity at sixty-five. It was in the very year, 1876, when the Nares expedition was making (from King's point of view) many of the same mistakes as the Franklin expedition had made. It was on the day, 4 February, which marked the forty-third anniversary of the receipt of orders by the Back party in 1833 to proceed down the Great Fish River; and the final illness, for the man who has since been called the "excitable" and "irascible" Dr. King, was four days of "serious apoplexy."[33] The illness, the day, and the year were appropriate.

The difficulty experienced by the Royal Navy in the Arctic stemmed from the absence not only of the navy's purpose, warfare, but of its definitive element, water, the latter condition occurring, however, not in a simple but in an ambiguous way. The arctic region was composed of what was now found, surprisingly, to be a very considerable and puzzling archipelago in which even the oceanic portion was composed not just of open sea but also of ice. It was in this context that polar exploration in peacetime had taken the navy's measure as no enemy fleet or combination of fleets had done in war, while in a more literal way the navy had been a chief agent in taking the measure of the Arctic by surveying rather than exploring it. As regards the puzzling relationship of land and sea, King William Island had been wrongly thought by most to be part of Boothia, while the disputed Boothia–North Somerset complex, earlier thought to be proved, unexpectedly and in its entirety, an isthmus, not an island, had now been proved in its northern portion an island, not a peninsula. Again, Prince of Wales Land, wrongly thought of by Browne and Kennedy as a part of North Somerset, had been shown to be separated from it. Further west, Banks Land was proved to be separated by a strait from Wollaston Land, which in its turn was shown to be a part of Victoria Land. Even where technically there was ocean, this was often so frozen over wide areas as, first, to conceal the relationship between land and water and, secondly, to make the area tantamount for travel purposes to land rather than open sea, or, according to M'Clintock, to give it features that belonged neither to one element nor the other.[34]

Confused and confusing truths about the relationship further south between land, open sea, and ice were true also of the Arctic further north. In this period evidence had been found in Wellington Channel and Smith Sound to provide hope, for those of maritime interests, of a wide and immeasurable open polar sea such as Wrangel had seen off Siberia, with, it was claimed, the additional attraction of plentiful animal life. Yet, although people had been, "occasionally . . . startled by announcements of open water," in fact, "a little further exploration . . . had proved these iceless spaces . . . to be very limited in extent . . . solely due to local and apparent causes, such as currents or tides" and "only . . . found in straits and not to seaward of an open coast-line." No "reliable indications" of a state of things similar to that which Wrangel had experienced off Siberia had been found.[35] Yet the finding of some open sea had had the effect, taken in conjunction with Franklin's instructions and the finds at Beechey Island, of diverting the navy's attention northward. In addition, the variability of open sea and ice conditions from year to year, as for example in Barrow Strait, had been important.

Franklin, his instructions, and the manner in which he followed them, both reflected and amplified this ambiguity. New to sea travel in the North American Arctic and proud of following orders, Franklin had not written his own instructions. Their basic tenor was to seek a continental passage but the thought of going north and west by way of an open polar sea had been added as an inserted postscript in a different hand. In meticulous obedience, Franklin had conformed to their main thrust by attempting a course southwest from Cape Walker; after that he had followed the post-script insertion by going up Wellington Channel, and then, relying at last on his own judgment, he had found and gone down Peel Sound, suggested but unproved before. Beechey Island, around which Franklin had now radiated, was an arctic crossroads, on the threshold of Wellington Channel, Barrow Strait, Peel Sound, and Prince Regent Inlet. Here the variety and speed of Franklin's advances had had a complicating effect. That he had arrived at Beechey Island for the first wintering after, not before, he went up Wellington Channel added to the difficulty that he had left no written record at the island; few if any thought that at Beechey Island he was on his way back from the channel rather than up it. This meant that there was now a new set of factors as confusing as the truth about Boothia–North Somerset itself and about the existence or nonexistence of open water in the north.

As already stated, with the loss of Franklin the task of arctic discovery had been changed not simply in degree but in kind. There had been only one sea expedition at the outset, Franklin's, and involvement of only one nation in one continent. Following his loss there was involvement of countries of three continents (Europe, North America, and Asia) in a search by ships of at least two nations (Great Britain and the United States), and by men of at least three nations (Great Britain, the United States, and France).

Two vessels, the *Erebus* and *Terror*, had been dispatched to find a passage in 1845, four ships to find them, and then a fifth ship to find two of these four in 1848–49; eight ships had been sent in the second, Austin phase of the search; and by 1854 there had been involved in all some twenty-two expeditions, a total of thirty-three ship winterings, and at least twenty ships. There had gone out ships searching for Franklin, base ships, ships tracking down rumours, and ships searching for ships that were searching for Franklin—all because he had once been searching for a passage. In addition there had been land expeditions. All this has the aura of a problem in multiplication, not in simple summation. Naval operations were under the Hydrographic Office and an alert hydrographer might have noted this acceleration in theoretical terms, that is, that there had been a transfer of the problem from one of linear or arithmetic progression, the search for a passage, to one of area or geometric progression, the search for Franklin. Or, to say the same thing in a somewhat different way, naval operations, being under the Hydrographic Office, had taken on a still more definite surveying aspect. In practical terms Franklin had been lost while he was seeking a passage; eventually, as King had predicted, one half of the Canadian Arctic, including three Northwest Passages, was found in the search for Franklin. Financially, there was a matching escalation. From the spending of some tens of thousands of pounds to send out Franklin, there was an expansion of outlay, by the navy alone, to more than half a million pounds.[36]

As already suggested, a further compounding of the situation had occurred through the use of steam. It is possible that without steam Franklin would not have arrived at Beechey Island for his first wintering after rather than before he had been up Wellington Channel. When in the following spring he left Beechey Island, steam may have lodged him more quickly than would otherwise have been the case in a very inaccessible region of the central Arctic, without hope of extrication even with steam. While it aided, steam had also probably complicated the task of searching for Franklin. By facilitating a quest into Wellington Channel and Smith Sound, it had seemed to emphasize the existence of an open polar sea, and given special credence to those who thought Franklin had sailed northward. In addition, a multitude of plans for other technological developments in, and of further suggestions for, arctic travel had poured into the Admiralty. Many of these were amusing, fantastic, or ridiculous; some were forerunners of eventual realistic improvements in travel, and there were even attempts to take to the air.[37] Probably all of them had, like steam, a delaying effect upon the search for Franklin, for time was spent in analysing them, yet they did not aid or shorten the search.

Another factor has also been mentioned. The very number of men and ships that had come to the Arctic, both before Franklin's last voyage and in the search for him, had encouraged the purveying of confused stories of white men both on the west coast, as in Pim's experience, and on the Atlantic side, as in the case of the Adam Beck story.[38] New discoveries, added to the aftermath of old ones, helped cause confusion; Rae's finds in Parker Bay, for example, were interpreted as having come from the old wreck of *Fury* through newly discovered Bellot Strait. Delay and uncertainty in finding the actual truth about rumours, and confused reports that arose through the expanding list of expeditions at one time or another present in the Arctic meant, as the reports were tracked down and investigated, still greater delay and a still greater diffusion of the search.

Psychologically, too, there was a multiple burgeoning. The search for Sir John Franklin became at home a national obsession as, increasingly, Franklin himself took on heroic stature. In the 1850s Alfred Tennyson, Franklin's nephew by marriage and his memorialist in Westminster Abbey, published *The Idylls of the King*. In these, Tennyson wrote, he wished to emphasize "the need for the Ideal" and "chivalrous feeling." The arctic voyages of this period, the poet said, represented an example in his own day of what he had in mind.[39] M'Clintock, having matched the scientific spirit of Tennyson's "Locksley Hall" in his steam training in the 1840s, showed in the Arctic in the 1850s a "chivalric spirit" and a consciousness of the "crusaders of old," a development which became still more apparent in the *Fox* voyage at the close of the decade. For by this time Franklin and his party had in the public mind something of the aura of the Holy Grail, Lady Franklin of the fair Elaine, and those searching for Franklin of the knights of the court of King Arthur.[40] At the very time when Rae's discovery had brought an end to the physical elaboration, there had flowered a psychological one, as there was sought a goal the clue to whose attainment had been all along not increasing complexity but greater simplicity.

Perhaps only some sense of "the Ideal" could explain the conduct of the ordinary seamen. On hummocky and serrated ice, loads of 200 lb. or more for each man were burdens for draft animals, not men. But there were no draft animals of the right size, so the men took their places as willing horses who were sometimes worked, or worked themselves, into a breakdown of health or even to death, suggesting that Rae's approach provided not only a more rapid means of travel but also a more humane one, and that the very availability of these men made possible a heavier approach which might otherwise have been avoided. Kellett was appalled at the hardships of sled travel for the men and developed, perhaps in part for this very reason, the "satellite sledge" for use in light reconnaissance work into small bays and inlets as an adjunct to main sledge parties.[41]

Meanwhile, because of its nature, the Hudson's Bay Company had been operating to a very marked degree with a more coastal emphasis, more indigenous travel methods, less expensively, on a smaller scale, and within a narrower circle around the scene of the disaster near the Back River than had the navy. In 1851 Rae had anticipated the crossing of a northern passage by arriving at Prince Albert Sound within striking distance of one of M'Clure's sled parties, and in the same year he might, if his aim had not been to find Franklin, have crossed Victoria Strait to reach Boothia, and so have added to knowledge of a coastal passage. Indeed, the company's contribution to the finding of coastline and of Franklin had in this period been out of all proportion to the small scale of its activity in comparison with that of the navy. Yet the Hudson's Bay Company had continued to be caught up in the elaborate approach of the navy. Rae had been delayed in his operations through the naval contact with Pullen in 1850, had been handicapped by the lack of identification by the navy of the finds he had brought home in 1852, and again, by speeding home in 1854, in part to get the navy to stop its search further north, had lost a crucial opportunity of finding out more about Franklin. To the last there was interference with the lesser but more effective agency by the larger but less effective one. Yet the company, like the navy, had been hampered by its lack of interest in the Back River, and it, too, had eventually given up the search. Although to a lesser extent, survey and accident, rather than design, had characterized the company's quest as well as that of the navy.

The role of the inland routes and the private agencies has already been touched upon. Some private ideas and parties were more technologically advanced or "far out" than those of the navy and company. For example, Sir John Ross had not only pioneered with steam machinery in the Arctic in 1829; he also brought there on his third voyage in 1850 such items as gongs to attract Franklin's notice, an instance of primitive or fantastic technology of the same genre as the multiple capricious suggestions which deluged the Admiralty. Again, from those outside the navy or the company, or those divorcing themselves temporarily from it, there had come activities that were widest of all of the mark. Examples are the abortive expedition of Pim to Russia and the expedition of Inglefield, a naval officer who, while on leave in 1852, made a summer foray into Smith Sound which was brilliant in itself but, like some activities of Pim, far wide of the mark. Private endeavours had also tended to be inconclusive through a lack of support or organization, as witnessed by the failure of Lady Franklin's first two parties by sea to get to the part of Boothia intended. Nevertheless, it was a private agent who had left the employ of the company, William Kennedy, who had shown an even more indigenous emphasis than that of the company explorer Rae. Furthermore, the more accurate ideas of where to search and the most effective action in the search itself had come from those outside the navy and the company, for example, John Brown, Lady Franklin, Richard King, and A. K. Isbister,[42] or else from those who had dissociated themselves to some extent from either the company or the navy, for example, Rae in 1853–54 and M'Clintock in 1857–59. In other words, those outside an institutional framework could go to either of the extremes. And of their number, as we have seen, it had been Richard King who had most persistently and coherently emphasized both an inland route and the west coast of Boothia (or a region just west of it) as the locale in which both to complete a passage and find Franklin.

It is a theme of historians of Canada that there has been a "metropolitan–hinterland" relationship in Canadian history, in part a relationship between the metropolitan country of Great Britain and British North America itself, considered as a hinterland. Great explorers, it has been said, come from the heart of civilization; on the other hand, it has also been said that those who travel by sea change their skies but not their minds.[43] It was Europeans who were making many of the discoveries in the Canadian Arctic; yet willingness and ability to adapt in travelling to a North American environment did have to be present for success. In the period 1818–60 the Royal Navy had represented European overall planning and technical excellence. Yet the navy had been slow in discerning important factors as regards arctic geography, strategy, and tactics, a weakness of which the story of the last Franklin party stood out as the most dramatic example. This was one extreme, a metropolitan one. On the other hand, in this period British North America's own contribution to the discovery of what would become its Arctic and a part of its own hinterland had been small. Examples of contributions by colonies of central and eastern British North America are the provision of one vessel, the *Isabel* of Inglefield, built in Prince Edward Island,[44] and many of the timbers of other arctic ships; and the presence at Lachine of the North American headquarters of the Hudson's Bay Company. There had also been the introduction to the arctic story, in the person of the Nova Scotian Sir Edward Belcher, of the most incompetent of the arctic naval commanders of the period. In the Northwest there had been the provision of personnel for Rae's and other parties, and of William Kennedy. Yet, for all his skill in indigenous travel methods,

Kennedy was a "a very simple fellow,"[45] who had shown insufficient over-all control and planning ability. His lack of knowledge of navigation had led to a split command with Bellot and a confusion, which consisted partly in a split between land and sea emphases, as the two commanders proceeded. All these factors represented another extreme, a hinterland one.

Between the two extremes were, on the other hand, such naval figures as Mecham, M'Clintock, and to an extent Pim. They showed the navy's ability to adapt. Thus M'Clintock said that over the course of time, as one travelled on the ice, one became "more of an animal";[46] one took on, that is, a more local and indigenous aspect, and gradually the navy did move towards use of native techniques in tactics of travel. A complex of skills was developed in which steam and increasingly indigenous methods were combined. Yet to the last, as already indicated in the account of the *Fox* voyage, and as the uncomfortable way in which Pim generally fitted into the naval pattern showed, navy personnel remained as regards indigenous skills behind those who had a more local North American emphasis, whether by birth or long experience. On the other hand (again between the two extremes of an exclusively home influence and a purely North American one), there were such men as King, Isbister, and Rae who, like certain naval figures, showed a combination of elements both metropolitan and hinterland. Their contribution gained added strength from the fact that it included not only indigenous skills and a light-party emphasis but also, to a considerable extent, accuracy of assessment concerning strategy. They were men who operated, sooner or later, in a private rather than an institutional capacity. To sum up, on the one hand, there were needed some of the travel techniques of the metropolitan region; on the other hand, these had to be employed very much in combination with the methods and skills of the hinterland region, and in specific relationship to its environment. A similar combination was necessary as regards planning and organization. There was need for a central element in these areas; yet if planning and organization were too centralized, especially within an institutional framework, expeditions could become too elaborate, strategy too optimistic, or some other note of unrealism could enter in. As well as central control, there had to be a good deal of individual initiative. In all, a creative combination of features from both sides of the Atlantic, worked out in the context of a minimum of necessary organization and a maximum of freedom of choice on the spot, were necessary ingredients for success in exploration in the Canadian Arctic in this period.

In this frame of reference, the navy's elaborate and methodical mode of operation had proved a very expensive way to discover a passage, and had failed to find Franklin; yet it had also resulted in an extensive mapping and occupation of the Canadian Arctic. The navy's eccentricities and wishful thinking as regards an Arctic that did not exist had resulted, both directly and by stimulation of others, in a huge survey of the Arctic that did. Coalition of the North West and Hudson's Bay Companies in 1821 had meant that during most of the period 1818–60 central and eastern British North America had been largely detached from a Northwest hinterland. Nevertheless, when this lost hinterland would in due course be handed back to a newly confederated and continental Canada, it would have attached to it a vast arctic domain. The navy had been largely responsible for opening up an important new region at a time when there had been no other agency to accomplish this, certainly not on so grand a scale.

There were two other noteworthy consequences of arctic exploration in this period. As Great Britain lost belief in a passage to the Orient through polar regions, even with the aid of steam, British interest in crossing North America by railway was growing. The Palliser expedition of 1857–60 to investigate the Northwest was in part a sequel to the failure to discover a useful passage further north. Similarly, the eventual building of the Canadian Pacific Railway was in part a sequel to the arctic rebuff. Sir William Van Horne, in charge of constructing the railway, possessed a large collection of books on the maritime quest for a passage—symbol of an interconnection between failure of a sea route and completion of a land one. In addition to surveying the Arctic, that is to say, the navy had turned attention southward from it. Indeed, the tale of Franklin and the searches for him had given to northern development a contrapuntal character. The course of arctic exploration during the early and mid-nineteenth century had burdened the region with an exaggeratedly frigid reputation, a metropolitan extreme. In reaction, there would come a twentieth-century "Stefansson syndrome" of the "friendly Arctic," an opposite and also exaggerated swing of the pendulum, to a hinterland extreme.[47] Probably the truth as to the real nature of the Arctic, and the means of coping with it, lay between the two extremes.

Appendix 1

M'CLURE AND KELLETT
AS FIRST DISCOVERERS OF A NORTHWEST PASSAGE

The strong sense that Franklin was the first discoverer of a Northwest Passage has its prelude in a remark by M'Clintock, who says of the labours of the Franklin expedition in the Arctic in 1845–46 that they brought the "addition to *our* charts of ... extensive lands." There was an assumption, in other words, that because Franklin and his men knew of these lands, therefore somehow those at home knew. This attitude was voiced regarding the Northwest Passage by Sir Roderick Murchison in his preface to the first edition of M'Clintock's account of the *Fox* voyage. "It is clear," Sir Roderick wrote of Franklin, "that he ... was *the first real discoverer of the Northwest Passage.* This great fact must therefore be inscribed upon the monument of Franklin."[1] In due course it was. A series of memorials, including the one in Westminster Abbey and the monument erected in Waterloo Place by unanimous vote of Parliament, describe Franklin as the man who completed discovery of the Northwest Passage. We are told also, in perhaps the best-known work on the Franklin expedition, that the "expedition was successful especially in making geographical discoveries." Cyriax writes of Franklin as discovering Wellington Channel, Peel Sound, Franklin Strait, the west coast of King William Land, Crozier Strait, and a Northwest Passage, adding that "no previous [Arctic] explorers had accomplished so much in so short a time." The same author also writes that "The Franklin expedition is universally acknowledged at the present day to have been the first to find a Northwest Passage," a sentiment which is repeated in almost the same words in the centenary article by Cyriax and Wordie.[2]

Yet in fact there was no direct "*addition* to *our* charts" by the Franklin expedition. For neither M'Clintock, the Admiralty, nor anyone in the United Kingdom was destined to see the charts of Franklin. They were to remain the private possession of the expedition itself, and possibly of Eskimos and their children, a point which is taken up by Cyriax himself. For besides saying that the expedition was a "brilliant success," Cyriax also calls it "a disastrous failure," adding that "it is to those who took part in the search" for Franklin, rather than to Franklin himself that "geographers are indebted for their knowledge of the lands and channels which were first explored by the Franklin expedition." And Cyriax himself, in writing of Sir James Ross's expedition of 1848–49 in search of Franklin, speaks of *Ross* as discovering Peel Sound.[3] Yet Franklin was discoverer of Peel Sound in exactly the same sense that he was the discoverer of a Northwest Passage; indeed, his finding of Peel Sound was a part of his finding of a Northwest Passage. Cyriax is therefore inconsistent in giving credit to Ross for discovery of the former and to Franklin for discovery of the latter.

These points underline the question of who were original discoverers, those who first saw the features, or those who both saw and reported them to London. Both sets of attitudes and statements by Cyriax cannot be true in the same sense. The ambiguity is resolved if one differentiates between survey and discovery. Franklin's expedition had been brilliant as a survey at the expense of being disastrous as discovery. In short, the more meaningful sense of discovery is the second one used by Cyriax.[4] For discovery is not a race conducted from a known point to an unknown one. It is the science of bringing the unknown in topography into the purview of the known, the acquirement of information about a hitherto unknown region by a discovering country. Until the country acquires the information discovery has not been completed.

It was through Ross's expedition that news of the existence of Peel Sound reached London, not through the expedition of Franklin—save only in the sense that Franklin's expedition had necessitated Ross's. The same is also true of the discovery of a Northwest Passage. The fact that for some years London *thought* M'Clure was the first discoverer of a passage is the proof, by definition of discovery, that he was, provided one also gives credit to Kellett for having made it possible for M'Clure to get news home of what it was that he had found. The most one can say for a claim in behalf of Franklin is that, by necessitating the searches for his party, and by so placing the party that to find it and convey home news of it was also to complete discovery of a passage, Franklin was a participant in discovery of both passages, the one known as his own and M'Clure's. His own actions led to the report, conveyed to London in 1859, that the Franklin party had been the first to see a passage. But by that time, of course, another passage had already been proved, taking away priority of discovery of this one. Franklin, so far as we can judge, initiated and very possibly delayed the discovery of the passage known as his own and by the same action initiated and promoted the discovery, prior to his own, of the M'Clure–Kellett passage.

This is more than a debating point. It seems to be interconnected with the loss of Franklin and the long failure of the searches for him. For successful exploration in the Arctic was the work of men who were very conscious of the necessity for a homeward movement as well as an outgoing one. Indeed, the homebound journey was often more difficult than the outward one. Effective exploration was the work of men who understood, as Thomas Simpson once put it, "that any further foolhardy perseverance [at the distance he was from his winter retreat] could only lead to loss of the whole party."[5] Had Franklin been instructed and attuned in his own mind to go as far as possible, to realistically assess the difficulties, and then return home, he would have been able to report what he had seen.

In the absence of this attitude, either at home or on the expedition, the discovery of Franklin's passage took fourteen years (1845–59). Otherwise it might have taken less, successors building upon what Franklin had done. At any rate Franklin, in that event, would not have hindered the discovery of a passage by making a search for himself necessary.

In short, the implicit sense of community in M'Clintock's remark — between the officers and crew of *Erebus* and *Terror* and their countrymen at home — showed admirable spirit, but not a grasp of the meaning of discovery. Very much to the contrary, M'Clintock's was an attitude by which the Admiralty search for a passage became a search for Franklin, and then, against the Admiralty's will but according to its bent, the search for Franklin became a survey of the Arctic.

Appendix 2

RAE ON FLAT SLEDS AND SLEDS WITH HIGH RUNNERS

After his trip of 1847 Rae made sure never again to use sledges with high runners. He used instead a type derived by the Hudson's Bay Company from the Indian toboggan. Rae said that while no runners were required for inland travel, there was a necessity on sea ice to have some runners, albeit very low ones. This was because sea ice, when there was no snow upon it, was "almost invariably covered with a moist semi-frozen film of strong salt brine." So the sledge which the Hudson's Bay Company used on the coast of Hudson Bay and the one which he used was flat with low "runners 2 inches wide and a half or three quarters of an inch high." Rae contrasted flat sledges with government or naval ones. These had high runners of eight or ten inches, and were of a type derived from Greenland Eskimos. Rae said that Eskimos did not use sledges like his because "they had not tough wood to make them of, and ... seldom or never went upon rough ice because they seldom or never found walrus or seals there"; therefore to follow the Eskimo mode was not necessarily appropriate.[1]

The sled with low runners, Rae said, while equal to one with high runners on the bare ice or hard snow, was far better when crossing rough ice "or overland where the snow is usually comparatively soft and deep; the flat sledge sliding over this, whilst the high runner sledge sinks more or less deeply," so that hauling it was difficult or so that it "stuck fast altogether, until lightened wholly or in part of its load." Rae spoke in this connection of an extremely fatiguing experience, when he and his party sank knee-deep at every step in spring snow that was not quite hard enough to bear the party's weight. "Fortunately," Rae says, "our flat sledges did not break through the crust as the high runner sledges would have done," which would have made the difficulties very much greater than they already were.[2]

Another advantage of the toboggan type of sleigh, in Rae's view, was the fact that in sledding one sometimes encountered "snow-waves or 'sastrugi'" which lay across the line of route. On his trip of 1853–54, for example, he came across waves which were "like those on water, steep on the *lee side* and not hard packed so that it was rather a stiff pull to take our sledges over them. I am certain that with loaded sledges of the high runner pattern such as are used by the Government

Expeditions, not more than four or five miles a day could have been made over such difficulties." Rae felt, as well, that a basic difficulty for sledges of the government arctic expeditions was that their runners were so narrow that (as the sailors who had to haul them said) they "buried themselves in the deep soft snow lying between the ice hummocks, giving immense trouble and labour in extracting them." By contrast, said Rae, his own "flat sledges in the form of the Indian 'toboggin'," not sinking in the snow, "having run down one hummock, ... by its own impetus went half-way up the next."[3]

Rae also wrote on the subject of adapting for naval use Rae's flat sledges with very low runners. Although the sledges of which he spoke were only fourteen inches wide, this width could be increased to at least three feet for eight men so as to carry 1,600 lb. or more if requisite. M'Clintock had claimed that Rae's type of sled would roll over readily; but when loaded in the ordinary way it would in fact have a greater stability than M'Clintock's own sled because the centre of gravity would be lower. On another occasion Rae said that the

sledge he had described was nearly 2 feet broad and would not turn over as Sir Leopold M'Clintock had ... asserted. If a man walked at the head of it he could prevent its turning over, and could keep it as steady as was necessary. In 1851 he travelled in a flat sledge only 14 inches wide where there was deep water, and got along very comfortably. These sledges had iron runners on them, which would work on hard snow or ice, but the moment they came to soft snow the flat part of the sledge prevented it from sinking.[4]

Indeed, said Rae, although M'Clintock had said "that Sir James Ross knew all about Hudson's Bay sledges and sledging" (Ross being M'Clintock's source of information on these matters), nevertheless this so-called knowledge on the part of Ross apparently came simply from hearsay, not experience. For Ross, so far as Rae knew, had not been in Hudson's Bay Company territory.[5]

Appendix 3

THE DOCUMENT FOUND AT POINT VICTORY IN 1859

The following is the text of the document found in 1859 at Point Victory on King William Island by Lieut. W. R. Hobson, RN, when serving under Capt. F. L. M'Clintock, RN, on the *Fox* voyage, 1857–59.[1] The record appears on one of the printed forms supplied to discovery ships for the purpose of being enclosed in bottles and thrown overboard at sea, in order to ascertain the set of the currents; any person finding such a record was requested to forward it to the secretary of the Admiralty, with a note of time and place. Upon this particular form there was written, apparently by Lieutenant Gore, the following:

28 of May, 1847. H. M. ships 'Erebus' and 'Terror' wintered in the ice in lat. 70° 5'N., long 98° 23'W.

Having wintered in 1846-7 at Beechey Island, in lat. 74° 43 28" N., long. 91° 39' 15" W., after having ascended Wellington Channel to lat. 77°, and returned by the west side of Cornwallis Island.

Sir John Franklin commanding the expedition.

All well.

Party consisting of 2 officers and 6 men left the ships on Monday 24th. May, 1847.

Gm. Gore, Lieut.

Chas. F. Des Voeux, Mate

In fact the *Erebus* and *Terror* had wintered at Beechey Island in 1845–46, not 1846–47, as "a glance at the date at the top and bottom of the record" shows. Around the margin of the paper another hand than Gore's had subsequently written:

April 25, 1848.- H.M. ships 'Terror' and 'Erebus' were deserted on the 22nd. April, 5 leagues N.N.W. of this, having been beset since 12th. September, 1846. The officers and crews, consisting of 105 souls, under the command of Captain F. R. M. Crozier, landed here in lat. 69° 37' 42" N., long. 98° 41' W.

Sir John Franklin died on the 11th. June, 1847; and the total loss by deaths in the expedition has been to this date 9 officers and 15 men.

(Signed)   (Signed)

    F. R. M. Crozier   *James Fitzjames*

  Captain and Senior Officer.   *Captain H.M.S. Erebus*

    and start on tomorrow, 26th., for Back's Fish River.

The marginal information was evidently written by Captain Fitzjames, excepting only the note stating when and where the members of the party planned to go, which was added by Captain Crozier. There is some additional marginal information relative to the transfer of the document, namely to the site of Sir James Ross's pillar, from a spot four miles northward, near Point Victory, where it had been originally deposited by Gore. The words "late" and "Commander" in reference to Gore in this added note show that Gore had been promoted, and had died, in the preceding twelve months.

Abbreviations

Adm	Admiralty Records, Public Record Office
Back, *Narrative*	George Back, *Narrative of the Arctic Land Expedition ... 1833–35* (London, 1836; reprint ed., Edmonton: Hurtig, 1970)
BM	British Museum
C.O.	Colonial Office Records, Public Record Office
DNB	*Dictionary of National Biography*
HBC	Hudson's Bay Company
ILN	*Illustrated London News*
King, *F. Exped.*	R. King, *The Franklin Expedition from First to Last* (London, 1855; revised ed., 1860)
King, *Narrative*	R. King, *Narrative of a Journey to the Shores of the Arctic Ocean*, 2 vols. (London, 1836)
M'Clintock, *Intrepid* Journal	Manuscript journal of F. L. M'Clintock in *Intrepid*, 1852–54, National Maritime Museum
NMM	National Maritime Museum, Greenwich
PP	Parliamentary Papers
PRO	Public Record Office
RAC	John Rae, *Rae's Arctic Correspondence, 1844–1855*, with introduction by J. M. Wordie and R. J. Cyriax. Vol. XVI of Hudson's Bay Record Society (London, 1953)
Rae "Achievements" Letter, Feb. 1856	"Voyages and Travels of Dr. Rae, In The Arctic Regions: Copy of a Letter from Dr. Rae to ----- February, 1856. London, February, 1856," in Wordie and Cyriax, Introduction, *Rae's Arctic Correspondence*, pp. xciii–c.
Rae, Autob. MS	Rae, Autobiographical manuscript, Scott Polar Research Institute, Cambridge
RGS	Royal Geographical Society
SPRI	Scott Polar Research Institute, Cambridge
Wonders, Introduction	W. C. Wonders, Introduction to Back, *Narrative* (1970)

Notes

CHAPTER 1

1. For an indication of the state of knowledge of the Arctic in 1818 see Map 1, reproduced from John Barrow, *A Chronological History of Voyages into the Arctic Regions*.

2. See V. Stefansson, *The Friendly Arctic*; idem, *Northwest to Fortune*; idem, *Great Adventures and Explorations from the Earliest Times to the Present*. For Neatby's viewpoint, see L. H. Neatby, *In Quest of the North West Passage*; idem, *The Search for Franklin*. For a well-known work of the same school as that of Neatby, see R. J. Cyriax, *Sir John Franklin's Last Arctic Expedition*.

3. Chief works of two seminal writers in this regard are H. A. Innis, *The Fur Trade in Canada* and D. G. Creighton, *The Commercial Empire of the St. Lawrence, 1760–1850*. On the school itself, see R. Winks, *Recent Trends and New Literature in Canadian History*, pp. 9–11; for the extent and location of the Shield see Map 2.

4. R. Glover, Introduction, *Cumberland and Hudson House Journals, 1775–82; First Series, 1775–79*, Publications of the H.B.R.S., XIV: xxv; W. J. Eccles, *The Canadian Frontier, 1534–1760*, p. 5.

5. Stefansson, *Northwest to Fortune*, pp. 102–6, 138–44; see also idem, *Not By Bread Alone*.

6. See "Pemmican and How To Make It," *Beaver* [295] (Summer 1964): 53–54; Rae, Autob. MS, pp. 877m–877n; H. H. Herstein, L. J. Hughes, and R. C. Kirbyson, *Challenge and Survival: The History of Canada*, p. 140; Sir John Richardson as quoted in A. Armstrong, *A Personal Narrative of the Discovery of the North-West Passage*, p. 258n. The quotation is from Herstein et al., p. 140.

7. A. M. Johnson, Introduction, *Saskatchewan Journals, 1795–1802*, Publications of the H.B.R.S., XXVI: lxxxviii–xc.

8. G. P. de T. Glazebrook, *A History of Transportation in Canada*, I, 21; E. E. Rich, *Montreal and The Fur Trade*, pp. 97–98; Glover, Introduction, XIV: xli–xlii.

9. On the York boat, see R. Glover, "York Boats," *Beaver* 279 (March 1949): 19–23; A. M. Johnson, "Mons. Maugenest Suggests ...," *Beaver* 287 (Summer 1956): 50–51; on its eclipse of the canoe, Glazebrook, *History of Transportation* II: 27–29.

10. Rich, *Montreal and the Fur Trade*, pp. 97–98.

11. P. D. Baird, *Expeditions to the Canadian Arctic*, pp. 2–3; Glyndwr Williams, *The British Search for the Northwest Passage in the Eighteenth Century*, p. 271; L. P. Kirwan, *A History of Polar Exploration*, pp. 88–97; N. M. Crouse, *The Search for the Northwest Passage*, pp. 24–37. See also W. C. Wonders, Preface, R. M'Clure, *The Discovery of the Northwest Passage* (reprint ed., 1967), pp. xvi–xvii; W. H. Hooper, "Voyage of the Isabella and Alexander in Search of a North-West Passage: 1818," MS diary, 2 vols., vol. A, pp. 1–3, RGS Archives.

12. Wonders, Introduction, p. xxxi.

13. Sir John Richardson, *Arctic Searching Expedition*, pp. 30–31.

14. Williams, *The British Search*, pp. 136–37.

15. Christopher Lloyd, *Mr. Barrow of the Admiralty: A Life of Sir John Barrow, 1764–1848*, esp. pp. 20 and 30; Sir John Barrow, *An Autobiographical Memoir of Sir John Barrow*; idem, *Voyages of Discovery and Research within the Arctic Regions*.

16. Parry to Lord Haddington, 18 Jan. 1845, Adm 7/187/3.

17. Augustus Petermann, "On the Geography of the Arctic Regions," *Athenaeum*, 22 Oct. 1853.

18. L. H. Neatby, *Conquest of the Last Frontier*, p. 16.

19. On Parry's second and third voyages, see W. E. Parry, *Journal of a Second Voyage*; G. F. Lyon, *The Private Journal ... during the recent voyage*; W. H. Hooper, "Diary of Wm. Hooper (Purser) Kept on Board *Fury*, Capt. W. E. Parry, 1821–23," MS diary, 2 vols., RGS Archives; W. E. Parry, *Journal of a Third Voyage*; and A. Parry, *Parry of the Arctic: The Life Story of Admiral Sir Edward Parry, 1790–1855*, in which the end map indicates how Parry stayed close to the shoreline on his second and third voyages.

20. C. Lloyd and W. L. S. Coulter, *Medicine and the Navy, 1200–1900*, IV, *1815–1900*, pp. 107–23.

21. Kirwan, *Polar Exploration*, p. 95.

22. Hooper, "Voyage of the Isabella and Alexander," vol. A, pp. 5–17, RGS Archives.

23. A. Parry, *Parry of the Arctic*, pp. 81 and 93; the quotation is from p. 81.

24. Kirwan, *Polar Exploration*, p. 95.

25. A. Parry, *Parry of the Arctic*, p. 82.

26. Stefansson, *The Friendly Arctic*, pp. 2–3.

27. A. Parry, *Parry of the Arctic*, p. 81. On sledging developments under Parry, see R. J. Cyriax, "Arctic Sledge Travelling by Officers of the Royal Navy, 1819–49," *Mariner's Mirror* XLIX: 127–31.

28. A. Parry, *Parry of the Arctic*, p. 82.

29. See a speech by Parry in 1853 (*Athenaeum*, 5 Nov. 1853), and similar comments by Sir George Sabine, one of Parry's officers on his first expedition (W. Kennedy, *A Short Narrative of the Second Voyage of Prince Albert*, p. 178).

30. F. L. M'Clintock, "Reminiscences of Arctic Ice-Travel ... With geological notes ... [by] the Rev. Samuel Haughton," *Royal Dublin Society Journal* I (1856–57): 217.

31. Kirwan, *Polar Exploration*, p. 95.

32. Quoted from Sir Clements Markham (*The Lands of Silence*) by A. Parry, *Parry of the Arctic*, p. 9.

33. For Franklin's two land journeys, see J. Franklin, *Narrative of a Journey to the Shores of the Polar Sea*; idem, *Narrative of a Second Expedition to the Shores of the Polar Sea*.

34. Sir Albert Hastings Markham, *Life of Sir John Franklin*, pp. 116–17. Franklin, however, also made use of the canoe to go to, and to travel in, the Arctic.

35. V. Hopwood, "Explorers by Land: To 1860" in C. F. Klinck, ed., *Literary History of Canada: Canadian Literature in English*, pp. 36–37. Wintering at Great Bear Lake, Franklin wrote long letters home on public events; as he and Back travelled separately they had a complicated system of exchanging home newspapers and periodicals (Franklin to Back, 22 Mar. 1827, quoted in Sotheby and Co., *Catalogue of Voyages and Travels*, nos. 34 and 35 (London, 19 and 20 May 1969), p. 93). This attitude of mind forms a contrast with that of John Rae, whose winter at Great Bear Lake (1850–51) was preoccupied, not with home affairs but with meticulous preparations for his journeys of 1851 (see below, chap. 6).

36. Quoted in E. E. Rich, *The History of the Hudson's Bay Company, 1670–1870*, Publications of the H.B.R.S., XXII: 381–82. Simpson had a similar view as regards the usefulness of army men in the Northwest (ibid., p. 381).

37. Rae to Simpson, 19 Nov. 1852, *RAC*, p. 233.

CHAPTER 2

1. L. P. Kirwan, *A History of Polar Exploration*, p. 109.

2. See J. Ross, *Treatise on Navigation by Steam*; G. Penn, *Up Funnel, Down Screw!*, p. 27.

3. See A. G. E. Jones, "The Duke of Cornwall's Harbour and Launceston and Victoria Railway Co. 1838–1849," mimeographed MS, March 1950, in E. Ross Collection; N. M. Crouse, *The Search for the Northwest Passage*, pp. 292–94.

4. Kirwan, *Polar Exploration*, p. 109; see also Penn, *Up Funnel, Down Screw!*, p. 13.

5. J. Braithwaite, *Supplement to Captain Sir John Ross's Narrative of a Second Voyage*, pp. 1–5; John Ross to James Ross, Glasgow, 27 Feb. 1829, in E. Ross Collection. The quotation is from Braithwaite, p. 4.

6. Edgar C. Smith'to *The Times*, 30 Oct. 1933.

7. John Ross, *Narrative of a Second Voyage in Search of a North-West Passage*, pp. 3–4.

8. J. Braithwaite, *Supplement to ... John Ross's Narrative*, pp. iin, 1–3; Ross, *Narrative of a Second Voyage*, p. 3; G. S. Graham, "The Transition from Paddle-Wheel to Screw Propeller," *Mariner's Mirror* XLIV: 40–41, 43. The quotation is from Ross, p. 3. That a Maudslay engine was supplied is evidenced by the finding of parts of it clearly marked "H. Maudslay of London" by the personnel of H.M.C.S. *Labrador* on a voyage into Victoria Harbour on 9 Sept. 1957 under the

command of Capt. T. C. Pullen (entry for 9 Sept. 1957 in private journal of Captain Pullen, as reported in a letter to the author, 9 Mar. 1967).

9. E. C. Smith to *The Times*, 30 Oct. 1933; also idem, "Some Episodes in early Ocean Steam Navigation," *Newcomen Society Transactions* VIII: 61–63. The plans of the *Victory* boilers are preserved at the Science Museum, London, in the *Notebooks* of Goodrich whom Smith calls "The Pepys of marine engineering."

10. W. Hooper, "Diary of Wm. Hooper ... on ... Fury ... 1821–23," vol. C, pp. 353–57, RGS Archives; King, *F. Exped.*, p. 183; Ross, *Narrative of a Second Voyage*, pp. 259–62 and map facing p. 262.

11. On James Ross's suspicion of Bellot Strait, see F. L. M'Clintock, *The Voyage of the Fox in Arctic Seas*, 5th ed., p. 153n, as cited in J. Wordie and R. Cyriax, Introduction, *RAC*, p. xxviin5. See also Ann Savours, "Sir James Clark Ross 1800–1862," *Geographical Journal* CXXVIII: 326; Ross, *Narrative of a Second Voyage*, p. 555, from which the quotation is taken.

12. These points are true despite a contrary statement in J. Wordie and R. Cyriax, Introduction, *RAC*, p. xxvii. The only believers in the peninsularity of Boothia before 1847 were Sir John Ross himself and Dr. Richard King; all other "Arctics," including Thomas Simpson, Franklin, and Rae believed before that time that Boothia was an island.

13. Ross, *Narrative of a Second Voyage*, chart facing p. [1]; L. H. Neatby, *The Search for Franklin*, pp. 71–72; on Ross's belief that King William's Land extended to Point Turnagain, see Wordie and Cyriax, Introduction, *RAC*, p. xxiii.

14. Ross, *Narrative of a Second Voyage*, p. 205. Parts of the machinery are to be seen today, however, at the Maritime Museum in Halifax, N.S.

15. E. C. Smith to *The Times*, 30 Oct. 1933; see also Braithwaite, *Supplement to ... John Ross's Narrative*; Sir John Ross, *Appendix to the Narrative of a Second Voyage*.

16. Ross, *Narrative of a Second Voyage*, pp. 3–7; P. D. Baird, *Expeditions to the Canadian Arctic*, p. 5; and S. Schmucker, ed., *Arctic Explorations and Discoveries during the Nineteenth Century*, pp. 86, 102–3, 131.

17. Back, *Narrative*, pp. 3–4, 638–66, 2, 13–17; F. L. M'Clintock, "On Arctic Sledge-travelling," *Proceedings of the Royal Geographical Society* XIX: 464–65; King, *Narrative*, II: 321.

18. George Back to Charles Back, 25 May 1820, in Sotheby and Co., *Catalogue 34 and 35* (London, May 19 and 20, 1969), p. 92.

19. *DNB*; George Back to Charles Back, 24 May 1820, read in the sale-rooms of Sotheby and Co., London, May 1969; R. Hood, quoted in King, *Narrative*, II: 182. There are other evidences of Back's small stature, as for example his uniform which remains in the family's possession (conversation with Mrs. A. W. Holmes, great-niece of Sir George Back, Strawberry Hill, May 1969).

20. See Neatby, *Search for Franklin*, pp. 87–88, from which the quotations are taken; on Back's relations with subordinates, see King, *Narrative*, I: 12; Back, *Narrative*, pp. 29–30, 422–23; Charles Ross to R. King, *F. Exped.*, p. xxxiv; Alexander Simpson, *The Life and Times of Thomas Simpson*, p. 106; for the sug-

gested contrast between Back's appearance and character, see F. Mowat, *Tundra*, caption between pp. 192 and 193; on a matter of discipline, entry by G. Back, 22 Sept. 1836, "Watch Exercise Book, Sept. 21, 1836, to Sept. 2, 1837" kept on board *Terror*, Back Papers, MS 395, folder concerning *Terror*, 1836–37, SPRI.

21. Back, *Narrative*, p. 17; King to Back, 14 Jan. 1833, SPRI; King to Secy. of the Admiralty, 18 Feb. 1850, King, *F. Exped.*, p. 79.

22. There is no entry of King's birth at Somerset House and *DNB* records simply "1811?". He was baptized on 16 May 1810 (Candidates Qualifications Books (Hall Registers) of the Court of Examiners of the Society of Apothecaries, Guildhall Library, MS 824/6, p. 9), and was nine years old when enrolled at St. Paul's School on 24 Jan. 1820 (letter of St. Paul's School Archivist to the author, 18 Dec. 1968). Combining these dates one concludes he was born between 24 Jan. and 16 May 1810. For details of King's parentage and early career see also Candidates Qualifications Books (Hall Registers) of the Court of Examiners of the Society of Apothecaries: Guildhall Library MSS 8241/6, p. 9; 8241, p. 756; 8249/2, fol. 103r; and 8206/4, fol. 67r.; the Register of Guy's Hospital; *Borough of Marylebone Mercury*, 12 Feb. 1876. He was not, incidentally, the Richard King who served as assistant surgeon aboard *Resolute* in the expedition to the Arctic under Capt. Horatio Austin in 1850–51.

23. See R. King to Dr. T. Hodgkin, 5 June 1840, Journal MSS. Files, RGS Archives; on King's contributions to Back's *Narrative*, see Back, *Narrative*, pp. 523–42, 563–94, and on King's medical ministrations, ibid., pp. 187–88; on King's humaneness, see King, *Narrative*, esp. II: 49–54 and 58–59, and King to Back, 14 Jan. 1833, SPRI; on King's belief that a medical training was an asset in arctic exploration, see King, *F. Exped.*, p. 32, and King to Sir John Philpot, 11 Feb. 1836, Belcher Collection, B CL 1, NMM.

24. The quotations are from entries for 11 and 15 Oct. 1845 in the MS diary of George Dann Banes, foreman shipwright and surveyor, who heard King speak at a Mechanics Institute in Liverpool on the dates named; on King's relations with the men of the Back party, see C. Ross to R. King, 7 Nov. 1836, in King, *F. Exped.*, p. xxxiv, and also letters from Peter Taylor and Alexander McLeod to King, ibid., pp. xxxv–xxxviii.

25. Wonders, Introduction, p. xiii, and H. E. McClure, "Barren Land Bugs," *Beaver* 267 (March 1937): 16; quotations on geology are from Wonders and those on biology and botany from McClure. For a succinct description of the barrens by King himself, see King, *Narrative*, I: 256–57.

26. See, on Hearne's evidence, R. King to Duke of Newcastle, 23 Jan. 1860, King, *F. Exped.* (1860), p. 269, quoting from *Geographical Journal* III: 70; on the Back trip, Back, *Narrative*, pp. 328, 331, 371, and also 319–20, 323, 325, 369; on Simpson's experience, T. Simpson, *Narrative of the Discoveries on the North Coast of America*, p. 365; on the Anderson trip, J. Anderson to G. Simpson, 17 Sept. 1855, PP, *Accounts and Papers*, 7856: 41 [2124]: 29, as well as "Chief Factor James Anderson's Back River Journal of 1855," *Canadian Field Naturalist* LIV: 12 and 108 from which the quotation is taken.

27. See Wonders, Introduction, pp. xii–xiv, from which the quotations are taken; on Indian fear of Eskimos, see R. King to Captain Washington, 8 May 1837, RGS Archives.

28. Back to W. G. Romaine, Secy. to the Admiralty, 3 June 1857, Holmes Collection; Wonders, Introduction, p. xxi; Back, *Narrative*, p. 7; Sir John Richardson, memorandum, "Members of the Expedition," n.d., RGS Archives.

29. King, *Narrative*, I: 37–39, 174; Back, *Narrative*, pp. 185–86. The quotations are from King, I: 174 and Back, pp. 185–86.

30. See Back, *Narrative*, pp. 188–89, 66–67, 87; on boats and canoes, King, *Narrative*, I: 117–18, 61, 113, 291; on King's plan, ibid., pp. 48, 49, 131–33.

31. King, *Narrative*, I: 184, 192–93; II: 290–91. The quotation is from I: 193.

32. Back, *Narrative*, pp. 75–76, 87, 106–7, 197–98; King, *Narrative*, I: 184–85. King's map of 1845 shows that in that year he still believed the Thelon, or Fish River as he called it, entered the Arctic to the east of Boothia.

33. See Back, *Narrative*, pp. 88, 190–91, 198–99, 205–6; King, *Narrative*, I: 160–61, from which the quotations are taken.

34. Back, *Narrative*, pp. 243–45, 635–37; Cyriax and Wordie, Introduction, *RAC*, p. xv; King, *Narrative*, I: 203, 208; Richardson, "Members of the Expedition," RGS Archives. The quotations are from Richardson and from King, I: 203.

35. On the instructions, see Back, *Narrative*, pp. 18–20; the quotations are from p. 19.

36. King, *Narrative*, I: 201, 202, 214, 216, 251–52; Back, *Narrative*, p. 247.

37. See King, *Narrative*, I: 216–17, 251–52, 291; II: 67–72, 310–11; Back, *Narrative*, pp. 236, 261–62, 316. The quotation is from King, II: 310–11. Back gives the weight of the boat as 3,360 lbs.

38. Back, *Narrative*, pp. 390, 20–21; the quotations are from pp. 21 and 390.

39. King, *Narrative*, I: 221–22.

40. King to Captain Washington, 8 May 1837, RGS Archives, from which the quotations are taken; Crouse, *Search for the Northwest Passage*, p. 347; Richardson, "Members of the Expedition," RGS Archives.

41. Back, *Narrative*, pp. 392–94, 407–8; the quotations are from pp. 407–8.

42. Crouse, *Search for a Northwest Passage*, p. 348, from which the quotation is taken; see also Back, *Narrative*, pp. 423–25.

43. Back, *Narrative*, pp. 408, 423–25, and the end map; the quotations are from pp. 408 and 425. See also Crouse, *Search for a Northwest Passage*, pp. 348–49.

44. The quotations are from Back, *Narrative*, pp. 16, 425.

45. See King to Hodgkin, 5 June 1840, Journal MSS Files, RGS Archives, from which the quotations are taken; King, *Narrative*, II: 26–28, 67–72, 310–11.

46. King, *Narrative*, II: 29, 320, 70–71; L. H. Neatby, *In Quest of the North West Passage*, pp. 113–14; Richardson, "Members of the Expedition," RGS Archives; Back, *Narrative*, pp. 16, 20; on King's cache at Montreal Island, see King to Hodgkin, 5 June 1840, Journal MSS Files, RGS Archives.

47. King, *Narrative*, II, 76–77, 284, 311–12; King to Hodgkin, 5 June 1840,

RGS Archives; Back, *Narrative*, pp. 463–72. The quotation is from King, II: 311–12.

48. Thomas Simpson to Alexander Simpson, 7 Mar. 1834, in A. Simpson, *Thomas Simpson*, p. 108; King to the Royal Geographical Society, [1836], in King, *Narrative*, II: 302.

CHAPTER 3

1. King, *Narrative*.

2. King to Sir John Philpot (editor of *The Naval and Military Gazette*), 11 Feb. 1836, Belcher Papers B Cl 1, NMM.

3. See at the RGS Archives: King to Captain Whittington, RN, 5 Jan. 1837; King to Dr. Hodgkin, 5 June 1840, Journal MSS Files; and "Richard King's Arctic Expedition Subscriptions," n.d. See also Ann Savours, "Sir James Clark Ross 1800–1862," *Geographical Journal* CXXVIII: 326; for a copy of the métis map, see King, *Narrative*, II: facing 289, and for the quotations, ibid., p. 292, and King to Hodgkin, 5 June 1840.

4. The quotations are from King to Hodgkin, 5 June 1840, RGS Archives, and King to Philpot, 11 Feb. 1836, Belcher Papers, NMM; see also *Naval and Military Gazette*, 30 Jan. and 6, 13 Feb. 1836.

5. For the naval men's proposals, see "Communications on a North-West Passage," *Journal of the Royal Geographical Society* VI: 34–50; for, respectively, King's plan and Dr. Hodgkin's letter to the Committee of the Geographical Society on King's behalf, see King, *Narrative*, II: 301–5 and ibid., pp. 292–301. See also King, *F. Exped.*, pp. xiv–xv; King to Hodgkin, 5 June 1840, RGS Archives. The quotation is from King, *Narrative*, II: 292.

6. See King, *Narrative*, II: 301–3, from which (p. 303) the quotation is taken; King to Philpot, 11 Feb. 1836, Belcher Papers.

7. See King, *Narrative*, II: 295–97; King, *F. Exped.*, pp. x and 13.

8. See King, *Narrative*, II: 295, 300; King, *F. Exped.*, pp. ix–x, xii.

9. See, for example, Back, *Narrative*, pp. 186–89.

10. King, *Narrative*, II: 298–99; C. J. Bartlett, *Great Britain and Sea Power, 1815–1853*, p. 36.

11. See Sir John Franklin, "Report of Sir John Franklin," [1836], as quoted in Richard King, "On the Unexplored Coast of North America," *London, Edinburgh and Dublin Philosophical Magazine and Journal of Science* XX (3rd ser.): 491–92. For the original MS of Franklin's report, see Library MSS, Sir John Franklin, no. 5, RGS Archives.

12. King, "On the Unexplored Coast of North America," pp. 492–94; see also idem, *F. Exped.*, pp. xiv, 188; King cited Back, *Narrative* (1836 ed.), pp. 81–86 and 152, as evidence that the area from Fond du Lac to the Thelon, and along the Thelon banks, was wooded.

13. See A. Simpson, *The Life and Travels of Thomas Simpson*, pp. 174–76; the quotations are from pp. 174–75. See also King, *Narrative*, II: 49–54.

14. See King to Captain Whittington, RN, 5 Jan. 1837, RGS Archives, from

which the quotations are taken; L. H. Neatby, *In Quest of the North West Passage*, p. 115.

15. London Post Office Directories; entry of death, Somerset House, 4 Feb. 1876; King, *F. Exped.*, p. 66; *Borough of Marylebone Mercury*, 12 Feb. 1876; *Athenaeum*, 12 Feb. 1876; letter of the Librarian of the Royal Anthropological Institute, London, to the author, 12 Aug. 1968; one of King's best-known medical works was *The Preservation of Infants in Delivery; Being an Exposition of the Chief Causes of Mortality in Still-Born Children* (London, 1847; 2nd ed., 1858).

16. On the accuracy of King's views, see: A. Simpson, *Thomas Simpson*, pp. 174–75; J. P. Kelsall, *The Migratory Barren-Ground Caribou of Canada*, pp. 106–7, 109–10, and end map. On King's reaction to criticism of his views, see: King, *Narrative*, I: 222; King to Hodgkin, 5 June 1840, RGS Archives; King, *F. Exped.*, pp. xxxiii–xxxviii. The quotations are from Kelsall, p. 106, and A. Simpson, p. 175.

17. King, *F. Exped.*, pp. 10–11.

18. See A. Simpson, *Thomas Simpson*, p. 176; L. H. Neatby, *The Search for Franklin*, pp. 88–89; V. Stefansson, *Northwest to Fortune*, p. 149, from which the quoted phrase is taken.

19. King to Hodgkin, 5 June 1840, RGS Archives; see also King to Lord Stanley, 20 Feb. 1845, as quoted in King, *F. Exped.*, p. 9, from which the phrase "intelligent traveller" is taken.

20. King to Lord Stanley, secretary of state for the colonies, 24 Jan. 1842, in King, "On the Unexplored Coast of North America," pp. 488–89.

21. See Wordie and Cyriax, Introduction, *RAC*, p. xxviii and n1; Neatby, *Search for Franklin*, p. 90; King to Hodgkin, 5 June 1840, RGS Archives.

22. King to Hodgkin, 5 June 1840, RGS Archives.

23. Thomas Simpson to George Simpson, 25 Oct. 1839, quoted in A. Simpson, *Thomas Simpson*, p. 340.

24. See Thomas Simpson to the Directors of the Company, 18 Oct. 1839, as quoted, ibid., pp. 340–42.

25. Governor and Committee of the Hudson's Bay Company to C. F. Duncan Finlayson, 4 Mar. 1840, HBC B. 235 1/b/4, f. 21; idem to idem, 3 June 1840, as quoted in A. Simpson, *Thomas Simpson*, pp. 343–44; see also HBC B. 235/b/4, f. 109.

26. George Simpson to Thomas Simpson, 4 June 1840, HBC D. 4/25, ff. 193, 191.

27. Ibid., ff. 193–94; see also G. Williams, *The British Search for the Northwest Passage in the Eighteenth Century*, pp. 136–37, and *RAC*, p. 5 and n5, where puzzlement that George Simpson could think Repulse Bay a strait fades before the additional evidence found in this letter to Thomas that he did not fully know the arctic story.

28. See Neatby, *Search for Franklin*, p. 48; on the attitude of the company and George Simpson towards the Back River, see: The Governor and Committee to Dease and Simpson, 31 May 1838, HBC B. 235/b/4, f. 43; G. Simpson to T.

Simpson, 2 July 1836, as quoted in T. Simpson, *Narrative of the Discoveries on the North Coast of America ... 1836–39*, p. 7; A. Simpson, *Thomas Simpson*, p. 337n.

29. George Simpson to Thomas Simpson, 4 June 1840, HBC D. 4/25, ff. 190–92.

30. T. Simpson to A. Simpson, 19 June 1833, as quoted in A. Simpson, *Thomas Simpson*, p. 106.

31. Neatby, *Search for Franklin*, pp. 88–89, from which the quotation is taken; see also R. M. Ballantyne, *Hudson's Bay* (Boston, 1859), p. 101; A. Simpson, *Thomas Simpson*, pp. 100–4.

32. See Neatby, *Search for Franklin*, p. 91, and Thomas Simpson to George Simpson, 25 Oct. 1839, as quoted in A. Simpson, *Thomas Simpson*, p. 339, from which the quotations are respectively taken.

33. George Simpson to D. Finlayson, 10 Sept. 1840, HBC D. 4/25, f. 196.

34. On the death of Thomas Simpson, see Stefansson, *Northwest to Fortune*, p. 151; Neatby, *In Quest of the North West Passage*, pp. 127–29; idem, *Search for Franklin*, p. 91. See also D. MacKay and W. K. Lamb, "More Light on Thomas Simpson," *Beaver* 269 (September 1938): 26–31; R. M. Ballantyne, *Hudson's Bay*, pp. 100–101; J. A. Stevenson, "The Unsolved Death of Thomas Simpson, Explorer," *Beaver* 266 (June 1935): 17–20, 64–66. The argument has been advanced that George Simpson was in some way implicated in his cousin's death and was reluctant thoroughly to investigate it (Stefansson, *Northwest to Fortune*, p. 151; Neatby, *Search for Franklin*, p. 91). At least the first of these charges appears to be answered in Neatby, ibid. The letters of George Simpson of 4 June and 10 September 1840, quoted above, detract from the basic charge rather than reinforce it.

35. George Simpson to C. F. Duncan Finlayson, 10 Sept. 1840 HBC D. 4/25, f. 197.

36. King to Lord Stanley, 24 Jan. 1842, "On the Unexplored Coast of North America," pp. 488–90; E. B. Wilbraham, Pte. Secy. to Lord Stanley, to King, 16 Feb. 1842, ibid. p. 490.

37. "King, Arctic Expeditions," n.d., holograph statement marked "Rec'd. 3 May 1842," RGS Archives.

38. King, "On the Unexplored Coast of North America," pp. 488–94; see also King to Hodgkin, 5 June 1840, and "King, Arctic Expeditions ... Rec'd. 3 May 1842," both in the RGS Archives. The quotations are from King, "On the Unexplored Coast of North America," pp. 488 and 491.

39. See King, *Narrative*, II: 26–27, 311–12; King to Lord Stanley, 24 Jan. 1842, in King, "On the Unexplored Coast of North America," p. 490.

40. See Farley Mowat, *Tundra*, p. 220, from which the quotation is taken; for King's fundamental view, see *inter alia*, King, *Narrative*, II: 294, 302–3, and King to Hodgkin, 5 June 1840, RGS Archives.

41. King to Hodgkin, 5 June 1840, RGS Archives.

42. See King, *Narrative*, II: 302–3, and King to Hodgkin, 5 June 1840, RGS

Archives, from which, respectively, the quotations are taken; on the greater navigability of a northern passage, see H. Larsen, *The North-West Passage, 1940–1942, and 1944*, pp. 8, [36], and 51.

43. See Savours, "Sir James Clark Ross 1800–1862," p. 327.

44. Hopwood, "Explorers by Land: To 1860," pp. 36–38; the quotations are from pp. 36–37.

45. In G. Back, "Sir George Back Diaries," holograph diaries, 1844–78, 25 vols., SPRI, there are numerous entries regarding social occasions; examples for the mid-1840s are at 10, 14, 17, 18 June 1844 and 5, 7, 15 Mar. 1845.

46. King, *Narrative*, II: 310.

47. Report of attitude and information of Dr. Hugh Rump, Norfolk, who knew King when Rump was a boy. (Note, 7 Dec. 1896, by the explorer H. W. Feilden in Feilden's copy of King's *Narrative*, now in Feilden Correspondence, RGS Archives; italics Feilden's.)

48. Back, *Narrative*, p. 179.

CHAPTER 4

1. See R. J. Cyriax and J. Wordie, "Centenary of the Sailing of Sir John Franklin with the *Erebus* and *Terror*," *Geographical Journal* CVI, nos. 5 and 6: 173–74.

2. See Barrow to the Admiralty and Council of the Royal Society, [mid-] December 1844, in C. R. Weld, *Arctic Expeditions: A Lecture*, p. 21, from which the quotation is taken; Barrow to Lord Haddington, 27 Dec. 1844, Adm 7/187/1, and Sir John Barrow, unpublished introduction to *Voyages of Discovery and Research*, in BM Add. MSS 35301 (Barrow Bequest, vol. II), p. 6.

3. Barrow to Admiralty and Council of the Royal Society, [mid-] December 1844, p. 21; Lord Northampton to Lord Haddington, 18 Jan. 1845, Adm 7/187/2; copy of a letter by Sir Edward Sabine, Adm 7/187/5; pars. 13–16, instructions to Franklin, 3 and 5 May 1845, Adm 7/187/8.

4. E. Sabine, preface to Admiral F. Von Wrangell, *Narrative of an Expedition to the Polar Sea in the Years 1820, 1821, 1822 and 1823*, ed. E. Sabine, pp. vi, vii, x–xiv; see also Barrow (27 Dec. 1844), Parry (18 Jan. 1845), and J. C. Ross (25 Jan. 1845) to Lord Haddington in, respectively, Adm 7/187/1, –/3, and –/5.

5. Parry (18 Jan. 1845), Franklin (24 Jan. 1845), J. C. Ross (25 Jan. 1845) to Lord Haddington in, respectively, Adm 7/187/3, –/4, and –/5; L. P. Kirwan, *A History of Polar Exploration*, p. 180; Barrow to Admiralty and Council of the Royal Society [mid-] December 1844, pp. 20–21.

6. See Kathleen Fitzpatrick, *Sir John Franklin in Tasmania, 1837–1843*, chaps. IX, XII, and, in the Epilogue, pp. 369–74, esp. p. 370; Sir John Franklin, *Narrative of Some Passages in the History of Van Diemann's Land*; E. Parry, *Memoirs of Rear-Admiral Sir W. Edward Parry*, p. 367.

7. See Franklin to Lord Haddington, 24 Jan. 1845, Adm 7/187/4; Franklin to Parry, 10 July 1845, as quoted in E. Parry, *Memoirs of Rear-Admiral Sir W. Edward Parry*, p. 311; Franklin to Richardson, 7 July 1845, MS 248/314, SPRI. See also, on Franklin and Peel Sound, Franklin to J. C. Ross, 10 Feb. 1845, and

accompanying memorandum, MSS 248/316/22 and 22a, SPRI; on Franklin and Simpson Strait, S. Osborn, *Stray Leaves from an Arctic Journal*, p. 292, and Capt. James Fitzjames, "Journal of James Fitzjames Aboard Erebus, 1845," 8 June 1845, *Nautical Magazine* XXI: 160.

8. See Franklin's instructions, 3 and 5 May, 1845, Adm 7/187/8, from which the quotations are taken; Barrow to Admiralty and Council of the Royal Society, [mid-] December 1844, pp. 19–20; Barrow (27 Dec. 1845), Parry (18 Jan. 1845), Franklin (24 Jan. 1845), and J. C. Ross (25 Jan. 1845) to Lord Haddington in, respectively, Adm 7/187/1, –/3, –/4, –/5.

9. Instructions by Sir George Simpson to John Rae in Simpson to Rae, 15 June 1846, as quoted in J. Rae, *Narrative of an Expedition to the Shores of the Arctic Sea in 1846 and 1847*, p. 15; the instructions in full are at pp. 14–17.

10. Ibid., in particular pars. 1 and 9 at pp. 14 and 17. See also Rae, Autob. MS, pp. 702–3; R. M. Ballantyne, *Hudson's Bay . . .* (1848), pp. 225–26, as quoted in Wordie and Cyriax, Introduction, *RAC*, pp. xix; on Sir George Simpson's and Rae's specific hope that Melville was peninsular, see George Simpson to Thomas Simpson, 4 June 1840, HBC D.4/25 f. 191, and Rae to Simpson, 25 Feb. 1845, *RAC*, p. 5, from which the quotation is taken; on Simpson's awareness of public interest in a passage, see also George Simpson to Thomas Simpson, 4 June 1840, f. 193, and Simpson to Rae, 1 Dec. 1853, *RAC*, p. 342.

11. See Wordie and Cyriax, Introduction, *RAC*, pp. xvi–xviii; and Rae, *Narrative*, p. 2.

12. See Rae, Autob. MS, chap. I, pp. 3, 5–6, 8–10; chap. II, esp. pp. 45–46, 53–54, 74–77, 80–86b.

13. On Rae's prowess as traveller and sportsman and Simpson's selection of him for these reasons, see Wordie and Cyriax, Introduction, *RAC*, pp. xvi–xviii; Rae, "Achievements Letter," Feb. 1856, p. xcvii; and Rae, Autob. MS, p. 204; on the delay while he learnt navigation, see Wordie and Cyriax, Introduction, *RAC*, pp. xviii, xxviii.

14. See Fitzjames, "Journal," 6 June 1845, pp. 159–60; Franklin to Parry, Whale Fish Island, 10 July 1845, as quoted in E. Parry, *Memoirs of Rear-Admiral Sir W. Edward Parry*, p. 312; Rae's instructions, Rae, *Narrative*, pp. 14–15; Rae to Feilden, 19 Apr. 1878, RGS Archives; Rae, *Narrative*, Appendix, pp. 199–217; the quotations are from Fitzjames and Franklin to Parry.

15. See King, *F. Exped.*, pp. 186–87, and King's sketch map, referred to in note 16 below; Count Eigil Knuth, *Archeology of the Musk-Ox Way*.

16. The chart, dated 31 Jan. 1845, was first reproduced in King, *F. Exped.*, between pp. 170 and 171.

17. For quotations and references which follow, save where otherwise stated, see King to Lord Stanley, 20 Feb. 1845, ibid., pp. 5–11; the original is not in the Colonial Office papers. King also at this time addressed three letters to Sir John Barrow, 21 Dec. 1844, and 8 and 31 Jan. 1845 (ibid., pp. 171–80, 180–88, 188–94), the originals of which are not in the Admiralty papers; much of what King wrote to Stanley is in his earlier letter to Barrow, 31 Jan. 1845, pp. 189–92.

18. King, *F. Exped.*, p. 195n.

19. King to Barrow, 21 Dec. 1844, ibid., pp. 178–79.

20. See plans of *Erebus* and *Terror*, NMM. Principal plans, Press Box 62: for *Erebus*, Regd. nos. 4434, 4436, 4437, 4438 and 6137; for *Terror*, Regd. nos. 4366, 6132, 6133A, and 6136; see esp. 6137 and 6132. See also description of the vessels in N. Wright, *The Quest for Franklin*, pp. 98–99 and *ILN*, 24 May 1845.

21. Sir John Ross, *The Rear Admiral Sir John Franklin*, pp. 14–15.

22. See J. C. Ross to Sir James Graham, 22 Jan. 1834, Sir James Ross Letter Book, S.L. 25, Office of the Hydrographer.

23. K. Barnes at Whitehall, Admiralty, to F. L. M'Clintock, 4 Jan. 1881, M'Clintock Papers, M Cl/45a, NMM; see also copy of minute, 15 Jan. 1848, Dept. of the Surveyor of the Navy, Adm 7/187.

24. For specifications and a description of Rae's boats, see Rae, Autob. MS, pp. 234, 240, and Rae, *Narrative*, pp. 4, 6; the quoted phrase is from Rae, Autob. MS, p. 240.

25. See "Footnotes to the Franklin Search," *Beaver* 285 (Spring 1955): 46–48; P. Halkett, *Boat-Cloak, or Cloak-Boat*, and Rae, *Narrative*, p. 176.

26. King to Barrow, 31 Jan. 1845, King, *F. Exped.*, pp. 189–91.

27. C. Bartlett, *Great Britain and Sea Power, 1815–1853*, esp. pp. 158–74, 219–35; see also G. S. Graham, "The Transition from Paddle-Wheel to Screw Propeller," *Mariner's Mirror* XLIV: [35]–48.

28. See Parry to Lord Haddington, 18 Jan. 1845, Adm 7/187/3; plans of *Erebus* and *Terror*, Press Box 62, nos. 6137 and 6132, NMM.

29. On lack of time, see Adm Ind. 12249/68/5a; for specifications of the engines, brief description, and trials, see, respectively, J. Bourne, *A Treatise on the Screw Propeller*, p. i; *ILN*, 24 May 1845; C. R. Weld, *Arctic Expeditions: A Lecture*, p. 26.

30. Fitzjames, "Journal," 10 July 1845, pp. 200–201.

31. Kirwan, *Polar Exploration*, p. 180. For details of provisioning of the Franklin expedition, see Victualling Dept., "Miscellanea," vol. 17, Adm 7/114/17; *ILN*, 24 May 1845.

32. Ross, *Rear Admiral Sir John Franklin*, p. 9; A. M'Murdo, quoted in Sir George Back, Back MS Diaries, 27 Feb. 1845, SPRI. Back himself recorded that "[Franklin] is to go on Polar Expedition!!! He is fifty-eight years old" (Back Diaries, 7 Feb. 1845).

33. Fitzjames, "Journal," 10 June 1845, p. 161; ibid., 1 July 1845, p. 199; ibid., p. 197 from which the quotation is taken.

34. On Franklin's progress, see R. J. Cyriax, *Sir John Franklin's Last Arctic Expedition*, p. 103, and M'Clintock, *Voyage of the "Fox"* (1859), pp. 283–84; on the steam machinery, see "1851 Lt. Sh. Osborn R.N. Note on Franklin," Journal MSS Arctic 1851 (Osborn), RGS Archives; on an open season, A. Lubbock, *The Arctic Whalers*, p. 345.

35. On suggested use of the boats, see Franklin to Richardson, Whale Fish Islands, 7 July 1845, 248/314, SPRI, and Lieutenant Le Vesconte, as cited in

A.B.B. (pseud.), "Reflections on Sir John Franklin's Expedition, and Where his Ships Were Most Probably Beset in the Ice," *Nautical Magazine* XXV, no. 3: 133; on Franklin's return to Barrow Strait, see A. Taylor, *Geographical Discovery and Exploration in the Queen Elizabeth Islands*, p. 32.

36. See *ILN*, 14 Oct. 1851; R. J. Cyriax, "Notes on Noel Wright's *New Light on Franklin*, Ipswich, 1949, and *Quest for Franklin*, London 1959," Library MSS, RGS Archives. See also, as the writer specifically referred to, S. Osborn, *Stray Leaves from an Arctic Journal*, pp. 297–99, 94–95.

37. M'Clintock, *Intrepid* Journal, pp. 99–100.

38. M'Clintock, *Voyage of the "Fox"* (1859), p. 287.

39. Cyriax, *Franklin's Last Arctic Expedition*, pp. 198, 123; in support of the speculations Cyriax cites (p. 123) "Report of Scientific Researches made during the late Arctic voyage of the yacht 'Fox'," in *Proceedings of the Royal Society* 10 (London, 1860): 148–51.

40. For the tonnages see, respectively, S. E. Morison, *The European Discovery of America*, p. 613, and Sir Edward Evans, *British Polar Explorers*, p. 24.

41. See Cyriax, *Franklin's Last Arctic Expedition*, pp. 123–25, 146n, 149.

42. The quotation is from ibid., p. 125; see also Sir Allen Young, *The Search for Sir John Franklin*, p. 41.

43. P. D. Baird, *Expeditions to the Canadian Arctic*, p. 7.

44. See M'Clintock, *Voyage of the "Fox"* (1881), pp. 246, 257.

45. See M'Clintock, *Intrepid* Journal, p. 233.

46. For a transcript of this document, and of the superinscriptions of April 1848, see M'Clintock, *Voyage of the "Fox"* (1859), pp. 283–84, 286.

47. W. Gibson, "Sir John Franklin's Last Voyage," *Beaver* 268 (June 1937): 50 and 52n; see also Cyriax and Wordie, "Centenary of the Sailing of Sir John Franklin," pp. 178–79.

48. V. Stefansson, *The Friendly Arctic* (1921), p. 323; see also Cyriax, *Franklin's Last Arctic Expedition*, p. 142.

49. The ships were subsequently lost. One of them "is believed to have foundered in Victoria Strait" and the other "seems to have drifted to O'Reilly Island, where she was found and ransacked by Eskimos before she too sank" (Cyriax and Wordie, "Centenary of the Sailing of Sir John Franklin," p. 179), although any drifting of a Franklin vessel to O'Reilly Island is doubted by L. A. Learmonth, retired chief trader, Hudson's Bay Company, and student of the Franklin party and searches (conversations with the author, Georgetown, Ont., 4–5 Sept. 1976). See also, on traces of the Franklin expedition, Wordie and Cyriax, Introduction, *RAC*, p. xxxix; R. J. Cyriax, "Recently Discovered Traces of the Franklin Expedition," *Geographical Journal* CXVII, pt. 2: [211]–214; and "Chart Showing ... King William Island [and] ... Positions of ... Relics [of] the ... Expedition under ... Franklin" (Admiralty Chart 5101).

50. On some of these factors and possible incentives, see Osborn, *Stray Leaves*, pp. 276, 292, and Cyriax, *Franklin's Last Arctic Expedition*, pp. 147–49; these sources do not, however, discuss effects of scurvy upon mental processes.

51. M'Clintock, *Voyage of the "Fox"* (1881), p. 252.

52. King, *Narrative*, II: 295–97; for evidence that the *Narrative* had been carried aboard *Erebus* and *Terror* see Cyriax, *Franklin's Last Arctic Expedition*, pp. 146n, 149.

53. Rae to Mrs. Vaughan, 16 May 1889, RGS Archives.

54. For the view that none of the Franklin party reached Montreal Island, see C. F. Hall to H. Grinnell, 20 June 1869, in J. E. Nourse, *Narrative of the Second Arctic Expedition by C. F. Hall*, p. 415.

55. Cyriax, *Franklin's Last Arctic Expedition*, pp. 164–65.

56. Cyriax and Wordie, "Centenary of the Sailing of Sir John Franklin," p. 180.

57. For a further discussion of these points, see Appendix 1.

58. Rae, *Narrative*, p. 13; *ILN*, 24 May 1845.

59. Rae, *Narrative*, p. 63.

60. Rae to Governor, Deputy Governor and Committee of the Hudson's Bay Company, 21 Sept. 1847, *RAC*, p. 53.

61. See Rae, *Narrative*, pp. 66–68; and J. and M. Bird, "John Rae's Stone House," *Beaver* 284 (March 1954): [34]–35.

62. See Rae, "Achievements" Letter, Feb. 1856, p. xcvii; and Rae to Governor …, 21 Sept. 1847, *RAC*, p. 55.

63. See Rae to Governor …, 21 Sept. 1847, *RAC*, pp. 55–56; the quotations are from pp. 56. See also Rae, *Narrative*, pp. 82–84.

64. Rae, *Narrative*, p. 89.

65. Ibid., pp. 91–92; Rae to Governor …, 21 Sept. 1847, *RAC*, p. 56.

66. Rae to Mrs. Vaughan, 16 May 1889, RGS Archives.

67. Rae, *Narrative*, pp. 100, 107, and 146 from which the quotation is taken.

68. Rae, Autob. MS, pp. 877m–877n.

69. On Rae's chronometers and estimation of distances, see Rae in discussion portion of G. Nares, "On the Navigation of Smith Sound as a *Route* to the Polar Sea," *Proceedings of the Royal Geographical Society* XXI: 285; on magnetic variation and scientific samples, see Rae to Feilden, 19 Apr. 1878, Library MSS, RGS Archives. See also Rae, *Narrative*, pp. 101, 102, 141.

70. Rae, *Narrative*, pp. 11–12; Rae to Governor …, 21 Sept. 1847, *RAC*, p. 58.

71. Rae, *Narrative*, pp. 117 and Arrowsmith map facing title page; Rae, discussion in G. Nares, "On the Navigation of Smith Sound," p. 285; *Athenaeum*, 20 Nov. 1847; Rae to Governor …, 21 Sept. 1847, *RAC*, p. 60.

72. Rae to Simpson, 10 Aug. 1847, *RAC*, pp. 40–41; Rae to Governor …, 21 Sept. 1847, ibid., p. 61; Rae, *Narrative*, p. 133.

73. Rae, *Narrative*, pp. 137–38.

74. Ibid., p. 142. This description suggests a lack of snowshoes.

75. Ibid., pp. 155–56, and Rae to Simpson, 10 Aug. 1847, *RAC*, p. 41, from which the quotation is taken.

76. V. Stefansson, "Rae's Arctic Correspondence," *Beaver* 284 (March 1954): 36–37; J. Rae, *Snow-Huts, Sledges and Sledge Journeys*, p. 5, from which total

distances and daily rates are taken; Rae, "Achievements" Letter, Feb. 1856, p. xcix, from which the length of new coastline is taken; see also Rae to Mrs. Vaughan, 16 May 1889, RGS Archives.

77. Rae to Simpson, 20 Sept. 1847, *RAC*, p. 45, from which the quotations are taken; Rae, *Narrative*, Appendix, pp. 199–217; see also Rae to Feilden, 19 Apr. 1878, Library MSS, RGS Archives.

78. Stefansson, "Rae's Arctic Correspondence," p. 36.

79. For Sir John Ross's reaction, see Rae to Simpson, 2 Nov. 1847, *RAC*, p. 68; for King's reaction, see King to Earl Grey, 25 Nov. 1847, C.O. 323/232, and also in *Athenaeum*, 27 Nov. 1847.

80. Rae to Sir George Back, 11 March 1848, MS 395 (unsorted), SPRI.

81. Rae, Autob. MS, quoted in A. Cooke, "The Autobiography of Dr. John Rae (1813–1893): A Preliminary Note," *Polar Record* XIV: 174; see also Rae to Simpson, 1 Aug. 1850, *RAC*, pp. 136–37.

82. See Rae to Sir Francis Beaufort, Methy Portage, 24 June 1850, and the chart, both in Misc. 19, folder 4, Hydrographer's Office; two rivers, the Arrowsmith and the Kellett, do in fact flow into the foot of Pelly Bay.

CHAPTER 5

1. King to Earl Grey, 10 June 1847, C.O. 323/232; printed versions of this letter are to be found in the *Atheneum*, 12 June 1847, and also in King, *F. Exped.*, pp. 12–28, in which King corrects the figure of 126 men involved to 138. See also Sir John Ross to the Admiralty, 27 Jan. and 9 Feb. 1847, PP, *Accounts and Papers*, 1847–48, vol. 41, no. 264.

2. King to Earl Grey, 10 June 1847, C.O. 323/232; King cites as his source for Franklin's instructions Barrow's "History of Arctic Expeditions" and changes this to "History of Arctic Voyages" in the printed version of his letter (King, *F. Exped.*, p. 14).

3. King to Earl Grey, 10 June 1847, C.O. 323/232.

4. Minutes by J. Stephen and B. Hawes, respectively, both on 12 June, and by Lord Grey on 14 June, all on King to Earl Grey, 10 June 1847.

5. See minute of 17 June, initialled "A. Bd.," identifiable by his handwriting as M. A. Blackwood, and see also minute of 21 June by Hawes; both minutes are on King to Earl Grey, 10 June 1847. See also draft of acknowledgment to King, 28 June 1847, and King to Earl Grey, 25 Nov. 1847, both in C.O. 323/232; King, *F. Exped.*, p. 29.

6. R. J. Cyriax, "Sir James Clark Ross and the Franklin Expedition," *Polar Record* III, no. 24: 536–37; minute by Mr. Edge for Surveyor, Dept. of Surveyor of the Navy, and minute relating to minutes regarding *Plover*, both of 16 Nov. 1847, Adm 7/187.

7. Sir John Richardson, *Arctic Searching Expedition* (1854), pp. 20, 22, 25; Cyriax, "Sir James Clark Ross and the Franklin Expedition," p. 537.

8. See letters of King to Earl Grey, 25 Nov., 8 Dec. (from which the quotation is taken), and 16 Dec. 1847, in C.O. 323/232, and (for 8 Dec.) 323/232 Misc. 2007;

printed versions of the letters are in the *Athenaeum*, 27 Nov., 11 Dec., and 18 Dec. 1847, and in King, *F. Exped.*, pp. 29–55; see also Cyriax, "Sir James Clark Ross and the Franklin Expedition," p. 537, and Richardson, *Arctic Searching Expedition*, p. 22.

9. King to Earl Grey, 8 Dec. 1847, C.O. 323/232 Misc. 2007, from which the quotations are taken; minutes on King to Grey, 25 Nov. and 8 Dec. 1847, and draft of letter to King, 7 Dec. 1847, C.O. 323/232; King to Hawes, 16 Dec. 1847, ibid.

10. King to Earl Grey, 16 Dec. 1847, C.O. 323/232.

11. *Nautical Standard*, 12 June 1847; see also King, *F. Exped.*, pp. xx and xxiii.

12. *Athenaeum*, 6 and 13 Nov. 1847; *Pictorial Times*, 4 Dec. 1847, as quoted in King, *F. Exped.*, p. xxiii.

13. King to Lords Commissioners of the Admiralty, 16 Feb. 1848, in King, *F. Exped.*, pp. 55–65; see also, for a copy of the same letter, PP, *Accounts and Papers*, 1847–48, vol. 41, no. 264, pp. 41–43 [203–5]. The original has not been found at the Public Record Office or elsewhere; see in this regard the account in chap. 8 of Beaufort calling upon Back with certain pamphlets of King.

14. King to Lords Commissioners, 16 Feb. 1848, pp. 55–56, quoting from "Barrow's Arctic Voyages, p. 11."

15. King to Lords Commissioners, 16 Feb. 1848, p. 57; see also Cyriax, "Sir James Clark Ross and the Franklin Expedition," p. 534.

16. King to Lords Commissioners, 16 Feb. 1848, pp. 61–64; the quotation is from p. 64.

17. Parry to Captain Hamilton, 23 Feb. 1848, PP, *Accounts and Papers*, 1847–48, vol. 41, no. 264, pp. 43–44 [205–6]; the quotations are from p. 44.

18. See Sir James Clark Ross to H. G. Ward, Admiralty, 29 Feb. 1848, PP, *Accounts and Papers*, 1847–48, vol. 41, no. 264, pp. 44–47 [206–9]; Cyriax, "Sir James Clark Ross and the Franklin Expedition," pp. 535–36.

19. Ross to Ward, 29 Feb. 1848, pp. 45–47 [207–9]; the quotations are from pp. 45–46, [207–8].

20. King to H. G. Ward, 3 Mar. 1848; Ward to King, 3 Mar. 1848; King to Lady Franklin, 29 Mar. 1848: all in King, *F. Exped.*, pp. 66–70; the quotations are from p. 69.

21. Cyriax, "Sir James Clark Ross and the Franklin Expedition," pp. 528–40, esp. 533–36; see also idem, *Sir John Franklin's Last Arctic Expedition*.

22. The quotations are from Cyriax, "Sir James Clark Ross and the Franklin Expedition," pp. 536, 534.

23. Ibid., pp. 530–31, and 535–36 from which the quotation is taken; see also J. C. Ross to Lord Haddington, 25 Jan. 1845, Adm 7/178/5.

24. On Ross's retirement, see L. P. Kirwan, *A History of Polar Exploration*, p. 178; on his health, see J. C. Ross, "Diary, 1847–8," MS journal in E. Ross Collection, 14–30 March 1847; on King, see diary of George Dann Banes, 11 and 15 Oct. 1845, and Feilden note, 7 Dec. 1896, RGS Archives.

25. For Anderson's trip, see below, chap. 8.

26. R. Cundy, MS, 1967, on his Back River trip, 1964, conducted to inspect the Dease and Simpson cairn, Castor and Pollux River, for Admiral Noel Wright, p. 56; see also the printed version of Cundy's judgment, idem, *Beacon Six*, p. 49.

27. See Admiralty Chart 5101, compiled by Lt. Cmdr. R. T. Gould, RN; C. Markham, *The Life of Admiral Sir Leopold McClintock*, p. 4, and idem, *The Lands of Silence*, p. 248.

28. See A. G. E. Jones, "Sir James Clark Ross and the Voyage of the *Enterprise* and *Investigator*, 1848–49," *Geographical Journal* CXXXVII, no. 2: [165]; and N. M. Crouse, *The Search for the Northwest Passage*, pp. 416–17.

29. See "Memoranda relating to ... Two Ships to proceed to Baffin's Bay," 16 Nov. 1847; copy of minute of 15 Jan. 1848, by Mr. Edge, Dept. of Surveyor of the Navy; and "Proposed Establishment" of *Enterprise* and *Investigator*, n.d.: all in Adm 7/187. See also Cyriax, "Sir James Clark Ross and the Franklin Expedition," p. 533; A. B. Lubbock, *The Arctic Whalers*, p. 347; for plans of the two vessels, see "Profile and Decks," *Enterprise* and *Investigator*, Draft Room, NMM; see also J. C. Ross, "Diary, 1847–8," 24 and 27 Nov. 1848; for the boats aboard *Erebus* and *Terror*, see K. Barnes to F. M'Clintock, 4 Jan. 1881, M'Clintock Papers, M Cl/45a, NMM; the quotations are from "Memoranda relating to ... Two Ships," 16 Nov. 1847.

30. *ILN*, 13 May 1848; minute of Surveyor Dept., 15 Jan. 1848, Adm 7/187; see also Alexander Armstrong, *A Personal Narrative of the Discovery of the North-West Passage*, pp. 6, 609–14. For a description of the Silvester stove see E. Parry, *Journal of a Second Voyage for the Discovery of a North-West Passage ... 1821–22–23*, pp. v–vi, and M'Clintock, "J. Silvester's Stove," McClintock notebook, 1849–52, M'Clintock Papers, MCL/338/MS 58/024, NMM. See also Jones, "Sir James Clark Ross and the Voyage of ... 1848–49," p. 171.

31. See J. C. Ross, "Diary 1847–48," 26 May, 11 July, and 25 Nov. 1847; *ILN*, 13 May 1848; "On the Introduction and Progressive Increase of Screw Propulsion in Her Majesty's Navy," Somerset House, May 1850, in Adm 7/614.

32. J. C. Ross, "Narrative of the Proceedings of Captain Sir James C. Ross, in command of the Expedition through Lancaster Sound and Barrow Straits," PP, *Accounts and Papers*, 1850, vol. 35, no. 107, p. 60 [238]; M'Clintock, *Enterprise Journal*, 15 Sept. 1848, MCL/9, NMM; see also ibid., 11, 12, and 13 Sept. 1848.

33. R. J. Cyriax, "Arctic Sledge Travelling by Officers of the Royal Navy, 1819–49," *Mariner's Mirror* XLIX: 138.

34. On deficiency of diet and a bent minutely to survey, see Jones, "Sir James Clark Ross and the Voyage of ... 1848–49," pp. 171, 174.

35. See J. Rae, *Snow-Huts, Sledges, and Sledge Journeys*, p. 5; F. M'Clintock, "Journal of Lt. M'Clintock in *Enterprise*, 1848–9: Rewritten and abbreviated," MS journal, p. 205, Library MSS, RGS Archives; see also: J. Rae, "Achievements" Letter, Feb. 1856, p. xciv; Rae to Mrs. Vaughan, 16 May 1889, RGS Archives; and Jones, "Sir James Clark Ross and the Voyage of ... 1848–49," pp. 175, 177. The quotations are from Rae, *Snow-Huts*, p. 5, and M'Clintock, p. 205, respectively.

36. Jones, "Sir James Clark Ross and the Voyage of ... 1848–49," p. 177; *Nautical Standard*, 10 Nov. 1849.

37. See Rae to Simpson, 16 Sept. 1848, *RAC*, p. 83, from which the quotation is taken. See also Rae to Simpson, 20 Sept., ibid., p. 87; Rae, Autob. MS, pp. 255–57, 264–65; Richardson, *Arctic Searching Expedition* (1854), pp. 36, 319–21.

38. Richardson, *Arctic Searching Expedition*, p. 306, from which the quoted phrases are taken. See also Rae to Simpson, 4 Nov. 1848, *RAC*, pp. 93–94; idem to idem, pp. 106–7; Rae, Autob. MS, p. 447.

39. Rae, Autob. MS, p. 447; G. M'Dougall, *The Eventful Voyage of H. M. Discovery Ship "Resolute"*, p. xxxiii; Jones, "Sir James Clark Ross and the Voyage of ... 1848–49," pp. 177–78; F. L. M'Clintock, "Reminiscences of Arctic Ice-Travel in Search of Sir John Franklin," *Royal Dublin Society Journal* I: 195–96.

40. Cyriax, "Sir James Clark Ross and the Franklin Expedition," p. 538; Jones, "Sir James Clark Ross and the Voyage of ... 1848–49," pp. 177–78; Rae to Mrs. Vaughan, 16 May 1889, RGS Archives; F. Woodward, *Portrait of Jane*, p. 270; King, *F. Exped.*, p. 72; *Nautical Standard*, 10 Nov. 1849. The quotations are from Jones, p. 178, Rae, King, and *Nautical Standard*.

41. M'Clintock, "Journal of Lt. M'Clintock," pp. 162–63, RGS Archives.

42. Parry to John Barrow, 24 Nov. 1849, extract copied in Lady Franklin's hand, MS 248/452/2, SPRI; Parry to Lady Franklin, 10 and 28 Nov., MS 248/452/5 and /6 respectively, SPRI; the quotation is from Parry to Barrow.

43. Cyriax, "Sir James Clark Ross and the Franklin Expedition," p. 538.

CHAPTER 6

1. King, *F. Exped.*, p. 75.

2. Richard King to the Secy. of the Admiralty, 18 Feb. 1850, Adm 7/188/12; see also King, *F. Exped.*, pp. 76–82 for a copy of this letter.

3. F. L. M'Clintock, "Reminiscences of Arctic Ice-Travel in Search of Sir John Franklin," *Royal Dublin Society Journal* I: 184.

4. Minute by Admiral Dundas, on King to Secy. of Admiralty, 18 Feb. 1850, Adm 7/188/12.

5. See F. H. Burns, "H.M.S. *Herald* in Search of Franklin," *Beaver* 294 (Autumn): 3–13, from which, citing Pim's journal, the quotations are taken.

6. Ibid., pp. 8–10, from which (p. 8) the quotation is taken; PP, *Accounts and Papers*, 1856, vol. 41 [2124], "Copy of the Journal of Lieutenant Bedford Pim, Her Majesty's brig 'Plover', from the 10th of March till the 29th of April, 1850," pp. 75–78; Rae to the Editor, *Northern Daily Express*, 17 Feb. 1856; see also the same newspaper, 23 Feb. 1856.

7. "Our Portrait Gallery, No. LXXII: Captain M'Clure, R.N.," *Dublin University Magazine* XLIII: 348–49.

8. J. H. Nelson, "Voyage of H.M.S. *Investigator* resulting in the Discovery of the North West Passage," MS diary, 2 vols., MS 848/1 and /2, SPRI: vol. I, pp. 19, 23, 39, 40, 43; L. H. Neatby, *The Search for Franklin*, p. 166; idem, in J.

Miertsching, *Frozen Ships: The Arctic Diary of Johann Miertsching, 1850–1854,* ed. and trans. L. H. Neatby, p. 66n. The phrase "Old Iron Bows" is from Nelson, vol. I, pp. 19, 43.

9. On Collinson, see L. P. Kirwan, *A History of Polar Exploration,* p. 189; upon M'Clure see Neatby, *Search for Franklin,* pp. 181, 182, 203, 207; idem in J. Miertsching, *Frozen Ships,* pp. 16n, 246–47. See also W. C. Wonders, Preface, R. M'Clure, *The Discovery of the North-West Passage* (reprint ed., 1967), pp. xxiii–xxiv, and "Our Portrait Gallery," p. 345.

10. "Our Portrait Gallery," p. 334; on Franklin's loss of a governorship, see above, chap. 4.

11. For the phrase, "Nelsons of discovery," see Kirwan, *Polar Exploration,* p. 184, citing the *Quarterly Review;* for details of M'Clure's early career, see "Our Portrait Gallery," pp. 334–35, 345; regarding M'Clure on the eve of departure, see ibid., p. 348 and Wonders, preface, *Discovery of the North-West Passage,* pp. xxiii–xxiv, quoting from Osborn at p. xxiii.

12. Nelson, "Voyage," vol. I, pp. 39–41; Neatby, *Search for Franklin,* pp. 169–70; "Our Portrait Gallery," pp. 348–49; the quotation is from Nelson, p. 41.

13. The quotation on carrying canvas is from "Our Portrait Gallery," p. 348; the others are from Nelson, "Voyage," vol. I, pp. 43–44.

14. See Nelson, "Voyage," vol. I, pp. 41–42; also "Our Portrait Gallery," p. 349, for report of a speech by Parry at King's Lynn, October 1853.

15. For this trip, see M'Clure, *Discovery of the North-West Passage,* pp. 125–29; see also, esp. on Court's party, Nelson, "Voyage," vol. I, pp. 87, 90; Neatby, *Search for Franklin,* pp. 175–77; A. Armstrong, *A Personal Narrative of the Discovery of the North-West Passage,* p. 272.

16. Nelson, "Voyage," vol. I, pp. 91–92.

17. See Neatby, *Search for Franklin,* p. 177; G. M'Dougall, *The Eventful Voyage of H.M. Discovery Ship "Resolute,"* pp. 271–72; Armstrong, *A Personal Narrative,* pp. 278–79 and 285, from which the quotations are taken; for Rae's comments, see Rae, Autob. MS, p. 855. See also Appendix 2.

18. "Our Portrait Gallery," pp. 351–52; the quotation is from p. 352, citing "Captain M'Clure's Despatches to the Admiralty."

19. Armstrong, *A Personal Narrative,* as cited in Neatby, *Search for Franklin,* pp. 185, 188.

20. *Nautical Standard,* 16 and 23 Feb., and 2 and 9 Mar. 1850; *Naval and Military Gazette,* 2 Mar. 1850; details of registry of *Intrepid,* Board of Trade, Cardiff; Rupert Jones Lists, NMM; plan of *Intrepid,* "Profile, showing the general fitments and mode of fortifying the Bows," signed by Oliver Lang, 28 Nov. 1851, NMM. The quotations are from *Nautical Standard* (2 March) and from the plan of *Intrepid.*

21. Nelson, "Voyage," vol. I, p. 254.

22. F. L. McClintock, "Track 'Enterprise', 1848–9," RGS Map Room; idem, "Journal of a Sledge Journey, 15 April–4 July, 1851," Adm 7/193/20, pp. 256–340, including "Report of Sledge Journey, 15 April–4 July, 1851," pp. 256

ff., and "Sledge Equipment," pp. 338–40; idem, "Reminiscences of Arctic Ice-Travel," pp. 196–214, from which (p. 196) the quotation is taken; see also *Athenaeum*, 7 Feb. 1852.

23. *Athenaeum*, 7 Feb. 1852; M'Clintock, "Reminiscences of Arctic Ice-Travel," p. 203; idem, "Journal of a Sledge Journey," 21 May 1851; the quotations are from these three references respectively.

24. M'Clintock, "Reminiscences of Arctic Ice-Travel," pp. 199–202, 208, 211–13; idem, "Journal of a Sledge Journey," 5 June 1851, and accompanying sketch; E. Parry, *Memoirs of Rear-Admiral Sir W. Edward Parry*, p. 366; King, *F. Exped.*, p. 85; the quotations are from M'Clintock, "Reminiscences," p. 202, Parry, and King.

25. M'Clintock, "Journal of a Sledge Journey," p. 264, and entry for 4 July, pp. 337 ff.; see also Rae, Autob. MS, pp. 877l–877m.

26. On the gutta percha boat, see M'Clintock, "Journal of a Sledge Journey," p. 338; on selection and increase of men, see ibid., and idem, "On Arctic Sledge-travelling," *Proceedings of the Royal Geographical Society* XIX: 478; on dehydrated potatoes, see R. Maclure [*sic*], *The Arctic Dispatches Containing an Account of the Discovery of the North-West Passage*, unnumbered pages following p. 111, and Rae, Autob. MS, pp. 868–69; on dispatch of sled parties, *Athenaeum*, 7 Feb. 1852.

27. For these criticisms see: Armstrong, *A Personal Narrative*, pp. 518–19; Rae, Autob. MS, p. 699; Woodward, *Portrait of Jane*, p. 280; *Athenaeum*, 7 Feb. 1852.

28. *Athenaeum*, 21 Aug. 1852; Neatby, *Search for Franklin*, pp. 140–42; R. J. Cyriax, *Sir John Franklin's Last Arctic Expedition*, p. 105 and note, citing PP, "Arctic Expeditions: Report of the Committee, etc.," London, 1851, p. 123; see also, for an account of the Penny expedition, P. C. Sutherland, *Journal of a Voyage in Baffin Bay and Barrow Strait*. The quotations are from the *Athenaeum* and Cyriax.

29. Neatby, *Search for Franklin*, p. 142; *Athenaeum*, 30 Mar. 1852, from which the quotation is taken.

30. Woodward, *Portrait of Jane*, pp. 279–80; King, *F. Exped.*, p. 84; *Athenaeum*, 7 Feb. 1852. The quotations are from King and the *Athenaeum*.

31. Rae to Simpson, 30 Aug. 1850 and 23 Apr. 1851, *RAC*, pp. 141 and 173 respectively; see also Rae, Autob. MS, pp. 495–96; on Rae's concern for his stamina, see Rae to Simpson, 2 Nov. 1850, *RAC*, p. 150.

32. Rae to Simpson, private, 10 June 1851, *RAC*, p. 193; Rae, "Achievements" Letter, Feb. 1856, p. xciv, from which the quotations are taken.

33. Rae, Autob. MS, pp. 491–94, 496–97, 500, 504, 510; Rae, "Achievements" Letter, Feb. 1856, p. xcv. See also Rae to Simpson, 2 Nov. 1850; Rae to Governor-in-Chief, Governor, Chief Factors and Chief Traders, Rupert's Land, 17 Apr. 1851; Rae to Simpson, 18 Apr. 1851: in *RAC*, pp. 152, 157, and 158–59 respectively.

34. See Rae, "Achievements" Letter, Feb. 1856, p. xcv, and *RAC*, p. 144n. See also Rae at Portage La Loche, to York Factory, 1 Aug. 1850; Rae to Governor,

Chief Factors and Chief Traders of the Northern Department, 28 Oct. 1850; Rae to Simpson, 30 Aug. and 2 Nov. 1850, and 23 Apr. 1851; Rae to Barclay, 27 Sept. 1851: all in *RAC*, pp. 138, 142–45, 150–51, 167, and 211. For a view of his boats (reproduced here), see Rae's sketch, "Ft. Conf.—Winter View 1850–51," ibid., facing p. 92; and see Rae, Autob. MS, pp. 494–95, 495n, 499, 504, 784. The quotation is from Rae to Barclay, 27 Sept. 1851, p. 211. Rae wrote Simpson that the first boat was turned off the stocks on 2 Nov. (Rae to Simpson, 2 Nov. 1850, p. 150); however, in his autobiography (which he usually wrote with his journals before him) Rae says that this event occurred on 30 Oct. (Rae, Autob. MS, p. 495); in what he says of case of portage, Rae is writing directly of a single boat, but his comment obviously applies to both boats.

35. See Rae to Simpson, 18 and 23 Apr. 1851; Rae to Governor-in-Chief, 17 Apr. 1851: in *RAC*, pp. 156, 157, 161, 167, 169. See also Rae, Autob. MS, pp. 491, 498, 503–5, 784, 877k, 877l; on mitts and gloves, see John Rae, "Treatment of Frost Bite," Library MSS, RGS Archives, and Rae, Autob. MS, pp. 877k and 877l. The quotations are from Rae to Governor-in-Chief, 17 Apr. 1851, and Rae to Simpson, 23 Apr. 1851, pp. 157, 167, 169.

36. See Rae, Autob. MS, pp. 503–10, 517; Rae to Governor-in-Chief, 17 Apr. 1851, *RAC*, p. 157; Rae to Simpson, 18 Apr. and 10 June 1851, ibid., pp. 161–63 and 181 respectively; the quotations are from Rae, Autob. MS, p. 510, and Rae to Simpson, 18 Apr. 1851, p. 161. See also, for Rae's later opinion of Beads, *RAC*, p. 352. By one account Rae had a total of seven dogs, including those for the fatigue party (Rae to Simpson, 10 June 1851, p. 181); by another he had only six dogs (Rae, Autob. MS, p. 508).

37. See Rae to Simpson, 10 June 1851, *RAC*, pp. 181–82. See also Rae, Autob. MS, pp. 508–9, 512, 516–19; the quotations are from pp. 517 and 519.

38. Rae, Autob. MS, pp. 509, 511, 519–21, 526–27; Rae to Simpson, 10 June 1851, *RAC*, pp. 186, 188; the quotations are from Rae, Autob. MS, pp. 511, 527 and Rae to Simpson, 10 June 1851, p. 188. For a reference to the satellite sledge, see chap. 8 below.

39. Rae to Simpson, 10 June 1851, *RAC*, pp. 188–90; the quotations are from pp. 188 and 190.

40. Ibid., pp. 189–90; Rae to Simpson, private, 10 June 1851, pp. 192–93; Rae, Autob. MS, p. 877n; the quotations are from *RAC*, pp. 190 and 192.

41. Rae, Autob. MS, pp. 510, 512, 516–17, 519, 877b–877c; Rae to Simpson, 10 June 1851, *RAC*, p. 183; Rae in discussion portion of Capt. B. Pim, "Plan for Further Search after the Remains of the Franklin Expedition," *Proceedings of the Royal Geographical Society* I, sec. VI: 215; the quotations are from Rae, Autob. MS, pp. 877b–877c.

42. On Wilbank Bay, see Rae, Autob. MS, p. 517; on Rae's exactness, V. Stefansson, *My Life with the Eskimo*, p. 304; on his sense of return, memorandum to H. A. McKenzie, 22 Apr. 1851, *RAC*, p. 165; on Haswell's proximity and Prince Albert Sound, see Wordie and Cyriax, Introduction, ibid., p. lxv, and M'Clure, *Discovery of the North-West Passage*, p. 185. McKenzie, the only

second-in-command Rae ever had, for "carelessness and inattention ... was put off duty before we reached the sea" (Rae, "Achievements" Letter, Feb. 1856, p. xcvii and note).

43. For Rae's times and distances, see Rae to Simpson, 10 June 1851, *RAC*, pp. 191–92, and Rae, "Achievements" Letter, Feb. 1856, p. xcviii; in the first of his computations (685) Rae speaks of geographical miles, in the second (1,080) he writes of statute miles. On Rae's lively letter to Simpson (10 June 1851, pp. 180–92), measures to dispatch it, and receipt of it, see Wordie and Cyriax, Introduction, *RAC*, p. lxv; Rae to Simpson, private, 10 June 1851, ibid., pp. 192–94; RGS Council Minute Book, 1841–53, RGS Archives, pp. 289, 291; and *RAC*, p. 194n.

44. Rae to Barclay, 27 Sept. 1851, *RAC*, pp. 197, 199–201, 203; Rae, Autob. MS, pp. 596a, 602–3; Admiralty Chart 5100.

45. Rae to Barclay, 27 Sept. 1851, *RAC*, pp. 202–6; Rae, Autob. MS, pp. 612–16.

46. Rae, Autob. MS, pp. 616, 621, 622, 624; Wordie and Cyriax, Introduction, *RAC*, p. lxvi; Rae to Barclay, 27 Sept. 1851, ibid., p. 208. Wordie and Cyriax reason circumstantially that Rae named Victoria Strait (p. 210n); Rae's autobiography confirms this (p. 621).

47. Wordie and Cyriax, Introduction, *RAC*, pp. lxvii–lxix; Rae, Autob. MS, pp. 625–28; the first and last quotations are from Wordie and Cyriax, p. lxviii, the second one from Rae, p. 628.

48. Rae to Barclay, 27 Sept. 1851, *RAC*, p. 212.

49. "Rae on the Eskimos," *Beaver* 284 (March 1954): 38–41; John Rae, *Arctic and Sub-Arctic Life*, pp. 8–12; memorandum of Rae to McKenzie, 22 Apr. 1851, *RAC*, p. 165; Rae, Autob. MS, p. 504. The quoted phrases and words are from, respectively, *Beaver*, p. 41; Rae to McKenzie, p. 165; Rae Autob. MS, p. 504.

50. Rae, Autob. MS, p. 622a; Rae, "Achievements" Letter, Feb. 1856, pp. xcviii–xcix; "Dr. John Rae *For the Founders Medal*," J. Arrowsmith, 5 Apr. 1852, to the Council of the RGS, Arrowsmith Correspondence, RGS Archives; the quotation is from Arrowsmith and the italics are his.

51. On Back Point, see Rae to Barclay, 27 Sept. 1851, p. 199; on support for a medal, see Back to the Council of the RGS, 5 Apr. 1852, Back Correspondence, 1851–60, RGS Archives; on the award itself, see *Journal of the Royal Geographical Society* XXII (1852): lviin, lviii.

52. See Rae to Barclay, 28 Mar. 1852, *RAC*, p. 214; on the naval investigation and Ross's feeling, Wordie and Cyriax, Introduction, *RAC*, pp. lxx–lxxi.

53. See Comdr. James Clark Ross to Sir James Graham, 22 Jan. 1834, Sir James Ross Letter Book, S.L. 25, Office of the Hydrographer; Kirwan, *Polar Exploration*, p. 178; Wordie and Cyriax, Introduction, *RAC*, p. lxx; on Bellot Strait and Rae's finds, *Athenaeum*, 3 Apr. 1852.

54. Wordie and Cyriax, Introduction, *RAC*, p. lxxi; James Fitzjames, "Journal of James Fitzjames Aboard Erebus, 1845," *Nautical Magazine* XXI, nos. 3 and 4 (1852); see also, on the handling of the letters, John Brown, *The Northwest Passage* (rev. ed., 1860), p. 253.

55. Rae to Barclay, 1 May 1852, *RAC*, p. 222; *Athenaeum*, 4 Dec. 1852; see also Wordie and Cyriax, Introduction, *RAC*, pp. lxxiv-lxxviii.

CHAPTER 7

1. J. H. Nelson, "Voyage of H.M.S. *Investigator*," vol. I, pp. 188–89, SPRI.

2. See J. Miertsching, *Frozen Ships: The Arctic Diary of Johann Miertsching, 1850–1854*, p. 151.

3. F. L. M'Clintock, *Voyage of the "Fox"* (1859), p. 284; A. Armstrong, *A Personal Narrative of the Discovery of the North-West Passage*, pp. 513, 516–17.

4. See Armstrong, *A Personal Narrative*, pp. 517–18 and 520, from which the quotation is taken. See also J. Brown, *The Northwest Passage and the Plans for the Search for Sir John Franklin* (1858), p. 305; Miertsching, *Frozen Ships*, pp. 162–63; L. H. Neatby, *The Search for Franklin*, p. 203.

5. M'Clintock, "Investigator's bundle of Yarns," *Intrepid* Journal, p. 271; Armstrong, *A Personal Narrative*, p. 521; John Brown, *The Northwest Passage* (1858), p. 305; Nelson, "Voyage," vol. I, p. 190; Pierre Berton, *The National Dream*, p. 250. The quotations are from Berton and Nelson.

6. Stephen Court, "Work and Remark Book of Stephen Court, 2nd. Master, H.M.S. Investigator. (Nov. 1, 1851–April 1, 1853)," MS journal in Hydrographer's Office, 5 Oct. 1852; see also Miertsching, *Frozen Ships*, p. 174; Armstrong, *A Personal Narrative*, p. 548.

7. M'Clintock, "Investigator's bundle of Yarns," p. 271.

8. Nelson, "Voyage," vol. I, pp. 203–4; Armstrong, *A Personal Narrative*, pp. 6, 523–52, 548–49, 554, 563, 608–14; Brown, *Northwest Passage* (1858), p. 307; see also Stephen Court, "Work and Remark Book," 28 Feb. and 19 Mar.–1 Apr. 1853. The quotation is from Nelson, "Voyage," vol. I, p. 204.

9. Armstrong, *A Personal Narrative*, pp. 500–503, 523–52.

10. M'Clintock, "Investigator's bundle of Yarns," p. 271.

11. Ibid., pp. 271–72, from which the quotation comes; see also p. 294 on the figures for game.

12. Rae, Autob. MS, pp. 861–861a; see also Neatby, *Search for Franklin*, p. 192.

13. Armstrong, *A Personal Narrative*, pp. 547, 555, 570; Nelson, "Voyage," vol. I, pp. 203–5; M'Clintock, *Intrepid* Journal, p. 233; the quotations are from Armstrong, p. 555, and M'Clintock.

14. "Personal Narrative of Lieutenant Gurny Cresswell," as quoted in "Our Portrait Gallery ... Captain M'Clure, R.N.," *Dublin University Magazine* XLIII: 352.

15. Nelson, "Voyage," vol. I, pp. 207, 216–17, from which the quotations are taken; "Stephen Court Remark Book," 1 Mar. 1853; Armstrong, *A Personal Narrative*, p. 558; see also M'Clintock, "Investigator's bundle of Yarns," pp. 272–73.

16. See "Stephen Court Remark Book," 4 Mar. and 7 Mar. to 1 Apr. 1853; Nelson, "Voyage," vol. I, pp. 213–14; Armstrong, *Narrative*, p. 559. See also, for an account of M'Clure's speech, G. F. M. M'Dougall, *The Eventful Voyage of ... "Resolute,"* pp. 274–75. The exact allowance consisted of 1¼ lb. of soft bread; ¾

lb. of preserved or salt meat; ¼ lb. of vegetables; 1 oz. of cocoa; ¼ oz. of tea; 1 oz. of lemon juice and sugar for the same and 1¹⁄₁₆ oz. of sugar for the tea and cocoa; 8 oz. of flour and 2 oz. of suet on salt beef days and ¼ pint of pease on pork days (Court entry, 15 Mar. 1853).

17. Lieut. B. C. T. Pim, RN, "Plan for the Investigation of the Northern coast of Siberia in search of the missing Franklin Expedition," Journal MSS, 1851, RGS Archives; n.d. but laid before RGS Council, and read at a society meeting, 10 Nov. 1851 (RGS Council Minute Book, 1841–53, RGS Archives, pp. 286, 289).

18. Sir Roderick Murchison to Annual Meeting, RGS, 24 May 1852, in *Journal of the Royal Geographical Society* XXII (1852): lxxiv.

19. Brown, *Northwest Passage* (1858), p. 217 and note.

20. See Count Nesselrode to Pim, 6/18 Dec. 1851 (translation), and Pim to [Sir Hamilton Seymour], St. Petersburg, 8/20 Dec. 1851, both in Pim, "Plan for the Investigation of ... Siberia"; Pim, memorandum at British Mission, St. Petersburg, 11/23 Dec. 1851, ibid.

21. Rear Admiral Matyischkin to Count Nesselrode: enclosure in letter of Count Nesselrode, St. Petersburg, 27 Dec. 1851 (translations); Count Nesselrode to Pim, 6/18 Dec. 1851 (translation); Sir Hamilton Seymour to Pim, 12 Jan. 1852: all in Pim, "Plan for the Investigation of ... Siberia."

22. See Back, "Sir George Back Diaries," 5 Mar. and 5 Apr. 1845, SPRI; PP, *Report from Select Committee on Arctic Expeditions*, 1854–55, vol. 7, no. 409, p. 18.

23. Murchison to Annual Meeting, RGS, 24 May 1852, pp. lxxiii–lxxiv; Pim, "Plan for the Investigation of ... Siberia."

24. Kellett, 5 Nov. 1851, "Arctic Expeditions, 1851, Report, and etc.," p. 168, as cited in Brown, *Northwest Passage* (rev. ed., 1860), pp. 201 and note, 202; R. Maguire, "Journal kept by Rochefort Maguire, Cmdr. on Board H.M.S. Plover on the Behring Straits Arctic Expedition ... 1852–54," MS journal, 2 vols., National Library of Ireland, vol. I, 3 Jan. 1852. See also report of RGS meeting, 8 Nov. 1852, in newsclipping, and "Extract of a letter from Captain Maguire of the Plover ... to Mr. Barrow," n.d., read at RGS meeting, 8 Nov. 1852, both in Kennedy Journal, MSS Files, RGS Archives.

25. Reports of RGS meeting, 8 Nov. 1852, in newsclipping, Kennedy Journal, MSS Files, RGS Archives and in *Naval and Military Gazette*, 13 Nov. 1852.

26. See "Report prepared by Lt. F. L. M'Clintock for Arctic Committee ... on the equipment ... for a sledge party of 1 officer and 10 men," prepared 7 Nov. 1851, enclosure no. 13, Arctic Committee Papers, vol. I (144(1)), 1851, Adm 7/612, pp. 7–20; PP, *Accounts and Papers*, 1852, vol. 50, no. 1435, *inter alia*, pp. xl–xli, 85–94, 154–64, 192–93.

27. F. L. M'Clintock, "Reminiscences of Arctic Ice-Travel," *Royal Dublin Society Journal* I: 184; W. Kennedy, *A Short Narrative of the Second Voyage of Prince Albert*, pp. 174–78. For a discussion of the issue of looking north or south which, on the whole, exonerates the navy, see R. J. Cyriax, *Sir John Franklin's Last Arctic Expedition*, pp. 81–83, and Neatby, *Search for Franklin*, pp. 196–97;

for more critical comments see Brown, *Northwest Passage* (1860), pp. 253–54; see also chap. 6 above.

28. King, *F. Exped.*, pp. 86–87, 89, 90: the words quoted are from pp. 86–87. Members of the Arctic Council were Beaufort, Parry, Richardson, James Clark Ross, Back, Sabine, Captain Hamilton, Beechey, Scoresby, and the junior John Barrow.

29. Neatby, *Search for Franklin*, p. 197.

30. King, *F. Exped.*, p. 91.

31. "Profile, showing the general fitments and mode of fortifying the Bows," "Plan of Upper Deck ... including diagonal doubling on the Deck," "Plan of Lower Deck and Hold," all of Arctic Schooners *Pioneer* and *Intrepid*, signed O. Lang, Woolwich Yard, 28 Nov. 1851, no. L.3991, NMM. *Pioneer* and *Intrepid* were sister ships. See also notes regarding *Intrepid*, M'Clintock Papers, McCl./25, NMM.

32. M'Clintock, *Intrepid* Journal, pp. 2–3, 7.

33. Ibid., 45, 51–55, 58–60; see also A. B. Lubbock, *The Arctic Whalers*, p. 355, from which the quoted phrase is taken.

34. Ibid., 30 June 1852, pp. 43–44; the quotation is from p. 44; see also the diagram, p. 44, and further references to docking, pp. 37, 48, 50, 51. See also M'Dougall, *Eventful Voyage of ... "Resolute,"* diagrams, pp. 51, 61.

35. M'Clintock, *Intrepid* Journal, pp. 21, 23, 30, 67–69, 73, 77–83; the quoted words are from p. 83.

36. Ibid., pp. 13–15, 51, 62–65, 73, 85, 87, 93; the quotation is from p. 85. See also M'Dougall, *Eventful Voyage of ... "Resolute,"* pp. 49, 51–53 (diagram, p. 52); Kellett to John Barrow, 21 Apr. and 2 May 1853, as quoted in R. Maclure, *The Arctic Dispatches ... of the North-West Passage*, p. 40.

37. M'Clintock, *Intrepid* Journal, pp. 99, 102–4, 107–8; the quotation is from pp. 102–3.

38. Kellett to John Barrow, 12 Apr. and 2 May 1853, p. 32; M'Clintock, *Intrepid* Journal, 16 Aug. 1852, pp. 110–12; see also M'Dougall, *Eventful Voyage of ... "Resolute,"* pp. 89–94. The quotations are from M'Clintock, pp. 111–12.

39. M'Clintock, *Intrepid* Journal, 17–19 Aug., pp. 113–21; the quotation is from p. 121.

40. Clements R. Markham, *Life of ... McClintock*, pp. 147–48.

41. See McClintock, "Reminiscences of Arctic Travel," p. 215; M'Clintock's comments on the paper by Dr. F. Nansen, "Journey Across the Inland Ice of Greenland from East to West," *Proceedings of the Royal Geographical Society* XI: 484, from which "baggage animals" comes; M'Clintock, *Intrepid* Journal, pp. 151–71, 178–200, from which (p. 179) the quotation on chivalry is taken.

42. McClintock, *Intrepid* Journal, 25 Oct. 1852, p. 204.

43. See Wordie and Cyriax, Introduction, *RAC*, p. c; see also Orders, 20 Sept. 1852, by Capt. H. Kellett, in Lieut. G. F. Mecham, "Journal of Her Majesty's Sledge *Discovery* detached from H.M.S. *Resolute*, 21 Sept.–14 Oct. 1852," Adm 7/198/3, ff. 27–28.

44. Mecham, "Journal of Sledge *Discovery*," ff. 29–31, 33–41; the quotation is from f. 40. See also M'Clintock, *Intrepid* Journal, p. 202.

45. Clements R. Markham, *The Arctic Navy List*, p. 3; Mecham, "Journal of Sledge *Discovery*," ff. 31, 41–42.

46. M'Clintock, *Intrepid* Journal, pp. 208–9, 227–28, and 249 which has the quoted phrase.

47. Ibid., 14 Mar. 1853, pp. 248–49; Pim, "Journal of Sled Trip," [March–April 1853], photostat from Adm 7/198, RGS Archives, p. 252. Although Pim's was the earliest spring journey by the navy thus far, William Kennedy, former Hudson's Bay Company employee, had never stopped travelling at all during the winter of 1851–52, on his expedition in the Boothia–North Somerset region (P. D. Baird, *Expeditions to the Canadian Arctic*, p. 7; Kennedy, *A Short Narrative*, pp. 61–88, especially pp. 82–83).

48. M'Clintock, *Intrepid* Journal, p. 251; N. M. Crouse, *The Search for the Northwest Passage*, p. 443; Miertsching, *Frozen Ships*, p. 189; Markham, *Life of ... McClintock*, p. 154; Pim, "Journal of Sled Trip," Adm 7/198, p. 263.

49. Pim, "Journal of Sled Trip," Adm 7/198, pp. 262–64.

50. Nelson, "Voyage," vol. I, pp. 217–18.

51. See Kellett to John Barrow, 12 Apr. and 2 May 1853, p. 39, which has the first quoted phrase; "Our Portrait Gallery," p. 354 and note, which quotes M'Clure directly.

52. Nelson, "Voyage," vol. I, p. 220.

53. Armstrong, *A Personal Narrative*, pp. xx–xxi, 559, 565–66, 568.

54. Neatby, *Search for Franklin*, p. 207; M'Clintock, *Intrepid* Journal, p. 280.

55. See Armstrong, *A Personal Narrative*, p. 570.

56. Nelson, "Voyage," vol. I, pp. 222–25; Armstrong, *A Personal Narrative*, p. 581; M'Clintock, *Intrepid* Journal, p. 273, from which the quotation is taken.

57. "Our Portrait Gallery," p. 355.

58. M'Dougall, *Eventful Voyage of ... "Resolute,"* p. 305 and note.

59. M'Clintock, *Intrepid* Journal, 20 Sept. 1853, p. 297.

60. Ibid., pp. 337–40.

61. Nelson, "Voyage," vol. I, pp. 249–50, 254, 258–59, and 273 from which the quotations are taken.

62. For the quoted phrases see, respectively, A. Petermann in "The Geography of the Arctic Regions," as quoted in the *Athenaeum*, 22 Oct. 1853, and Sir George Simpson to John Rae, 13 June 1854, *RAC*, p. 342. One attempt at commercial use of the passage was the *Manhattan* voyage of 1969.

63. M'Clintock, "Reminiscences of Arctic Ice-Travel," p. 217; M'Clintock, *Intrepid* Journal, 18 July 1854, p. 364.

64. Kellett to John Barrow, 12 Apr. to 2 May 1853, p. 38; see also Armstrong, *A Personal Narrative*, pp. 578–79.

65. See "Arctic Service, 1818–1856," Names of Arctic Ships and Crew Numbers, John Washington, Hydrographer, 14 Jan. 1857, Adm 1/5685; on Mecham, Markham, *Arctic Navy List*, p. 36.

66. F. L. M'Clintock, "On Arctic Sledge-travelling," *Proceedings of the Royal Geographical Society* XIX: 464–65.

67. PP, *Report From Select Committee on Arctic Expeditions*, 1854–55, vol. 7, no. 409, pp. v–vi.

68. Markham, *Life of ... McClintock*, p. 8.

69. PP, *Report From Select Committee on Arctic Expeditions*, 1854–55, vol. 7, no. 409, p. 6. On M'Clure and Kellett as first discoverers of a passage, see Appendix 1.

70. Rae to editor of *Northern Daily Express*, 17 Feb. 1856; see also letter from E.G., unaddressed, n.d., B Cl 1, Belcher Collection, NMM.

71. *Nautical Standard*, 12 June 1847.

72. For criticism of Pim, see M'Clintock, *Intrepid* Journal, p. 280, and Markham, *Life of ... McClintock*, p. 155; the quotation is from M'Clintock, "On Arctic Sledge-travelling," p. 478.

73. On Pim's insurance, see King to Dr. McCormick, RN, 29 June 1858, in BM Add. MSS 42580 (Sherborn Autographs), f. 248; on Pim when King died, see *Borough of Marylebone Mercury*, 12 Feb. 1876.

74. On the reaction of parties at Beechey Island, see M'Clintock, *Intrepid* Journal, pp. 373–74, and on Admiralty abandonment of the search, *London Gazette*, 20 Jan. 1854, as cited in Wordie and Cyriax, Introduction, *RAC*, p. lxxxviin6; the quotation is from M'Clintock, p. 374.

CHAPTER 8

1. See Rae, Autob. MS, pp. 753–894; Rae to Mrs. Vaughan, 16 May 1889, RGS Archives; Wordie and Cyriax, Introduction, *RAC*, pp. lxxii–lxxxiii.

2. Wordie and Cyriax, Introduction, *RAC*, pp. lxxx–lxxxi.

3. See Murchison to Council and Members of the RGS, 10 Nov. 1854; Murchison to Shaw, secretary to the Royal Geographical Society, Brighton, 2 Nov. (italics Murchison's) and 8 Nov. 1854; Murchison to Lord Ellesmere, 5 Nov. 1854, all in Murchison Correspondence, RGS Archives. The quotations are from these sources. See also, on criticism of Rae relating to lack of information and alleged cannibalism, Wordie and Cyriax, Introduction, *RAC*, pp. lxxxiii–iv, lxxxvii–viii.

4. Murchison to Council and Members of the RGS, 10 Nov. 1854; Murchison to Shaw, 8 Nov. (confidential), 12, and 19 Nov. 1854, Murchison Correspondence, RGS Archives (italics Murchison's).

5. G. Back, Back Diaries, 24, 25, 26, 27, and 30 Oct. 1854, SPRI; the quotation is from the entry for 30 Oct. All of King's letters to Sir John Barrow in 1844 and 1845 are missing from the Admiralty Papers in the PRO, possibly owing to a general "weeding" for this period or to the letters having been taken out of the Admiralty Papers on this or some other occasion and not restored. King's letters to the Colonial Office in the same period are in the PRO and provide interesting marginal comments.

6. G. Back, Back Diaries, 8 Nov. 1854, SPRI.

7. For accounts of this trip, see "Extracts from Anderson's Arctic Journal," *Journal of the Royal Geographical Society* XXVI: 18–25; XXVII: [321]–28. See also "Chief Factor J. Anderson's Journal of 1855," *Canadian Field Naturalist* LIV: [63]–67, 84–89, 107–9, 125–26; LV, 9–11, 21–26, 38–44; James Anderson to Sir George Simpson, 17 Sept. 1855, in PP, *Accounts and Papers*, 1856, vol. 41, no. 2124, pp. 25–29.

8. King, *F. Exped.*, pp. 211–12, 198n.

9. On a possible sighting of one of Franklin's vessels, see introduction by S. Mickle to James Anderson, *The Hudson Bay Expedition in Search of Sir John Franklin*, pp. 15–16. On potential embarrassment and Rae's view that Anderson made a faster trip than Back because the river was now known, see Rae to Back, 29 Jan. 1856, Holmes Collection.

10. See King, *F. Exped.* (1860) at pp. 29–47, 48–75; King to Lords Commissioners of the Admiralty, 21 Apr. 1856, in PP, *Accounts and Papers*, 1856, vol. 41, no. 2124, pp. 82–85; the quotation is from p. 85.

11. See memoranda of John Washington, 2 June 1856, John Barrow to Sir Robert Peel and other Admiralty officials, 24 Jan. 1846, and Sir Robert Peel, 6 June 1856, as well as other correspondence, in Adm 7/200/9; PP, *Accounts and Papers*, vol. 41, no. 2124, pp. 57–58, 88.

12. See memoranda of John Barrow, 24 Jan. 1846, and Sir Robert Peel, 6 June 1856, Adm 7/200/9; the list on Peel's memorandum reads as follows: 1-Pim; 2-Penny; 3-Garland; 4-Cheyne; 5-M'Cormick; 6-King; 7-Rae.

13. See King to the Lords of the Admiralty, 21 Jan. 1856, Adm 7/200/4; and PP, Accounts and Papers, 1856, vol. 41, no. 2124, pp. 31–34. For the same letter misdated 23 Jan., see King, *F. Exped.*, pp. 212–24. See also John Brown, *The North West Passage* (rev. ed., 1860), p. 425.

14. King, *F. Exped.* (1860), p. 71; King and Pim to the Admiralty, 8 Dec. 1856, quoted in Brown, *Northwest Passage* (1860), pp. 433–34, from which (p. 434) the quotation is taken. See also B. Pim, *An Earnest Appeal to the British Public on Behalf of the Missing Arctic Expedition*, and for an earlier proposal by the same officer envisaging the use of dogs as well as steam, idem, "Plan for Further Search after the Remains of the Franklin Expedition," *Proceedings of the Royal Geographical Society* I: 209–15.

15. Lady Franklin to Sir Charles Wood, 4 Apr. 1857, Adm 1/5688.

16. Ibid.; Lady Franklin to Secy. of the Admiralty, 21 Apr. 1857, Adm 1/5688.

17. Minute on Lady Franklin to Sir Charles Wood, 4 Apr. 1857, Adm 1/5688; a letter from the Admiralty was written to Lady Franklin on 8 April. See also M'Clintock to Sir James Ross, 10 Apr. 1857, E. Ross Collection.

18. M'Clintock to Sir James Ross, 4 Apr. 1857, copy, E. Ross Collection.

19. M'Clintock to Sir James Ross, 10 Apr. 1857, ibid.; minutes on Lady Franklin to Secy. of the Admiralty, 21 Apr. 1857, Adm 1/5688.

20. Lady Franklin to Secy. of the Admiralty, 21 Apr. 1857, Adm 1/5688.

21. L. P. Kirwan, *A History of Polar Exploration*, p. 192; prospectus for auction of *Fox* at Royal Exchange, 10 Nov. 1859, McCl/22b, and plans of the *Fox*, McCl/25, M'Clintock Papers, NMM.

22. On M'Clintock's formal training in steam in 1842, see three notebooks in, respectively, McCl/28/29/30, McClintock Papers, NMM; on steam training in 1855, see ibid., McCl/32.

23. Dr. Walker, quoted in Clements R. Markham, *Life of ... M'Clintock*, p. 242.

24. William Kennedy, *A Short Narrative of the Second Voyage of Prince Albert*, pp. 66–67, 78–80, 94–95; Kennedy to Lady Franklin, 10 Oct. 1852, in PP, *Accounts and Papers*, 1852–53, vol. 60, no. 82, p. 29; W. Kennedy, "Report on the Return of ... Prince Albert ... from the Arctic Regions. Read Nov. 8, 1852," *Journal of the Royal Geographical Society* XXIII: 125. Kennedy had served in Labrador and learnt Eskimo methods there (see *RAC*, p. 233n1; Kennedy, *A Short Narrative*, p. 37; *Athenaeum*, 16 Oct. 1852; *Winnipeg Free Press*, 27 Jan. 1890).

25. Rae, *Snow-Huts, Sledges and Sledge Journeys*, pp. 1–2; V. Stefansson, *The Friendly Arctic*, p. 176; see also Rae, Autob. MS, pp. 877d, 877i–877k.

26. For accounts of the *Fox* voyage, see M'Clintock, *Voyage of the "Fox"* (1859); Markham, *Life of ... McClintock*, pp. 193–245; A. Young, *The Search for Sir John Franklin*; F. L. M'Clintock, "Journal of the 'Fox', April 1857–Dec. 1858," MS journal, NMM; see also M'Clintock, *Voyage of the "Fox"* (5th ed., 1881).

27. On King's style, see Brown, *Northwest Passage* (1860), p. 81, and Sir John Franklin, "Report on Mr. King's project of surveying the north-west coast of America," [1836], Library MSS, RGS Archives; on Rae's and M'Clintock's, see V. Hopwood, "Explorers By Land: To 1860," in C. F. Klinck, ed., *Literary History of Canada*, pp. 38 and 40, from which the quotations are taken.

28. G. Williams, *The British Search for the Northwest Passage in the Eighteenth Century*, p. 271.

29. Markham, *Life of ... McClintock*, p. 239; see also M'Clintock, *Voyage of the "Fox"* (1859), p. xii.

30. Humboldt as quoted in S. E. Morison, *The European Discovery of America: The Northern Voyages, A.D. 500–1600*, p. 81.

31. King, *F. Exped.* (1860).

32. See J. E. Nourse, *Narrative of the Second Arctic Expedition by C. F. Hall*, p. 415.

33. See entry of death, 4 Feb. 1876, Somerset House.

34. F. L. M'Clintock, "On Arctic Sledge-travelling," *Proceedings of the Royal Geographical Society* XIX: 464.

35. See reports of meetings of the RGS on 9 Feb. and 22 Mar. 1852 in the *Athenaeum*, 6 Mar. and 3 Apr. 1852; M'Clintock, "On Arctic Sledge-travelling," p. 475, from which the quotations are taken.

36. The probable cost of government Franklin searches and of government aid to other searches for Franklin, up to and including the estimates voted for 1856–57 was £610,520.13s.8d. (Accounts General Report to the Admiralty, 11 Feb. 1857, prepared for the First Lord agreeably with the Accounts General Memorandum of 13 Jan. 1857, Adm 1/5685). King claimed that total costs up to

1860, including privately supported searches, were over £2,000,000 (King, *F. Exped.* [1860], p. 258).

37. See Adm 7/608 for the vast number of technical and other suggestions.

38. On the Adam Beck story, leading to the Inglefield expedition, see L. H. Neatby, *The Search for Franklin*, pp. 125–26, 230–33.

39. Alfred Tennyson quoted in Hallam Tennyson, *Memoir of Tennyson*, as cited in W. E. Houghton, *The Victorian Frame of Mind, 1830–1870*, p. 317 and n40.

40. See in this regard Markham, *Life of ... McClintock*, p. 239; Brown, *Northwest Passage* (1860), Sequel, p. 16.

41. The sledge was five feet long and 14 lb. in weight (Neatby, *Search for Franklin*, p. 209). On the satellite sledge, see M'Clintock, *Intrepid* Journal, 17 Mar. 1853, pp. 250–51; G. F. M. M'Dougall, *The Eventful Voyage of ... "Resolute,"* pp. 204–5. Of satellite sledges M'Clintock wrote: "Small sledges called Satellites have been made for the extended parties, the idea is to select a few of the best walkers of the party; and leaving the remainder encamped where game is likely to be found, to push on for a few days with only a blanket bag each, travelling perhaps 20 miles a day. I proposed the telescopic plan but the idea of a small sledge instead of carrying the provisions etc. is Captain Kellett's" (M'Clintock, p. 250).

42. John Brown was a constant critic of the idea that Franklin had sailed northwards, and did name the general region in which the Franklin vessels became beset, although he never agreed with King's projects for reaching the Franklin party. A. K. Isbister (1822–83) was, like his uncle William Kennedy, a half-breed; he made a career in England, where he knew Hodgkin and King, and as early as 1847 he named the Boothia area as a place to search for Franklin and advocated a route which Rae himself later looked upon favourably (see A. Isbister to the Secy. of the Admiralty, 18 Apr. 1856, in PP, *Accounts and Papers*, 1856, vol. 41, no. 2124, p. 86; and letter of A. Isbister, 14 Dec. 1847, *Athenaeum*, 18 Dec. 1847).

43. See A. R. M. Lower, *Colony to Nation: A History of Canada* (Toronto: Longmans, Green, 1946), p. 2; Horace, *Epistles*, I.xi.27 ("Caelum, non animum, mutant qui trans mare currunt").

44. Capt. Donald Beatson to Sir Roderick Murchison, undated and unsigned letter, read before the RGS, c. February–March 1852, RGS Journal MSS; even as regards this vessel, one of its voyages, conducted by Kennedy, was largely paid for by funds from Van'Diemen's Land (Frances J. Woodward, *Portrait of Jane*, p. 284).

45. Woodward, *Portrait of Jane*, p. 277.

46. F. L. M'Clintock, "Reminiscences of Arctic Ice-Travel," *Royal Dublin Society Journal* I: 224.

47. The phrase "Stefansson syndrome" is that of John Holmes, in the foreword to R. St. J. Macdonald, ed., *The Arctic Frontier*, p. [iv]; it is employed here in a somewhat different sense. The phrase "friendly Arctic" is the title of a book by Stefansson himself.

APPENDIX 1

1. F. L. M'Clintock, *The Voyage of the "Fox"* (1859), p. 285 (italics supplied); ibid., preface by Sir Roderick Murchison, pp. xiv–xv (italics Murchison's).

2. See R. J. Cyriax, *Sir John Franklin's Last Arctic Expedition*, pp. 197–98, from which the quotations are taken, and 201 ff.; Cyriax and Wordie, "Centenary of the Sailing of Sir John Franklin," *Geographical Journal* CVI, nos. 5 and 6: 180.

3. See Cyriax, *Franklin's Last Arctic Expedition*, p. 197, from which the quotation is taken; idem, "Sir James Clark Ross and the Franklin Expedition," *Polar Record* III, no. 24: 538–39.

4 P. D. Baird (in *Expeditions to the Canadian Arctic*) essentially agrees with the second of Cyriax's attitudes. Despite Baird's statement that his criterion of discovery is the first sighting of a given coastline (p. 8), his real criterion is the first sighting *and reporting* of one. For example, he gives J. C. Ross, not Franklin, credit for discovery of the North Somerset coast of Peel Sound; and M'Clintock and Rae, not Franklin, are given credit for discovery of other final links in a coastal passage (see map, pp. 8–9).

5. See John Stuart to Richard King, 31 Dec. 1835, as quoted in King, *Narrative*, II: 307; see also the dispatch (from which the quotation is taken) of Thomas Simpson to the Hudson's Bay Company, *Times*, 18 Apr. 1840, as quoted in King to Earl Gray, 8 Dec. 1847, C.O. 323/232 and in King, *F. Exped.*, p. 47.

APPENDIX 2

1. Rae in discussion portion of G. Nares, "On the Navigation of Smith Sound as a Route to the Polar Sea," *Proceedings of the Royal Geographical Society* XXI: 286–87; Wordie and Cyriax, Introduction, *RAC*, p. c; John Rae, *Snow-Huts, Sledges and Sledge Journeys*, pp. 1 and 4. For the quotations, see ibid., p. 4, and Rae, in Nares, p. 286.

2. Rae, *Snow-Huts*, p. 1, and idem, Autob. MS, p. 893; the quotations are from these sources respectively.

3. Rae, Autob. MS, p. 889, and idem, in discussion portion of F. Nansen, "Journey Across the Inland Ice of Greenland from East to West," *Proceedings of the Royal Geographical Society* XI: 485; the quotations on snow waves and deep snow are from these respectively.

4. Rae, *Snow-Huts*, p. 3; idem, in discussion portion of F. L. M'Clintock, "On Arctic Sledge-travelling," *Proceedings of the Royal Geographical Society* XIX: 479, from which the quotation is taken.

5. Rae, *Snow-huts*, p. 4.

APPENDIX 3

1. This account of the document is based upon F. L. M'Clintock's in *The Voyage of the "Fox"* (1859), pp. 283–87, from which the text is taken; the facsimile facing p. 283 of the same work is here reproduced (plate 8).

Bibliography

I. MANUSCRIPT SOURCES

A. Public Record Office

(i) ADMIRALTY

Logs and journals of naval discovery vessels early in the period are in the Adm 55/ and Adm 56/series: Parry in *Fury*, *Hecla*, and *Griper*, 1819–20; John Ross in *Isabella*; and J. C. Ross in *Investigator* and *Enterprise* are in Adm 55/. Parry in *Fury* and *Hecla* in 1824–25 are in Adm 56/.

The central source for the period 1845–60 is the Adm 7/ series which was printed in the Parliamentary Papers for the period. Vol. 1 in the series is Admiralty Secretary's Department Miscellanea. Vols. 2–14 are Adm 7/187 (vol. 2) to Adm 7/200 (vol. 14), forming a run that covers the period 1845–56. The chief items used were:

Adm 7/187. The last Franklin expedition.
Adm 7/188. James Clark Ross expedition, 1848–49.
Adm 7/190. Penny expedition, 1850–51.
Adm 7/191. Rae expedition, 1850–51.
Adm 7/193. Austin expedition, 1850–51.
Adm 7/195 and –/199. M'Clure expedition, 1850–54.
Adm 7/198. Kellett expedition, 1852–54, including Pim's sled journey, 1853.
Adm 7/200. Anderson expedition, 1855.

Also used were:
Adm 1/1582. Correspondence relating to the Back expedition, 1833–35.
Adm 1/2433, –/2435, –/2436. Correspondence relating to Sir John Ross's expedition, 1829–33.
Adm 1/5642, –/5688. Correspondence relating to Richard King.
Adm 1/5676. List of ships in arctic exploration.
Adm 1/5679, –/5685, –/5688. Correspondence relating to the Arctic Medal.
Adm 1/5684, –/5696, –/5714, –/5718, –/5726, –/5738, –/5743, –/5754. Correspondence relating to M'Clintock, 1857–60.

Adm 1/5685. Probable cost of search expeditions for Franklin.

Adm 1/5688. Correspondence of Lady Franklin, 1857.

Adm 7/200. The award of the Franklin search prize.

Adm 7/608. Suggestions for the relief of Franklin.

Adm 7/612, –/613. Reports of M'Clintock on travelling methods.

Adm 7/614. The use of steam.

(ii) COLONIAL OFFICE

Records of Franklin's expedition, 1819–23 are in C.O. 6/15; and of his expedition, 1825–27 in C.O. 6/16 and 6/17. C.O. 323/232 contains letters of Richard King to the Colonial Office in the period, 1847–48, with marginal comments.

B. Hudson's Bay Company Archives

Note: For Sir George Simpson's letters to John Rae in the D series and Rae's writings in the E series, see also below, II, Printed Sources.

Sources used were:

A1/60–62. Minute Books. Decisions by the committee regarding Dease and Simpson and matters relating to the Admiralty, Colonial Office, the prime minister and the RGS.

A6/25. Correspondence Books Outwards. Correspondence concerning Dease and Simpson.

B 200/a/24. A copy of Stewart's journal.

B 200/a/31. The Anderson journal, 1855.

B 235/b/4. Correspondence relating to Dease and Simpson and Russian exploration, 1839, and to the Back expedition in *Terror*, 1836.

B 239/k. The Anderson expedition.

E 15/1. Franklin's second arctic expedition: Accounts and miscellaneous, 1824–28.

E 15/2. Back's first expedition: Accounts, correspondence, and contracts, 1832–35.

E 15/3, –/8, –/9. Correspondence concerning Rae's first (1844–47), second (1850–53), and third (1852–55) expeditions. See also *RAC*.

E 15/4. Franklin's last expedition: Circular letters and miscellaneous, 1848–54.

E 15/5. Richardson's expedition, 1847–50. See also *RAC*.

The letters of George Simpson to Thomas Simpson, 4 June 1840, and of George Simpson to C. F. Finlayson on Thomas Simpson's death are in D 4/25, ff. 190–94 and ff. 196–97 respectively.

C. The British Museum

Add. MSS. contain the Barrow Bequest of John Barrow, son of Sir John Barrow, numbered Add. MSS. 35, 300–35, 309, of which the following are the most important:

301. Sir John Barrow, "History of Arctic Voyages," manuscript.
302. Idem. Autobiography manuscript.
303. Idem. Supplemental biographical memoir.
306. Letters from arctic officers, including Austin, Penny, and Kennedy expeditions, 1852–54, including letters of Pim, M'Clintock, and Kellett.
308. Letters and papers of, or relating to, Collinson, M'Clure, Maguire, Kennedy, and Lady Franklin.
309. Papers relating to the *Fox* expedition, 1859–61.

Add. MSS. 42, 712. The John Brown Correspondence.
Add. MSS. 49, 599. Wood Correspondence, General; this is relevant to Lord Halifax's views and activities as first lord of the Admiralty at the time of the *Fox* expedition.
Add. MSS. 42, 580. Sherborn Autographs has correspondence of Richard King.

D. The Royal Geographical Society
There is a large amount of manuscript material in the Archives of the Royal Geographical Society. Correspondence is arranged in correspondence blocks in the Archives, for example, for Sir George Back for the years 1831–40, 1841–50, 1851–60, etc. There are other correspondence blocks for: J. Arrowsmith, Sir John Franklin, R. King, F. L. M'Clintock, Sir Roderick Murchison, S. Osborn, B. Pim, J. Rae, Sir James Ross, Sir John Ross, etc. Other materials in the Archives are:

Committee Minute Book, 1841–65.
Council Minute Books, 1841–53; 1853–59; 1859–67.
Letter Books, 1844–50; 1850–59.

Hooper, W. H. "Voyage of the Isabella and Alexander in Search of a North-West Passage: 1818." Manuscript diary. 2 vols.
———. "Diary of Wm. Hooper (Purser) Kept on Board *Fury*, Capt. W. E. Parry, 1821–23." Manuscript diary. 2 vols.
Kennedy, Wm. Journal MSS. Files.
King, R. Journal MSS. Files.
M'Clintock, F. L. "Journal of Lt. M'Clintock in *Enterprise*, 1848–9: Rewritten and abbreviated." Manuscript journal in Library MSS. This includes the sled journey, not in the journals at NMM or PRO.

Of special use were the following:
Pim's "Plan for the Investigation of the Northern Coast of Siberia," in Journal MSS. Files; and the correspondence relating to that plan in the Murchison and Pim correspondence.
Rae to Mrs. Catherine Vaughan, 16 May 1889.
King to Dr. T. Hodgkin, 5 June 1840, in Journal MSS. Files.

E. The National Maritime Museum
The following were of special use:

M'Clintock, F. Manuscript journal in *Enterprise* with J. C. Ross, 1848–49.
——. Manuscript journal in *Assistance* with Austin, 1850–51.
——. Manuscript journal in *Intrepid*, 1852–54.
——. Manuscript journal "Journal of the 'Fox', April 1857–Dec. 1858."

Also from the M'Clintock Papers:

McCl/22b and –/25. *Fox.*
McCl/28, –/29, –/30, and –/32. Steam.
McCl/45a. The Franklin and J. C. Ross expeditions.
McCl/338. M'Clintock notebook.

The Belcher Papers.

The Draft Room. Plans of:

Erebus and *Terror*
Investigator
Intrepid and *Pioneer*
Fox

F. The Scott Polar Research Institute
MS 248. The Lefroy Bequest. Lady Franklin Journals and Correspondence; the Cracroft Correspondence; letters of Franklin, Parry, etc. MS 395: Folder on Back in *Terror* in 1836, including Back, "Watch Exercise Book, Sept. 21, 1836 to Sept. 2, 1837" kept on board *Terror.*
MS 395. Back, "Sir George Back Diaries." Manuscript diaries, 1844–78. 25 vols.
MS 748/1 and 2. Nelson, J. H., "Voyage of H.M.S. *Investigator* resulting in the Discovery of the North West Passage." Manuscript diary. 2 vols.
Rae, John. "The Autobiography of Dr. John Rae." Manuscript autobiography, written by Rae with his journals before him, covering Rae's early life and most of his expeditions.

G. The Office of the Hydrographer
Correspondence of Beaufort, Belcher, Collinson, M'Clintock, M'Clure, Osborn, Pullen, Rae, Richards, James Ross, John Ross, and Washington. See Abstract of Letters, 1848–56, and especially Miscellaneous Files nos. 1, 2, 12, and 19.
Court, Stephen. "Work and Remark Book of Stephen Court, 2nd. Master H.M.S. Investigator. (Nov. 1, 1851–April, 1853)." Manuscript journal.
Charts and tracks of expeditions of Parry, Franklin, and James Ross.

H. The National Library of Ireland
Maguire, R. "Journal kept by Rochefort Maguire, Cmdr. on Board H.M.S. Plover on the Behring Straits Arctic Expedition, 1852–54." Manuscript journal. 2 vols.

I. Other Libraries and Archives
The Guildhall Library.
Guy's Hospital Archives.
The National Register of Archives.
The Wellcome Medical Library.

J. Private Collections
Banes Diary. "Diary of George Dann Banes." Manuscript diary of George Dann
Banes (1802–74), foreman shipwright, Chatham, and surveyor of the first iron-
clad navy, London, Glasgow, and Birkenhead; in the possession of Mr. G. E.
Banes, Bishops Stortford, Herts.
Holmes Collection. Correspondence to and from Sir George Back in the possession
of Mrs. A. W. Holmes, Strawberry Hill, Middlesex.
E. Ross Collection. Correspondence to and from Sir James Ross and Sir John Ross,
and other Ross Papers, in the possession of Miss Esther Ross, Kensington,
London.
Private manuscript of Robert Cundy, Esq., on his Back River trip, 1964, for
Admiral Noel Wright, to visit T. Simpson's Castor and Pollux cairn (later pub-
lished as *Beacon Six*; see sec. II B below).

II. PRINTED SOURCES

A. Official
The Admiralty series Adm 7/187–200 and other Admiralty Papers are available in
the Parliamentary Papers or House of Commons Sessional Papers. A guide was
published in *Arctic Bibliography*, vol. 8, items 45212–45250. The following is a
selective list:

Reports from Committees, 1834, vol. 18, no. 250. Report on Captain Ross's Voy-
age. (45213)
Estimates and Accounts, 1834, vol. 42, no. 493. Grant of £5,000 to Capt. John
Ross. (45214)
Accounts and Papers, Estimates, 1846, vol. 26, no. 51. (45215)
Accounts and Papers, 1847–48, vol. 41, no. 264. Instructions and correspondence,
Franklin and Franklin Relief. (45216)
Accounts and Papers, 1847–48, vol. 41, no. 386. Instructions to Sir James Clark
Ross. (45217)
Accounts and Papers, 1849, vol. 31, no. 152. Equipping of *North Star* to take
supplies to *Investigator* and *Enterprise*. (45218)
Accounts and Papers, 1849, vol. 32, no. 188. Progress dispatches from three
Franklin search expeditions: James C. Ross; J. Richardson; Moore and Kellett.
(45219)

Accounts and Papers, 1849, vol. 32, no. 188–II. Comments on proposal to send ship to Lancaster Sound to resupply Capt. Ross. (45220)

Accounts and Papers, 1849, vol. 32, no. 497. Report of Richardson's boat expedition. (45222)

Accounts and Papers, 1850, vol. 35, no. 107. Accounts of Franklin search expeditions under Ross and Saunders; Kellett, Moore, and Collinson; reports of whaling expeditions; proposed expeditions to Bering and Barrow Straits. (45223)

Accounts and Papers, 1850, vol. 35, no. 368. Cost of purchase and refit of *Resolute, Assistance, Pioneer*, and *Intrepid*; also cost of purchase and refit of *Lady Franklin* and *Sophia*. (45224)

Reports and Papers, 1850, vol. 35, no. 397. Admiralty instructions to Captains William Penny (*Lady Franklin*), James Saunders (*North Star*), and H. T. Austin (*Resolute*). (45225)

Accounts and Papers, 1851, vol. 33, no. 97. Reports on Arctic Expeditions, 1849–50. (45226)

Accounts and Papers, 1852, vol. 50, no. 1435. Results of inquiry by Arctic Committee into thoroughness of Austin's and Penny's search for Franklin. (45227)

Accounts and Papers, 1852, vol. 50, no. 1436. Extensive reports by sledgers from Austin's expedition of 1850–51. (45228)

Accounts and Papers, 1852, vol. 50, no. 1449. Major documents. Reports (1850–52) of expeditions under Collinson, De Haven, Ross, Austin, and Penny; reports by Rae of his expedition to SW Victoria Island; numerous letters. (45229)

Accounts and Papers, 1852, vol. 30, no. 14. Supplementary estimate, 1850–51, covering cost of Franklin search expeditions under Austin and Penny. (45230)

Accounts and Papers, 1852, vol. 50, no. 115. Contains Penny's letter protesting Admiralty's refusal to use his services in renewed Franklin search; also letters on rumour of Franklin expedition at Byron Bay. (45232)

Accounts and Papers, 1852, vol. 50, no. 248. Copy of report of Rae on Arctic searching expedition under his command. (45233)

Accounts and Papers, 1852, vol. 50, no. 317. Admiralty orders for Belcher to proceed to Lancaster Sound, establishing *North Star* as depot ship at Beechey Island. (45234)

Accounts and Papers, 1854–55, vol. 44, no. 489. Data on the Arctic Committee. (45237)

Accounts and Papers, 1852–53, vol. 60, no. 82. Reports of arrival of Belcher's Expedition on Beechey Island; Kennedy's and Inglefield's reports. (45238)

Accounts and Papers, 1854, vol. 42, no. 1725. Early report of Belcher's Expedition. (45241)

Accounts and Papers, 1854, vol. 42, no. 129. Lady Franklin's protest against Admiralty's removal from Navy List in 1854 of names of members of the Franklin expedition as having died in Her Majesty's service. (45242)

Accounts and Papers, 1854–55, vol. 35, no. 1898. Mainly reports arising out of Belcher's expedition. (45245)

Accounts and Papers, 1854–55, vol. 31, no. 140. Appropriation to McClure et al for discovery of Northwest Passage; appropriation for erection of monument to memory of Franklin. (45246)

Report from Committees, 1854–55, vol. 7, no. 409. List of members, report, and proceedings of committee appointed to recommend awards for Northwest Passage discovery. (45248)

Accounts and Papers, 1856, vol. 41, no. 2124. Correspondence on Hudson's Bay Company's expedition under Anderson and Stewart, and Franklin relics. (45249)

Accounts and Papers, 1857–58, vol. 60, no. 2416. Letters and newspaper account of recovery of the *Resolute*. (45250)

B. Published Journals, Memoirs, Correspondence etc.

Anderson, James. "Chief Factor James Anderson's Back River Journal of 1855." *The Canadian Field Naturalist* LIV (May–Dec. 1940): [63]–67, 84–89, 107–109, 125–26; LV (Jan.–March 1941), 9–11, 21–26, 38–44.

[———]. "Extracts from Anderson's Arctic Journal." *Journal of the Royal Geographical Society* XXVI (1856): 18–25; XXVII (1857), [321]–28.

Armstrong, Alexander. *A Personal Narrative of the Discovery of the North-West Passage*. London, 1857.

Back, Sir George. *Narrative of an Expedition in H.M.S. "Terror"*. London, 1838.

———. *Narrative of the Arctic Land Expedition to the Mouth of the Great Fish River*. London, 1836; reprint ed., Edmonton, Alta.: Hurtig, 1970.

Ballantyne, R. M. *Hudson's Bay: Or Every-Day Life in the Wilds of North America during Six Years' Residence in the Territories of the Hon. Hudson's Bay Company*. Boston, 1859; 2nd ed. London, 1848.

Barrow, Sir John. *An Autobiographical Memoir of Sir John Barrow*. London, 1847.

Braithwaite, John. *Supplement to Sir John Ross's Narrative of a Second Voyage*. London, 1835.

Cundy, Robert. *Beacon Six*. London: Eyre and Spottiswoode, 1970.

Fitzjames, James. "Journal of James Fitzjames Aboard Erebus, 1845" (letters to Mr. and Mrs. William Coningham). *Nautical Magazine and Naval Chronicle* XXI, nos. 3 and 4 (1852): 158–65, 195–201; also privately printed.

Franklin, John. *Narrative of a Journey to the Shores of the Polar Sea*. London, 1823.

———. *Narrative of a Second Expedition to the Shores of the Polar Sea*. London, 1828.

———. *Narrative of Some Passages in the History of Van Diemann's Land*. London, 1845.

Inglefield, E. A. *A Summer Search for Franklin: With a Peep into the Polar Basin*. London, 1853.

Kennedy, William. *A Short Narrative of the Second Voyage of the "Prince Albert"*. London, 1853.

————. "Report on the Return of Lady Franklin's vessel the Prince Albert, under the command of Mr. Wm. Kennedy, from the Arctic Regions." *Journal of the Royal Geographical Society* XXIII (1853): 122–29, with chart by Arrowsmith.

King, Richard. *Narrative of a Journey to the Shores of the Arctic Ocean, in 1833, 1834 and 1835.* 2 vols. London, 1836.

————. *The Franklin Expedition from First to Last.* London, 1855; rev. ed., London, 1860.

Larsen, Henry. *The North-West Passage, 1940–42 and 1944.* Ottawa: Queen's Printer, 1958.

Lyon, G. F. *The Private Journal of Captain G. F. Lyon, of H.M.S. Hecla, during the Recent Voyage of Discovery under Captain Parry.* London, 1824.

M'Dougall, G. F. M. *The Eventful Voyage of H.M. Discovery Ship "Resolute" to the Arctic Regions in Search of Sir John Franklin in 1852, 1853.* London, 1857.

M'Clintock, F. L. "On Arctic Sledge-travelling." *Proceedings of the Royal Geographical Society* XIX (1875): 464–79.

————. "Reminiscences of Arctic Ice-Travel in Search of Sir John Franklin and his companions. With geological notes and illustrations [by] the Rev. Samuel Haughton." *Royal Dublin Society Journal* I (1856–57): 183–250.

————. *The Voyage of the "Fox" in the Arctic Seas: A Narrative of the Discovery of the Fate of Sir John Franklin and His Companions.* London, 1859; 5th ed., London, 1881.

Maclure, R. *The Arctic Dispatches Containing an Account of the Discovery of the North-West Passage.* London, n.d. [1853].

M'Clure, R. *The Discovery of the North-West Passage.* Edited by S. Osborn. London, 1856; reprint ed., with preface by W. C. Wonders, Edmonton, Alta.: Hurtig, 1967.

Miertsching, J. *Frozen Ships: The Arctic Diary of Johann Miertsching, 1850–1854.* Translated and edited by L. H. Neatby. Toronto: Macmillan of Canada, 1967.

Nansen, F. "Journey Across the Inland Ice of Greenland from East to West." *Proceedings of the Royal Geographical Society* XI (1889): 479–87.

Osborn, S. *Stray Leaves from an Arctic Journal.* rev. ed. London, 1865.

Parry, E. *Memoirs of Rear-Admiral Sir W. Edward Parry.* 2nd ed. London, 1857.

Parry, W. E. *Journal of a Voyage for the Discovery of a North-West Passage.* London, 1821.

————. *Journal of a Second Voyage for the Discovery of a North-West Passage in 1821–22–23.* London, 1824–25.

————. *Journal of a Third Voyage for the Discovery of a North-West Passage in 1824–25.* London, 1826.

Rae, John. *John Rae's Correspondence with the Hudson's Bay Company on Arctic Exploration, 1844–1855.* Edited by E. E. Rich and A. M. Johnson, with introduction by J. M. Wordie and R. J. Cyriax. Publications of the Hudson's Bay Record Society, vol. XVI. London: Hudson's Bay Record Society, 1953.

————. *Narrative of an Expedition to the Shores of the Arctic Sea in 1846 and 1847*. London, 1850.

————. *Snow-huts, Sledges and Sledge Journeys*. (Pamphlet dated 24 June 1875 at the Scientific Club, London; an autographed copy is at the Library of the Royal Geographical Society). n.p., n.d.

Richardson, Sir John. *Arctic Searching Expedition*. London, 1851; New York, 1854.

Ross, John. *A Voyage of Discovery in H.M.S. Isabella and Alexander*. London, 1819.

————. *Appendix to the Narrative of a Second Voyage*. London, 1835.

————. *Narrative of a Second Voyage in Search of a North-West Passage*. London, 1835.

————. *The Rear Admiral Sir John Franklin: A Narrative of the Circumstances and Causes which Led to the Failure of the Searching Expeditions [for] Sir John Franklin*. 2nd ed. London, 1855.

Simpson, Alexander. *The Life and Travels of Thomas Simpson*. London, 1845.

Simpson, Thomas. *Narrative of the Discoveries on the North Coast of America during the Years 1836–39*. London, 1843.

Sotheby and Co. *Catalogue of Voyages and Travels*. Nos. 34 and 35 (19 and 20 May 1969). London, 1969.

Stefansson, Vilhjalmur. *The Friendly Arctic*. New York: Macmillan, 1921; new ed., 1944.

————. *My Life With the Eskimos*. New York: Macmillan, 1913.

Sutherland, P. C. *Journal of a Voyage in Baffin Bay and Barrow Strait*. London, 1852.

Von Wrangell, F. *Narrative of an Expedition to the Polar Sea in the Years 1820, 1821, 1822 and 1823*. Edited by E. Sabine. 2nd ed. London, 1844.

Young, Allen. *The Search for Sir John Franklin: From the Journal of Allen Young*. London, 1875.

III. SECONDARY WORKS

A. Books and Pamphlets

Anderson, James. *The Hudson Bay Expedition in Search of Sir John Franklin*. Introduction by S. Mickle. Reprinted from Transaction no. 20 of the Canadian Women's Historical Society. Toronto: Canadiana House, 1969.

Baird, P. D. *Expeditions to the Canadian Arctic*. Reprinted from *Beaver* (March, June, and September 1949). Winnipeg, Man.: The Hudson's Bay Company, n.d.

Barrow, Sir John. *A Chronological History of Voyages into the Arctic Regions*. London, 1818.

———. *Voyages of Discovery and Research within the Arctic Regions from 1818 to the Present*. London, 1846.

Bartlett, C. J. *Great Britain and Sea Power, 1815–1853*. Oxford: Clarendon Press, 1963.

Berton, Pierre. *The National Dream*. Toronto: McClelland and Stewart, 1970.

Bourne, John. *A Treatise on the Screw Propeller, with Various Suggestions of Improvement*. London, 1852.

Brown, John. *The Northwest Passage and the Plans for the Search for Sir John Franklin*. London, 1858; rev. ed., London, 1860.

Caswell, J. E. *Arctic Frontiers: United States Explorations in the Far North*. Norman: University of Oklahoma Press, 1956.

Creighton, D. G. *The Commercial Empire of the St. Lawrence, 1760–1850*. Toronto: The Ryerson Press, 1937.

Crouse, N. M. *The Search for the Northwest Passage*. New York: Columbia University Press, 1934.

Cyriax, R. J. *Sir John Franklin's Last Arctic Expedition: A Chapter in the History of the Royal Navy*. London: Methuen, 1939.

Eccles, W. J. *The Canadian Frontier, 1534–1760*. New York and Toronto: Holt, Rinehart and Winston, 1969.

Evans, Admiral Sir Edward. *British Polar Explorers*. London: Collins, 1943.

Fitzpatrick, Kathleen. *Sir John Franklin in Tasmania, 1837–1843*. Melbourne: Melbourne University Press, 1949.

Glazebrook, G. P. de T. *A History of Transportation in Canada*. 2 vols. Paperback ed. Toronto: McClelland and Stewart, 1964.

Glover, R., ed. *Cumberland and Hudson House Journals, 1775–82*, first series, *1775–79*. Publications of the Hudson's Bay Record Society, vol. XIV. London: The Hudson's Bay Record Society, 1951.

Halkett, Peter. *Boat-Cloak, or Cloak-Boat, Constructed of Macintosh India Rubber Cloth, with Paddle, Umbrella, Sail, Bellows, etc.* Richmond, 1848.

Herstein, H. H.; Hughes, L. J.; and Kirbyson, R. C. *Challenge and Survival: The History of Canada*. Scarborough, Ont.: Prentice-Hall of Canada, 1970.

Hopwood, V. "Explorers By Land: To 1860," in Klinck, C. F. ed. *Literary History of Canada: Canadian Literature in English*. Toronto: University of Toronto Press, 1965.

Houghton, W. E. *The Victorian Frame of Mind, 1830–1870*. New Haven: Yale University Press, 1957.

Innis, H. A. *The Fur Trade in Canada*. New Haven: Yale University Press, 1930.

Johnson, A. M., ed. *Saskatchewan Journals, 1795–1802*. Publications of the Hudson Bay Record Society, vol. XXVI. London: The Hudson's Bay Record Society, 1967.

Kelsall, John P. *The Migratory Barren-Ground Caribou of Canada*. Department of Indian Affairs and Northern Development, Canadian Wildlife Service. Ottawa: Queen's Printer, 1968.

King, R. *The Preservation of Infants in Delivery; Being an Exposition of the Chief Causes of Mortality in Still-Born Children.* London, 1847; 2nd ed. London, 1858.

Kirwan, L. P. *A History of Polar Exploration.* London: Penguin Books, 1962.

Knuth, Count Eigil. *Archeology of the Musk-Ox Way.* Paris: Ecole pratique des hautes études, 1967.

Lloyd, Christopher. *Mr. Barrow of the Admiralty: A Life of Sir John Barrow, 1764–1848.* London: Collins, 1970.

Lloyd, C. and Coulter, W. L. S. *Medicine and the Navy, 1200–1900,* vol. IV, *1815–1900.* London: Livingstone, 1963.

Lubbock, A. B. *The Arctic Whalers.* Glasgow: Brown, Son and Ferguson, 1937.

Macdonald, R. St. J., ed. *The Arctic Frontier.* Toronto: University of Toronto Press, 1966.

Markham, Sir Albert Hastings. *Life of Sir John Franklin.* London, 1891.

Markham, Clements R. *The Arctic Navy List.* London, 1875.

——. *The Lands of Silence.* Cambridge: The University Press, 1921.

——. *The Life of Admiral Sir Leopold McClintock.* London: John Murray, 1909.

Morison, S. E. *The European Discovery of America: The Northern Voyages, A.D. 500–1600.* New York: Oxford University Press, 1971.

Mowat, Farley. *Tundra: Selections from the Great Accounts of Arctic Voyages.* Toronto: McClelland and Stewart, 1973.

Neatby, L. H. *Conquest of the Last Frontier.* Athens, Ohio: Ohio University Press, 1966.

——. *In Quest of the North West Passage.* New York: Crowell, 1958.

——. *The Search for Franklin.* London: Arthur Barker, 1970.

Nourse, J. E. *Narrative of the Second Arctic Expedition by C. F. Hall.* Washington, D.C., 1879.

Parry, A. *Parry of the Arctic: The Life Story of Admiral Sir Edward Parry, 1790–1855.* London: Chatto and Windus, 1963.

Penn, G. *Up Funnel, Down Screw!* London: Hollis and Carter, 1955.

Pim, B. *An Earnest Appeal to the British Public on Behalf of the Missing Arctic Expedition.* 4th ed. London, 1857.

Rae, John. *Arctic and Sub-Arctic Life.* Address delivered to the Royal Institution of Great Britain, 27 April 1877. London, [1877].

Rich, E. E. *The History of the Hudson's Bay Company, 1670–1870.* Publications of the Hudson Bay Record Society, vols. XXI and XXII. London: Hudson's Bay Record Society, 1958–59.

——. *Montreal and the Fur Trade.* Montreal: McGill University Press, 1966.

Richardson, Sir John. *The Polar Regions.* London, 1861.

Ross, Sir John. *Treatise on Navigation by Steam.* London, 1828.

Schmucker, S., ed. *Arctic Explorations and Discoveries during the Nineteenth Century.* New York, 1860.

Stefansson, Vilhjalmur. *Great Adventures and Explorations from the Earliest Times to the Present.* rev. ed. New York: Dial Press, 1966.

——. *Northwest to Fortune.* New York: Duell, Sloan and Pearce, 1958.

——. *Not By Bread Alone.* New York: Macmillan, 1946.

Taylor, Andrew. *Geographical Discovery and Exploration in the Queen Elizabeth Islands.* Department of Mines and Technical Surveys, Geographical Branch, Memoir 3. Ottawa: Queen's Printer, 1955.

Weld, C. R. *Arctic Expeditions: A Lecture.* London, 1850.

Whalley, George. *The Legend of John Hornby.* London: John Murray, 1962.

Williams, Glyndwr. *The British Search for the Northwest Passage in the Eighteenth Century.* London: Longmans, 1962.

Winks, Robin. *Recent Trends and New Literature in Canadian History.* Washington: Service Center for Teachers of History, 1959.

Woodward, Frances J. *Portrait of Jane: A Life of Lady Franklin.* London: Hodder and Stoughton, 1951.

Wright, Noel. *The Quest for Franklin.* London: Heinemann, 1959.

B. Articles

A.B.B. (pseud.). "Reflections on Sir John Franklin's Expedition and Where his Ships Were Most Probably Beset in the Ice." *Nautical Magazine and Naval Chronicle* XXV (March 1856): 121–47.

Bird, J. and M. "John Rae's Stone House." *Beaver* 284 (March 1954): [34]–35.

Burns, F. H. "H.M.S. *Herald* in Search of Franklin." *Beaver* 294 (Autumn 1963): 3–13.

"Communications on a North-West Passage." *Journal of the Royal Geographical Society* VI (1835): 34–50.

Cooke, A. "The Autobiography of Dr. John Rae (1813–93): A Preliminary Note." *Polar Record* XIV (1968): 173–77.

Cyriax, R. J. "Arctic Sledge Travelling by Officers of the Royal Navy, 1819–49." *Mariner's Mirror* XLIX (May 1963): 127–42.

——. "Sir James Clark Ross and the Franklin Expedition." *Polar Record* III (July 1942): 528–40.

——. "Recently Discovered Traces of the Franklin Expedition." *Geographical Journal* CXVII (June 1951): [211]–14.

——. and Wordie, J. M. "Centenary of the Sailing of Sir John Franklin with *Erebus* and *Terror.*" *Geographical Journal* CVI (November–December 1945): 169–97.

"Footnotes to the Franklin Search." *Beaver* 285 (Spring 1955): 46–48.

Gibson, William. "Sir John Franklin's Last Voyage." *Beaver* 268 (June 1937): 44–75.

Glover, R. "York Boats." *Beaver* 279 (March 1949): 19–23.

Graham, G. S. "The Transition from Paddle-Wheel to Screw Propeller." *Mariner's Mirror* XLIV, no. 1 (1958): [35]–48.

Johnson, A. M. "Mons. Maugenest Suggests ...." *Beaver* 287 (Summer 1956): 50–51.

Jones, A. G. E. "Sir James Clark Ross and the Voyages of the *Enterprise* and *Investigator*, 1848–49." *Geographical Journal* 137 (June 1971): [165]– 79.

King, R. "On the Unexplored Coast of North America." *London, Edinburgh and Dublin Philosophical Magazine and Journal of Science*, 3rd series XX (January–June 1842): 488–94.

Lower, A. R. M. "The Metropolitan and the Provincial." *Queen's Quarterly* 76 (Winter 1969): 577–90.

MacKay, D., and Lamb, W. K. "More Light on Thomas Simpson." *Beaver* 269 (September 1938): 26–31.

Pim, B. "Plan for Further Search after the Remains of the Franklin Expedition." *Proceedings of the Royal Geographical Society* I (1856): 209–15.

McClure, H. E. "Barren Land Bugs." *Beaver* 267 (March 1937): 16–17.

Marsh, D. B. "The Mudding of Sledge Runners." *Polar Record* IV (1943–46): 139–40 and illustration facing p. 140.

Nares, G. S. "On the Navigation of Smith Sound as a Route to the Polar Sea." *Proceedings of the Royal Geographical Society* XXI (1877): 274–88.

"Our Portrait Gallery. No. LXXII: Captain M'Clure, R.N." *Dublin University Magazine* XLIII (March 1854): 334–58.

"Pemmican and How To Make It." *Beaver* [295] (Summer 1964): 53–54.

Petermann, A. "On The Geography of the Arctic Regions." *Athenaeum*, 22 Oct. 1853.

"Rae on the Eskimos." *Beaver* 284 (March 1954): 38–41.

Savours, Ann. "Sir James Clark Ross, 1800–1862." *Geographical Journal* CXXVIII (September 1962): 325–27.

Smith, E. C. "Some Episodes in Early Ocean Steam Navigation." *Newcomen Society Transactions* VIII (1928): 61–63.

Stefansson, V. "Rae's Arctic Correspondence." *Beaver* 284 (March 1954): 36–37.

Stevenson, J. A. "The Unsolved Death of Thomas Simpson, Explorer." *Beaver* 266 (June 1935): 17–20, 64–66.

V. MAPS

Maps consulted include those in the Office of the Hydrographer, in the Map Room of the Royal Geographical Society, in the British Museum, and at the Library of the University of London. Of particular use has been Admiralty Chart 5101, "Chart showing the vicinity of King William Island ... ," compiled by Lt. Cmdr. R. T. Gould, RN (The Admiralty, London, 1927), and also Admiralty Chart 5100, "Discoveries in the Arctic Sea: 1616–1927; Reproduction of Former Admiralty Chart No. 2118, Published 1855 with Corrections to 1927; Additional North West

Passage Tracks to 1954" (The Admiralty, London, 1956). See also the reproduction of part of a map on which John Rae marked his own discoveries, in *The Beaver* 284 (March 1954): 30–31; and the delineation of arctic discoveries for 1818–60 in Baird, *Expeditions*, pp. [8]–[9]. For the extent of the Canadian Shield see *Geological Map of the Arctic* (Symposium on Arctic Geology, Calgary, Alta., 1960); *Principal Mineral Areas of Canada* (Map 900A, Department of Energy, Mines and Resources, 26th ed., Ottawa, 1976); and *Geological Map of Canada* (Geological Survey of Canada, Ottawa, 1969). For the Barren Ground Region, the Tree Line in 1959 and the Thelon Game Sanctuary, see J. P. Kelsall, *The Migratory Barren-Ground Caribou of Canada* (end map).

The narratives of the explorers of this period have useful charts showing their tracks and discoveries, as for example, John Ross, *Narrative of a Second Voyage*, facing p. [1]; Rae, *Narrative of an Expedition*, facing title page; and T. Simpson, *Narrative of the Discoveries on the North Coast of America ... 1836–39*, facing title page.

The Hydrographer's Office has charts of the following: Parry, "Discoveries of ... *Hecla* and *Griper*," 1819–20; "The Eastern Coast of Prince Regent Inlet ... June 1852"; land expeditions of Franklin, Richardson, Back (1833) and Back (in *Terror*, 1836); voyage of J. C. Ross in *Enterprise* 1848–49); of *Enterprise*, Collinson (1851–54); M'Clure, *Investigator* (1850–53); Austin's expedition (1850–51); Belcher's expedition (1852–54); and *Herald* and *Plover* (1848–54); *Fox* (1859).

The Map Room of the Royal Geographical Society has among other arctic maps the following:

F. L. M'Clintock: Track of *Enterprise*, 1848–49, showing a supposed route travelled by Franklin to Bering Strait by a coastal and by a Wellington Channel route.

Track of *Fox*, 1857–59 (engraved by Stanfords for *Cornhill* Magazine).

A. Petermann: Penny's expedition of 1850–51.

J. Arrowsmith: Discoveries in the Arctic Seas between Baffin Bay and Melville Island, 1850–51 (published 1852).

T. Simpson: Routes through the Barren Lands to the Coppermine River, 1837–39.

"Mr. Findlay on the Probable Course Pursued By Sir John Franklin, 1856."

Index